UNLEASH YOUR TRANSFORMATION

MARCO VAN KALLEVEEN
PETER KOIJEN

UNLEASH YOUR
TRANSFORMATION

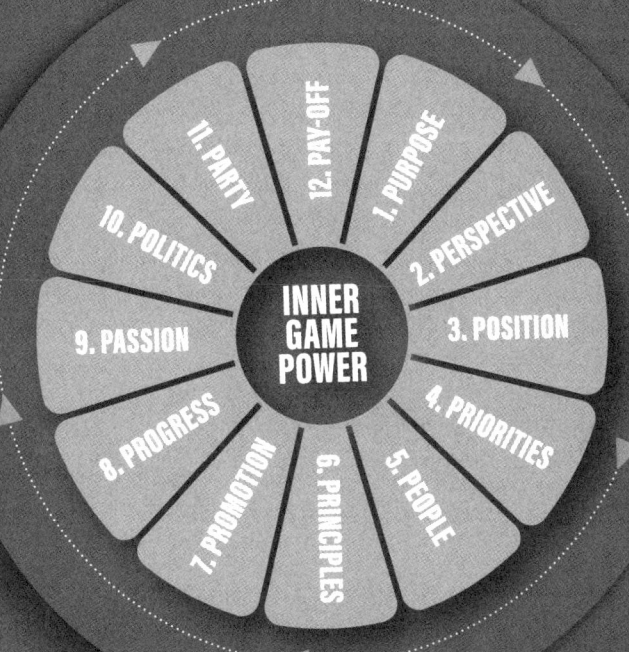

USING THE POWER OF THE FLYWHEEL
TO TRANSFORM YOUR BUSINESS

ForbesBooks

Copyright © 2022 by Marco van Kalleveen.

All rights reserved. No part of this book may be used or reproduced in any manner whatsoever without prior written consent of the author, except as provided by the United States of America copyright law.

Published by ForbesBooks, Charleston, South Carolina.
Member of Advantage Media Group.

ForbesBooks is a registered trademark, and the ForbesBooks colophon is a trademark of Forbes Media, LLC.

Printed in the United States of America.

10 9 8 7 6 5 4 3 2 1

ISBN: 978-1-64225-317-7
LCCN: 2022903231

Cover design by Analisa Smith.
Layout design by Wesley Strickland.

This custom publication is intended to provide accurate information and the opinions of the author in regard to the subject matter covered. It is sold with the understanding that the publisher, Advantage|ForbesBooks, is not engaged in rendering legal, financial, or professional services of any kind. If legal advice or other expert assistance is required, the reader is advised to seek the services of a competent professional.

 Advantage Media Group is proud to be a part of the Tree Neutral® program. Tree Neutral offsets the number of trees consumed in the production and printing of this book by taking proactive steps such as planting trees in direct proportion to the number of trees used to print books. To learn more about Tree Neutral, please visit **www.treeneutral.com**.

Since 1917, Forbes has remained steadfast in its mission to serve as the defining voice of entrepreneurial capitalism. ForbesBooks, launched in 2016 through a partnership with Advantage Media Group, furthers that aim by helping business and thought leaders bring their stories, passion, and knowledge to the forefront in custom books. Opinions expressed by ForbesBooks authors are their own. To be considered for publication, please visit **www.forbesbooks.com**.

In memory of Peter Koijen.

CONTENTS

PREFACE 1

INTRODUCTION. 5

CHAPTER 1. 25
PURPOSE

CHAPTER 2. 47
PERSPECTIVE

CHAPTER 3 67
POSITION

CHAPTER 4. 87
PRIORITIES

CHAPTER 5. 109
PEOPLE

CHAPTER 6. 131
PRINCIPLES

CHAPTER 7. 159
PROMOTION

CHAPTER 8 183
PROGRESS

CHAPTER 9 205
PASSION

CHAPTER 10 225
POLITICS

CHAPTER 11 249
PARTY

CHAPTER 12 267
PAY-OFF

CHAPTER 13 293
THE INNER GAME

CHAPTER 14 317
CONCLUSION: END OF THE BOOK, START OF THE JOURNEY

ACKNOWLEDGMENTS 329
ABOUT THE AUTHORS 333

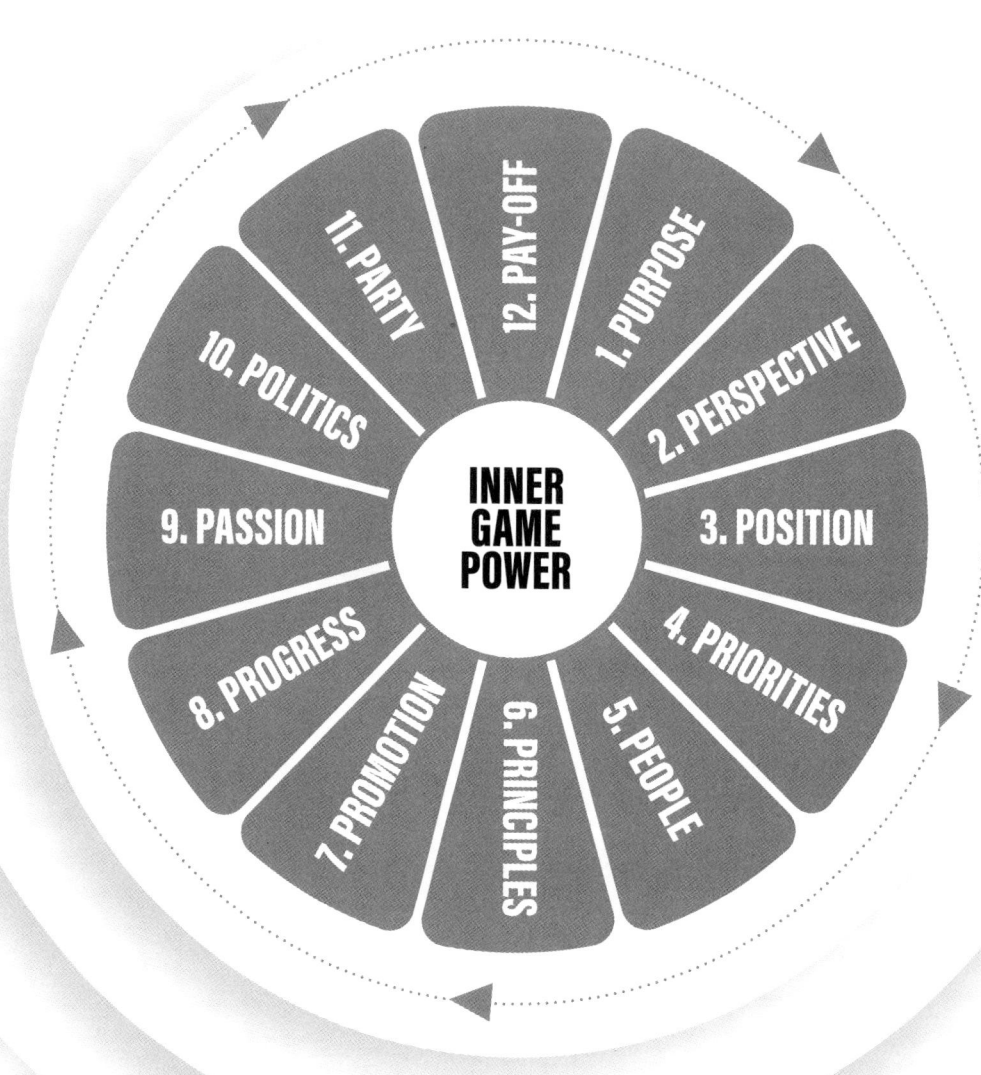

PREFACE

This book is meant for any leader—from CEO to business owner, department head, or team leader, essentially anybody who either is currently transforming their business or part of it or has the ambition to transform and stay ahead. The world is changing at an undeniably rapid pace. Disruptive technology shifts such as digitalization, globalization, sustainability demands, and new generational views on the role of business in society are just a few examples of change drivers. Are these changes good or bad for your organization? It all depends. On the one hand, disruptions are an opportunity when leaders transform their businesses and take advantage of the pace of change. On the other hand, for those who transform too slowly, an existential threat might loom on the horizon.

However, transforming is easier said than done. According to recent McKinsey & Company research, 70 percent of all business transformations struggle to succeed with their transformational efforts,[1] although there are also remarkable examples of success. Take, for example, the stories of well-known companies like Apple, Disney,

---

[1] M. Bucy et al., "The 'How' of Transformation," McKinsey & Company (2016).

Zappos, Microsoft, Starbucks, Salesforce, Tesla, and Instagram, which were able to successfully transform themselves.

Were these leadership teams just lucky, did they possess extraordinary talents, or did they follow certain approaches and principles to make their transformations take off? While the first two—luck and talent—can, of course, be helpful, we believe that there are specific, widely applicable approaches you can use to propel a transformation forward. These cover multiple angles of a transformation and can be pictured as a status-quo-defying Flywheel of Transformation.

This book is the outcome of a decades-long professional quest to discover, apply, and share these transformational principles. Marco's quest has led him through an MBA at Harvard Business School to a partnership at McKinsey & Company, where he advised a multitude of forward-thinking businesses that ranged from *Fortune* 500 companies to Silicon Valley start-ups. He served as senior vice president at Bain Capital, one of the leading private equity investors, before leading multiple successful transformations as a management board member and CEO of several international public and private equity-owned businesses. During this journey he developed the concept of the Flywheel of Transformation. The idea of this book took shape when he was regularly asked to speak about this topic and wanted to evolve the flywheel concept to the next level to underpin it with the latest research as well as well-known practical case examples.

At the start of the book journey, it was clear to Marco that to succeed in a transformation, enhancing a leader's inner game is fundamental as well because leading change is challenging and requires leaders to bring their best. He felt privileged that he could convince Peter Koijen to join the book project as coauthor. Peter had focused for decades on empowering leaders' inner game with his own coaching firm, after a career as an international leader in HR and cultural transformations, and was an authority in this field.

Three years later the Flywheel of Transformation concept was finalized. This tool will give you a practical framework for your own organization's transformation. It lays out twelve integral forces an organization can strengthen in order to propel a transformation forward. In this book you will find the codified learnings of decades of practical experience from both Marco and Peter, as well as real-life case examples from Apple, Starbucks, Microsoft, Instagram, etc. and the latest research from key business journals, all boiled down in the Flywheel of Transformation tool.

The next chapter provides a bird's-eye view of the flywheel. Then in the next twelve chapters, we describe each of the twelve forces, how you can assess your organization's status of them, and how you can power them up. Every chapter starts with an inspiring real-life case study from well-known companies. Finally, we have dedicated a chapter on how to strengthen your inner game as a leader.

Whether you read this book from end to end or simply focus on the specific chapters that might strengthen your own flywheel the most or read the inspiring starting cases of each chapter, we hope that you will find it helpful in your own transformation journey. Now let's dive into the flywheel concept.

INTRODUCTION

Change is the law of life. And those who look only to the past and present are certain to miss the future.
—JOHN F. KENNEDY

In a transformational challenge, there are many forces leaning against success. The status quo has a lot of inertia, which means change is hard. "Everybody loves progress, but nobody likes to change" is a famous quote for a reason. An innumerable number of case studies and research have proved that the majority of transformations fail and don't fly. Often it seems as if the status quo is too strong to be broken. Making progress, however, isn't impossible, and it isn't a game of chance. Making change happen against the odds is really what leadership is all about.

Next to the painful stories of businesses that were not able to adapt and transform fast enough, there are also truly inspiring examples of companies that transformed successfully, rising out of challenging environments. There are famous examples like Netflix, Zappos, Tesla, Instagram, Apple, and Virgin but also many smaller, less-known businesses. Was it all just luck? Supertalented leadership teams? Or is there something more to it? There are clear patterns that, if applied drastically, increase the chances of transforming an organization.

For decades we have, in different ways, focused our careers on discovering, applying, and sharing best practices to transform organizations. On top of this, we went on an extended quest researching best practices in transformation, reviewing latest research and case studies, and covering more than a hundred articles and books to underpin our insights.

To create inertia-defying transformational momentum, there are clear patterns in the strategies successful leaders and their teams use to create the momentum of change. We have found twelve distinct patterns that are almost always present (and working in concert) in successful change patterns. These concepts combine to form what we call the Flywheel of Transformation. Next to creating the flywheel, it's important that a leader bring his or her best mental health, physical health, and lifestyle during a change effort. We have dubbed these internal elements as the "inner game."

In this introductory chapter, we aim to give you a bird's-eye view of the Transformational Flywheel and the inner game before bringing each concept to life as its own dedicated chapter containing real-life case studies, insights from research, and practical tools a leader can use in the following chapters.

The Flywheel of Transformation

What is the Flywheel of Transformation? Based on our own experiences and on our research into successful (as well as not-so-successful) transformations, we recognized that successful transformation utilized twelve forces to create odds-defying strength. In the figure on the next page you can see the overview of the Flywheel of Transformation. As you can see, each of the wings starts with the letter *P*, which is both memorable and indicative of the power each wing contains. You might recognize several of these wings—like purpose and priorities—but others like promotion and party might seem less familiar.

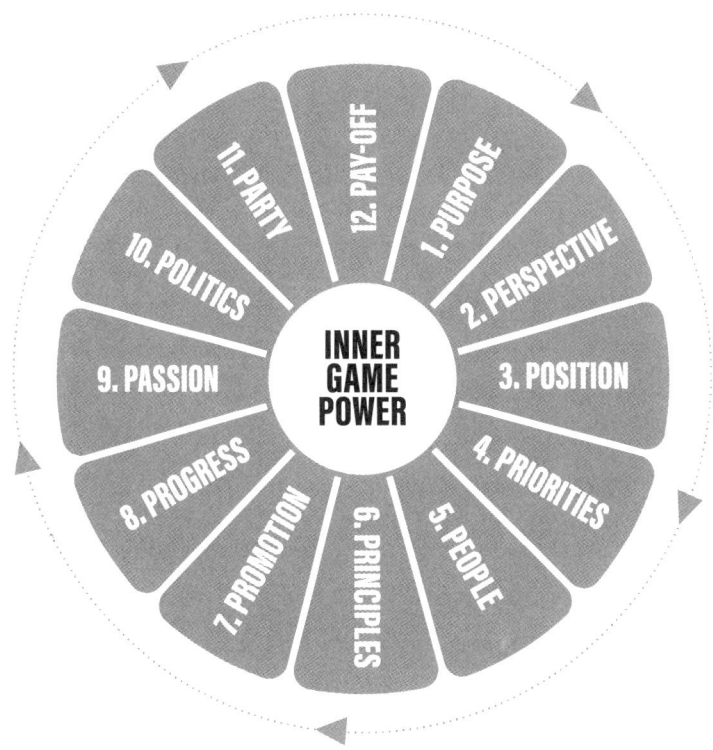

The Definition of the Twelve Wings

Although we describe each wing in detail in the following chapters, here we present a short summary so you can have a bird's-eye view. You might already be asking yourself which of the wings are at full power in your current organization and which have the potential for growth and increased velocity. Since these wings generate the most power when they work together, it is useful to have a knowledge of them all even as you read on for greater detail and specific strategies.

7

1. **Purpose.** Purpose is the foundation of successful transformations. A strong purpose is the reason an organization exists, and it can often be written as a sentence with the following structure: "We do X to help others do Y." Is your purpose clear and compelling? Does it provide meaning, and is it a genuine driving force for the organization? When Steve Jobs returned to Apple in 1997, the company was teetering on the edge of bankruptcy. He used the journey of defining and communicating Apple's purpose, a need to "think different." This purpose inspired a wildly successful transformation away from the PC market. Is your team and organization working to transform the business in service of a higher cause? Is the purpose of your organization fully embraced by the leadership and vital to strategy? Is that purpose motivating and guiding and more than a mere statement written across the top of an annual report?

2. **Perspective.** How accurate are the market and business beliefs on which an organization and its leadership team operate? Are they based on insightful views of how the market is changing and what this change means? The power of this wing is at its lowest when dated beliefs from past eras of success have become religious precepts from which an organization cannot diverge. This makes a business blind to new opportunities and threats. Blockbuster's assumption, for instance, was that dominating VHS rental stores was the way to defend their leading position in the home video market. This inaccurate assumption allowed a small DVD mailing service to seize the emerging opportunity of livestreaming video. Netflix's success was built on the way the upstart company looked at the current market trends and opportunities differently from the established players. Are there trends that you're missing or

misinterpreting? How eagerly are you hunting for new insights and pressure testing your current beliefs?

3. **Position.** Every organization has either implicitly or explicitly defined future target market position. Your future position is a combination of the answer to the following two questions: "Where to play?" and "How to win?" If a future position is not defined, it is, then, by default a fact that the current position will also be the future position. This is likely to cause problems given the ever-changing nature of market environment trends. The more correct, clearer, and more compelling this future position is, the more power this wing will have in the flywheel. When Howard Schultz stepped back in at Starbucks as CEO in 2008, the company had rapidly been losing its way. Schultz reformed the company by defining a clear way to win in the market once again—that Starbucks would secure its place in the future by radically strengthening its value proposition toward customers, breaking dated beliefs. As a result they achieved an unprecedented successful transformation.

4. **People.** As Jim Collins described in his book *Good to Great*, this wing is all about getting the right people in the right seats on the bus—and the wrong people off the bus. Does the leadership of your organization consist of the right inside and outside talent? Is it operating as a high-performing, unified team, or is every person fighting for their own fiefdom within the business? When Satya Nadella took over as CEO of Microsoft in 2014, he faced a company that desperately needed to shift gears. Besides re-creating a compelling purpose and a clear target position based on new market beliefs, Nadella assembled a completely new transformation-oriented management team by recruiting targeted

outsiders who had a proven track record while also promoting internal change agents. From day one he also invested in creating a successful team dynamic by using external experts to drive an incredible transformation.

5. **Priorities.** Setting priorities is absolutely key during a transformation. This is, of course, common sense, but it is essential to note that successful transformation leaders set only a handful of priorities and make them clear and compelling, and they communicate them often. Effective leaders also keep these priorities consistent, engineer them so that they cascade through the organization, and measure progress against them. Strong priorities are aligned with the purpose, perspective, and position. When Robert Iger wanted to step up from COO to CEO at the Walt Disney Company, he defined a set of clear priorities intended to transform Disney to meet shifting market trends and with the ambition of propelling Disney in the lead again. This not only convinced the supervisory board to hire him but it also gave the organization a clear direction. For years he focused on these priorities, which enabled him to dramatically change Disney and reclaim its crown as the leader of its industry. How powerful are your priorities? How clear are they? How constant? Does your organization understand these priorities and put energy behind them with force and commitment? Conversely is it possible that there are too many priorities that are changed often?

6. **Principles.** In the context of the flywheel, *principles* are defined as the key values and behaviors a company adheres to in support of a transformation, in other words the culture of a company. Principles can become a thriving force or put a hand brake on change. As Peter Drucker once said, "Culture eats strategy for

breakfast." Leaders of successful transformations need to have a clear view of where and how to shift the values to make them future fit. Tony Hsieh used defined, uncompromising principles to transform Zappos from a struggling online shoe retailer into the successful juggernaut it is today. One of the key drivers of his success was codifying the magic service culture of Zappos in operating principles. How well do the principles or values of your organization propel your business? Are they nebulous, abstract concepts, or are they actionable and specific?

7. **Promotion.** We have defined *promotion* as both the internal and external communications of the what, why, and how of the business engaging in a transformation. Successful transformational leaders invest heavily in communicating their strategies and intentions to all employees and stakeholders. This promotion cannot occur just once via a presentation or a newsletter but must instead happen consistently throughout the transformation process. When Salesforce CEO Marc Benioff transformed a small start-up operating out of his house into a multibillion industry, he communicated intensively, all the time, and often in quite innovative ways—like at the Dreamforce conference—so that everyone inside and outside the company knew the current and future position of Salesforce. He also gave every employee easy-to-digest note cards with key information on what Salesforce stood for, what it was doing, and what their message to the public encompassed. How effectively do you communicate both inside and outside your organization?

8. **Progress.** *Progress* is defined as the power of execution and the ability to make things happen. You can have everything in order—a great purpose, a clear perspective, a magnetic future

position, a great leadership team, a well-defined culture, and great communication—but the rubber truly hits the road with execution. The strength of this wing in the flywheel can range from weak execution to progress powerhouses. 3G Capital, one of the largest investor groups in the world, started as a small stock brokerage in Brazil and eventually developed a very aggressive execution approach based on KPI targets, a meritocracy, incentives, planning, and rigorous performance management. They then used this incredible ability to execute progress to transform a brewery in Brazil into an entity that was able to acquire Interbrew, Budweiser, and Miller and consolidate a position in the global beer market. How strong is your progress wing? Do you have the execution power that will allow you to transform?

9. **Passion.** Passion is the fuel of any great transformation. It is needed to convince others to join the transformation journey and leave the comfort zone of the known. Passion creates the drive to continue forward even when one is facing hurdles or setbacks. When Nike founder Phil Knight almost lost his fledgling, grassroots running shoe import business because his main Japanese supplier wanted to switch to another distributor in the United States, it was his passion for running and sports (and that of his carefully selected team of mostly former athletes) that drove him to create Nike. They used the setback of almost losing a supplier to create an opportunity by creating their own shoe brand and propelling it to become one of the most valuable brands in the world. How passionate is your organization about what they do for their customers?

10. **Politics.** In the context of the Flywheel of Transformation, politics refers to managing the interests and goodwill of important

stakeholders who are needed for the change journey. Politics also involves managing the internal power allocation within an organization. Successfully managing politics is essential for creating the sustained momentum necessary in a transformation. Managing these forces before difficulties arise is critical. When Kevin Systrom and Mike Krieger sold Instagram to Facebook for $1 billion and then, together with their workforce of twelve employees, arrived at Facebook's gigantic campus, they found themselves in a totally foreign political situation. Over the next few years, they succeeded in building Instagram into a powerhouse, while other companies Facebook had acquired failed. Their success, at least in part, can be attributed to their ability to navigate the initially hostile political environment at Facebook while also managing politics well with key stakeholders. How well are you aligning all the key stakeholders of your organization?

11. **Party.** Celebrating progress and achieving milestones is important in any transformation. Like in soccer, players celebrate every goal in a game and every game won instead of waiting until the end of a season. All the successful transformations we have studied or been a part of involved a lot of celebration of progress milestones. Richard Branson, the founder of Virgin, is one of the all-time greats when it comes to celebration. Both party and fun have been key in the companies he set up—companies that would go on to transform industries. Does your organization celebrate small wins as well as larger successes?

12. **Pay-off.** In the context of the Flywheel of Transformation, pay-off refers to how well the transformation creates value for all key stakeholders, from customers to employees to suppliers to investors to community. If a transformation doesn't create

value to any of these groups in equilibrium, it will be difficult to succeed. Danny Meyer, one of New York's leading restaurant entrepreneurs, has made this one of his keys to success. In all of his successful restaurants—of which he has several—he creates magic by first making his team happy and only then following this with his customers, then his community, then his suppliers, and finally his investors. Creating value for all key stakeholders is critical in a transformation. Is your transformation creating value for all these groups? Is that value maintained when the going gets tough?

The Order of the Wings in the Flywheel

There is a logic to the order of the flywheel. Without, for example, a clear purpose, clear perspectives, and a targeted future position, it becomes challenging to set the right priorities. Without knowing your priorities, it becomes extremely challenging to create the right leadership to deliver on these priorities. Having a lot of passion but not having a disciplined progress execution approach might lead to an organization spinning its wheels. As you can see, there is an order to the twelve wings of the flywheel. This doesn't mean, however, that you always should strengthen your transformation in the order indicated on the flywheel. It's more important to diagnose where your biggest improvement opportunities are in the flywheel.

THE FOUR POWER LEVELS BY WING

Now that we have given an overview of each of the twelve wings, let's introduce another aspect of the Transformational Flywheel. For each of the flywheel wings, we have defined four levels of power that are represented by their height on the vertical axis of their flywheel wing. In each of the following chapters, we are explicit about what is required to evaluate and subsequently strengthen one's performance on each wing.

Combining the twelve wings with their four possible power levels gives one the ability to evaluate their organization in relation to the full Transformational Flywheel. At the outset of many transformations, several wings might have no power, and it is likely that only a few will be at full transformative power. This is normal and should serve as inspiration to strengthen one's flywheel using the steps in subsequent chapters.

The flywheel is designed to get a broad set of the wings powering your organization to at least strong power (but ideally transformative power). These power levels will be evaluated using specific questions and reflection. Take, for example, the purpose wing. If you have only a somewhat defined purpose for your organization or if your company's purpose is written down on your documents but only paid lip service, your company will fall into the no power or some power tiers of strength. On the other hand, if you have a clearly defined and powerful purpose, one that is inspiring the organization, your purpose wing will be on the strong or transformative level.

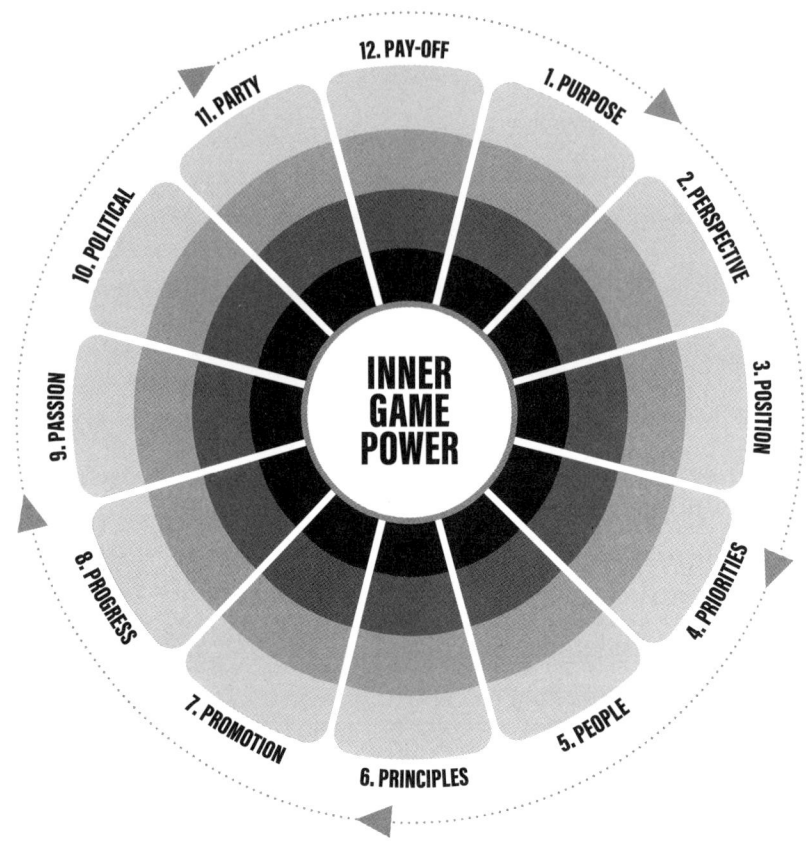

THE FLYWHEEL PATTERNS

Once you have evaluated the state of your current Transformational Flywheel force by wing, it is worth checking it against some of the common flywheel patterns that typically restrain a flywheel from reaching its full transformative power. Here are a few patterns that might describe your starting point.

The "Some Power" Flywheel

All the flywheel wings are somewhat powered by the actions of the leadership team, but they have not yet reached the odds-defying strength needed for your organization to make a transformation happen. This flywheel configuration might feel like one is doing the right things but that these efforts are not yielding proportional results.

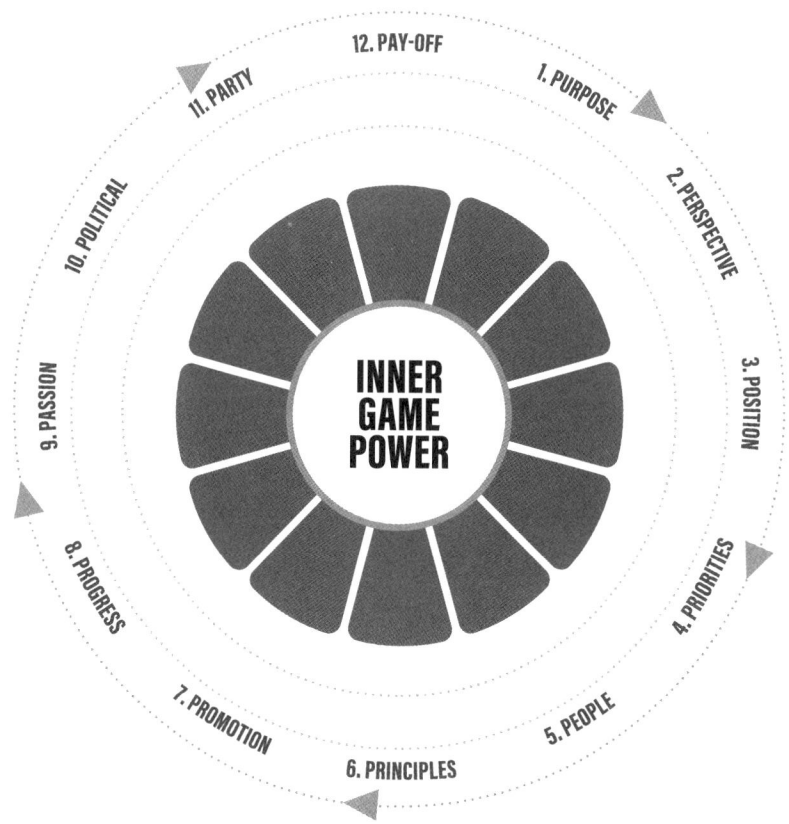

The "Unbalanced" Flywheel

In this situation the leadership has been focused on creating power in only a few wings. It hasn't become a flywheel, a condition that involves a positive feedback loop of increasing power, so there is a consistent loss of momentum. The underdeveloped nature of several wings is sapping power from the stronger wings, as, for example, a lack of priorities impedes effective progress, or a lack of purpose impedes the ability to promote the endeavors of the organization.

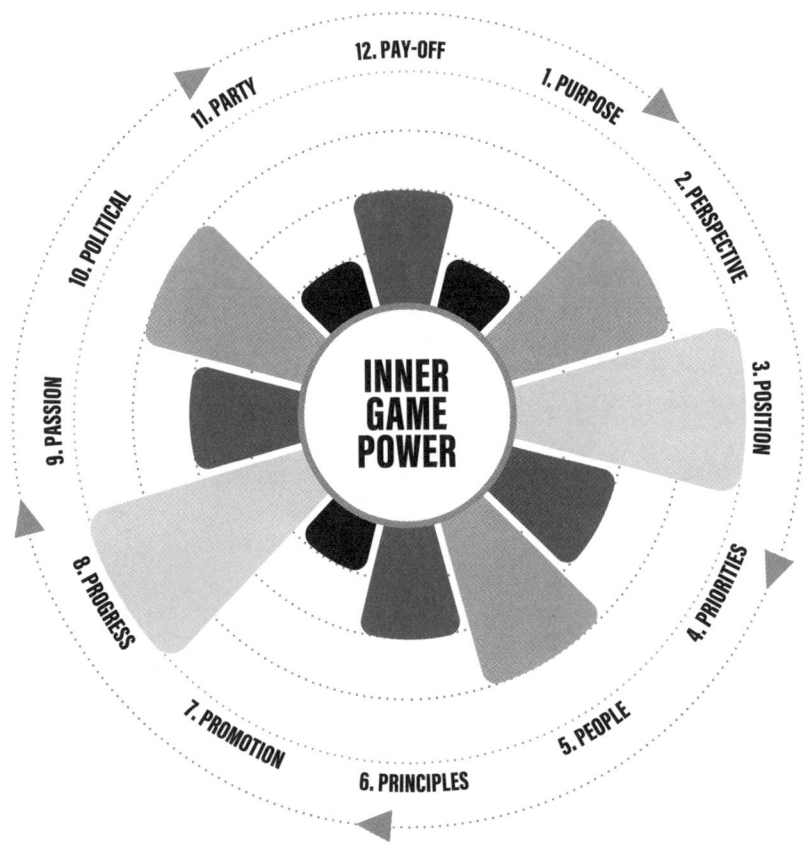

The Out-of-Sync Flywheel

This is the pattern where a lot of wings are strong or transformative, but they are not congruent, for example, if the leadership team has a lot of passion for the purpose but not for making progress. This condition might also arise if there are strong principles/values within an organization, but these values don't match the ideas that will be needed to reach a targeted position. Another company might find that their targeted future position is not aligned with their purpose. Many wings are reliant on each other for strength, so organizations must ensure that they are taking a holistic approach to their transformation efforts.

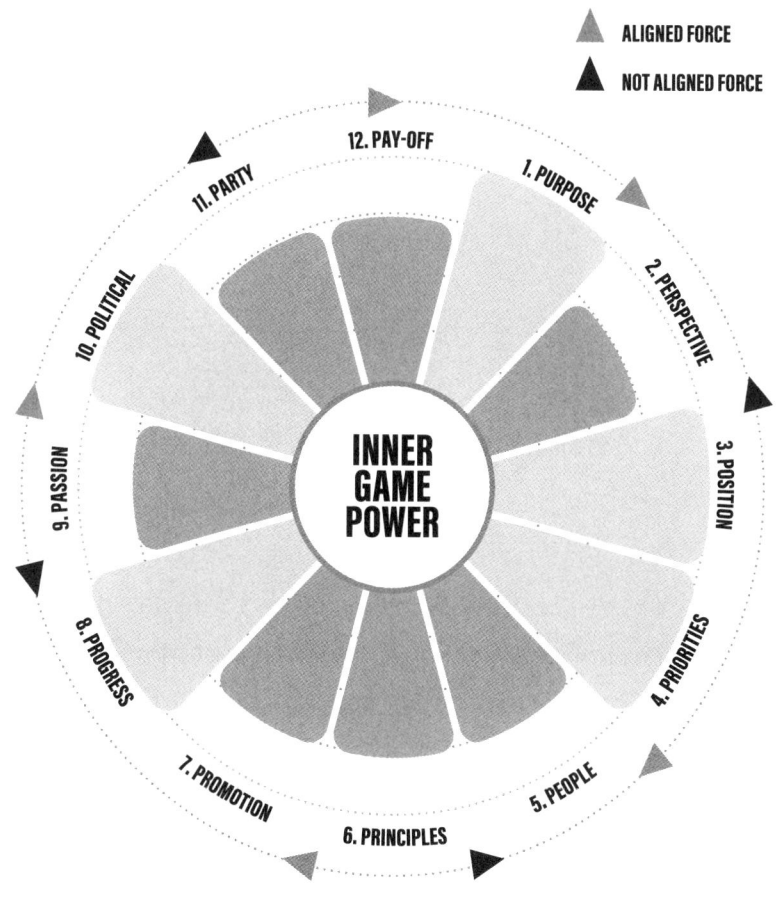

The Full Force Flywheel of Transformation

This is the pattern where almost all wings are at transformative strength and are congruent with each other, creating the gravity-defying strength to overcome the status quo. With this stage a transformation is literally flying.

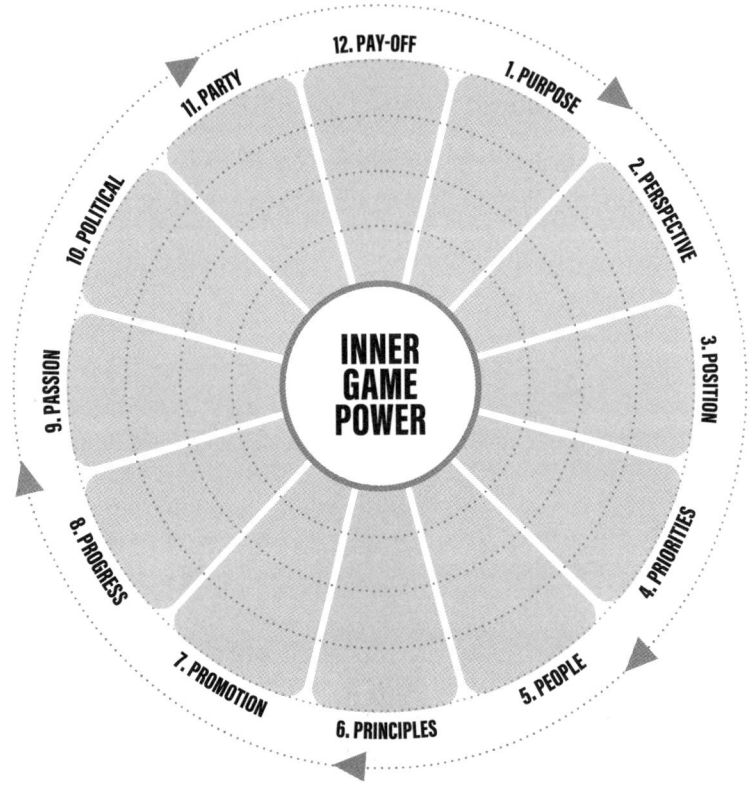

If you feel that not every wing in your flywheel is at full force or if you are just curious about our transformational method, we invite you to the next chapters, where you can learn about each of the wings, examine case studies on leading companies, and make use of our own experiences as transformation leaders. The following chapters examine the what, why, and how of transformations and provide you with a diagnostic for determining the current strength of each flywheel wing in your organization.

INTRODUCTION

Winning the Inner Game

At the center of the Transformational Flywheel is what we call the inner game. The inner game refers to the strength, capability, and flexibility of our body, mind, and emotions. Transforming an organization is challenging. Leaders who are able to bring their A game by mastering these aspects of their performance will find that they can better empower their flywheel.

So what are the different aspects of a strong inner game? Although there are many different aspects and qualifications that one might examine, we have found the following six aspects of the inner game to be critical for unlocking a leader's potential for leading and motivating a transformation.

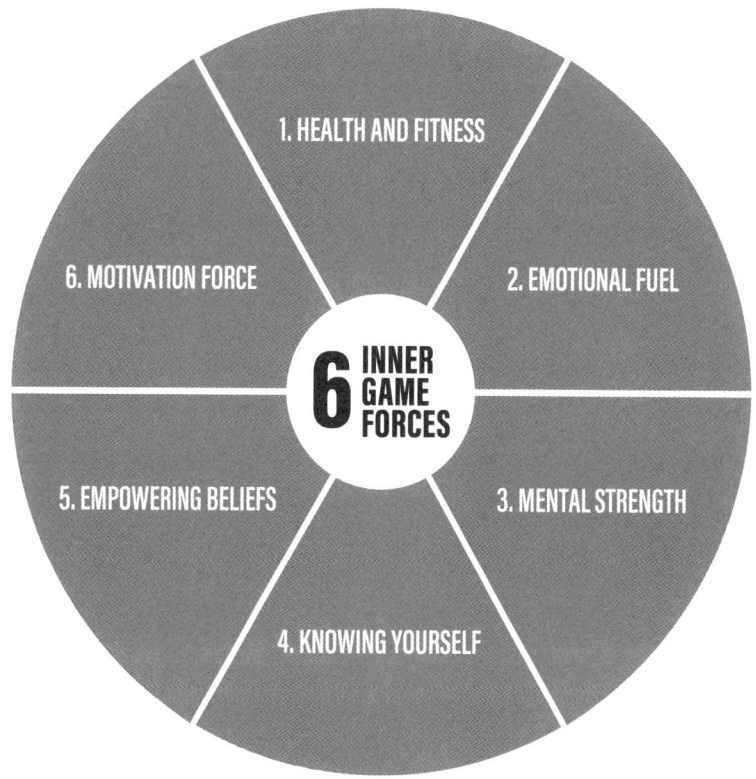

1. **Health and Fitness.** Most successful leaders prioritize their physical health and vitality. Whether it's through fitness, nutritious eating, or other healthy behaviors, the leaders who invest in their physical well-being will reap rewards. By investing in your health, fitness, strength, flexibility, and resulting vitality, you can optimize your energy and endurance. How strong are your health, fitness, strength, and flexibility? How will you rate the vitality your lifestyle grants you?

2. **Emotional Fuel.** How are your emotional fitness and your vitality? Leaders who are able to operate in a positive and productive emotional state can deal with challenges more positively and better motivate the people around them. If you are frequently stressed, worried, and angry, then it is challenging to succeed in driving a change program forward. Are you consistently living in an empowered state?

3. **Mental Strength**. Mental toughness as a leader is important in a transformational situation. It's the capacity as a leader for dealing with stressors, challenges, and pressures while continuing to present their best performance, irrespective of the circumstances in which they find themselves.[2] Mental toughness is the ability to conquer adversity and emerge stronger. Do you have ways to enhance your mental strength?

4. **Knowing Yourself.** Every person has a unique personality. Are you aware of your personality characteristics as well as those of the key people around you? Are you aware of what parts of those personalities will be helpful for succeeding with the change program? Are you able to anticipate those traits that might harm the effort?

---

2   P. Clough et al., "Mental Toughness: The Concept and Management," in *Solutions in Sport Psychology*, ed. I. Cockerill (2002).

5. **Empowering Beliefs**. We, as human beings, are inherently biased. When we embark on any kind of transformational journey, we begin it with all kinds of beliefs and values. How do you judge and interpret the world? Do you hold empowering beliefs regarding yourself, your team, the business, your industry? Or do you hold limiting, disempowering beliefs?

6. **Motivation Force**. How strong and empowering are your motivation and your drive to make your transformation happen? Are you fully committed and empowered? As a leader you can work on enhancing your motivation by, for instance, focusing on the benefits your transformation will create for both yourself and your stakeholders.

Your inner game has a direct impact on making use of the transformational flywheel. We provide a deep-dive chapter at the end of the book in which you can focus on how you can evaluate and improve your inner game.

How to Read and Use This Book

The book is made so that it can be experienced in multiple ways. You can, of course, read it from front to back to get all of our insights on the flywheel, its wings, and the inner game. Alternatively you can go straight to the specific wing chapters about which you are most curious or to those chapters where you sense that the biggest impact can be made on your transformation.

The linear journey through the flywheel begins with the first wing, purpose, a concept that is fundamental not just to transformation but also to having a healthy, directed, and fundamentally meaningful organization.

INNER GAME POWER

1. PURPOSE
2. PERSPECTIVE
3. POSITION
4. PRIORITIES
5. PEOPLE
6. PRINCIPLES
7. PROMOTION
8. PROGRESS
9. PASSION
10. POLITICAL
11. PARTY
12. PAY-OFF

CHAPTER 1

PURPOSE

When you're surrounded by people who share a passionate commitment around a common purpose, anything is possible.
—HOWARD SCHULTZ, CEO OF STARBUCKS

1.1 INTRODUCTION: APPLE

When Steve Jobs was asked to return to Apple as CEO in 1997, the company had lost its way.[3] He'd been forced to depart in 1985, after a disagreement with the board, and over the twelve years that he was absent, Apple's product offering had sprawled. The company had lost its way. For many of Apple's once loyal customers, the company had lost its attraction. Apple was losing the PC war on all sides, and sales were dropping fast.[4] With the losses stacking up and the stock price at an all-time low, many feared the company was facing bankruptcy.

---

3   W. Isaacson, *Steve Jobs* (New York: Simon & Schuster, 2011).
4   J. Nicas, "Apple Is Worth $1,000,000,000,000. Two Decades Ago, It Was Almost Bankrupt," *New York Times*, 2020.

When Jobs returned, he did what most would normally do in a turnaround. He dramatically simplified the product offering, he restructured the organization, and he managed costs to ensure the company survived. Yet he was also working on something behind the scenes, something that many didn't see at the time: Job's real target was not only to keep Apple alive but also for the company to thrive again.

> They had to go beyond solely selling goods and services and making profit. Apple had to stand for something again.

To achieve this goal, Jobs knew he had to go beyond the traditional business "turn-around playbook." He knew that great companies have a clear and compelling purpose to exist and that Apple had stepped away from theirs. They had to go beyond solely selling goods and services and making profit. Apple had to stand for something again.

While leading the hectic turnaround, he went on a quest to explore Apple's purpose. Clearly Apple didn't exist to make gray PCs with certain processing capacities. So why, then, did the company exist? Taking his time, he explored this question while reflecting on Apple's past and asking many at the company the very same question.

After months of this disciplined pursuit and in parallel with all his busy activities, he concluded that Apple was founded on a simple premise—that people with passion can change the world for the better. Apple simply existed to help them.[5] That was the driving force behind *why* their developers and engineers came to work each day. That was why they had gotten business in the first place. And that was what would bring them into the future.

To bring this statement alive, Apple decided to come up with a bold campaign. After kicking several ideas around and finding a new agency, Apple filmed what would become known as the beginning of the company's second coming, the "Think different" campaign. In the TV advertisement, a narrator says, "The people who are crazy enough to think they can change the world are the ones who do." The ad features shots of misfits and innovators like Albert Einstein, Richard Branson, Muhammad Ali, and Charlie Chaplin—all the while not showing a single Apple product. The only mention of the company was their rainbow-colored logo at the end with the words *think different* beneath it.

This campaign set Apple's transformation in motion and is still seen as one of the best brand campaigns of all time. However, it was one thing to rebrand the company; it was another to steer Apple's future based on this purpose. Jobs knew that Apple must find or, better yet, create a new market in which it could win—it needed a different future position. His perspective was that the commoditizing PC market was not the area to express such creativity. Driven by the purpose of empowering those crazy enough to change the world, Jobs asked himself, what exactly were such people passionate about, and how could Apple empower them?

---

5   S. Jobs, "To Me Marketing Is All about Values" (California, 1997).

Apple came to the conclusion that people were truly passionate about music. They then went on a journey to develop the unique concept that people could legally buy music online. They also, in tandem, developed an attractive device that could be used to listen to an almost unlimited number of songs they'd purchased online. iTunes and the iPod revolutionized the music industry. The iPhone and the iPad followed, opening up whole new markets by allowing passionate people to pursue their interests.

When Jobs came back to Apple in 1996, the company was close to bankruptcy. By the time he resigned in 2011—as he was losing the battle with pancreatic cancer—Apple had surpassed Exxon as the most valuable company in the world.[6]

The purpose wing is the foundation for creating a transformational flywheel. In this chapter, we will define *purpose*, lay out why it's a key element in a transformation, and give some practical ways to define a purpose and bring it to life.

1.2 What Is the Purpose Wing on the Flywheel of Transformation?

What does *organizational purpose* mean? In simple terms it is the answer to the question "Why does an organization exist?" According to Robert E. Quinn and Anjan V. Thakor in the *Harvard Business*

---

[6] A. Satariano, "Apple Overtakes Exxon Becoming World's Most Valuable Company," Bloomberg, 2011.

Review (*HBR*), purpose moves away from economic exchanges and reflects something more inspirational.[7]

Many organizations have begun to realize that purpose is necessary. However, too many have formulated their purpose as abstracts that appeal to sentiments, as generic as motherhood and apple pie. These statements often end up only being used as a sentence in an annual report. In a 2019 McKinsey & Company survey of over one thousand participants, while 82 percent affirmed the importance of purpose, only 42 percent reported that their company's stated purpose had much practical effect. This disconnect reflects "a purpose gap."[8] Thus, the question is not whether you have formulated a purpose but whether it has the potential to capture the hearts and minds of employees, customers, suppliers, and investors. In order to bridge this gap, organizations must bring their purpose to life.[9]

So what are the characteristics of a great purpose statement? Although there is no defined purpose playbook, we have found that powerful purpose statements have certain characteristics. A powerful purpose statement is as follows:

- Short, often kept to just one sentence
- Not generic or full of buzzwords
- Exclusive and does not appeal to everybody
- Striking and should be appealing to both the heart and the mind
- About what you can do for others

---

[7] R. Quinn et al., "Creating a Purpose-Driven Organization: How to Get Employees to Bring Their Smarts and Energy to Work," *Harvard Business Review*, 2018.

[8] Gast et al., "Purpose: Shifting from Why to How," McKinsey & Company, 2020.

[9] Carlisi et al., "Purpose with the Power to Transform Your Organization," Boston Consulting Group, 2017.

- Congruent with the unique strength and position of the organization

A good purpose is exclusive. It may not appeal to your heart or mind in particular, but it intends to capture a different, specific target audience. For inspiration here are a few examples of purpose statements that illustrate these characteristics.

- Starbucks: "To inspire and nurture human spirit—one person, one cup, and one neighborhood at a time"
- Google: "To organize the world's information and make it universally accessible and useful"
- Greenpeace: "To ensure the ability of the earth to nurture life in all its diversity"
- Bayer: "Science for a better life"
- Facebook: "To give people the power to share and make the world more open and connected"
- Airbnb: "To make people around the world feel like they can belong everywhere"
- Nike: "To bring inspiration and motivation to every athlete in the world—if you have a body, you are an athlete"

Of course, just having a compelling and defined purpose doesn't in itself become a driving force in your Flywheel of Transformation. It's only when that purpose comes to life in policy and action that it can be a guiding light for the organization. The Apple case demonstrates that the well-defined purpose can cause a cascade of results in the organization itself.

MARCO: PURPOSE AS A CATALYST FOR TRANSFORMATION

The first time I realized the power of purpose was when I was a student a long time ago. I had the privilege of being elected as the president of the leading student association, the EFR. It was one of the largest student unions in Europe, with more than three thousand members and an organization of more than two hundred active students. It organized yearly a lot of events such as a leading business conference that attracted the captains of industry, foreign study trips, seminars and workshops, a monthly magazine, and many other ambitious programs. For many years the student association had held a kind of monopoly position on these events, and as a result, the organization had become a bit complacent, just continuing to do what was done each year before. However, several new student bodies had been launched, and they were now fighting for the attention of the students with more innovative concepts than the EFR. We needed to break through this complacency if the EFR was to stay competitive.

Every year a whole new board of eight students was elected to run the association full time. After our new board was elected, I thought it would be good to bring the new leadership team together for an off-site to plan the university year ahead but also to have some fun. At this off-site at one of the parents' tiny vacation cabins, we spent some time on a SWOT analysis of the student association. There were some brutal facts glaring at us. I asked the question that would determine what we would do with our year at the helm: would we use last year's playbook, or would we take some risks to make it a transformative year that once again propelled the association to an unrivaled leadership position? Most of us wanted to make it an unforgettable leadership year.

Before we started to decide on our goals, our activities portfolio, and who should do what tasks, I placed the topic of purpose on the agenda. What was our purpose as an organization actually? In preparation for the off-site meeting, I had looked at old founding documents and spoken with former leaders to try to get a sense of why the EFR existed in the first place. Our purpose was to be found in connecting the business world with the academic world we represented. At this kickoff meeting, we embraced the phrase "bridging the gap between theory and practice"; nobody else had this mission. We felt excited about it; it fit our history and would provide us some guidance. We felt empowered to make some bold choices—including stopping a range of traditional activities and boldly launching some new ones. Some of the big activities included competing head-on with a new student organization by organizing the biggest campus recruiting days, as well as by launching a Pan-European student exchange program with other leading universities. Our rallying cry became "Let's bridge the gap," and we soon produced caps and stickers that brandished this slogan.

The journey of change was not easy, but in the end, it was rewarding. After the off-site we went back and laid out our plans to our supervisory. We got a lot of pushback and complaints that we were striving for too much change. However, with the force of our purpose, the honesty of our brutal fact analysis, and our excitement, we convinced them and went ahead. At the end of the year, we succeeded (with certain ups and downs) in transforming the student association, which was propelled forward for many years afterward. But maybe more importantly, having these brought the team together during the year with a sense of serving something bigger.

1.3 Why Is It Important to Have a Strong Purpose Wing?

A prominent purpose is a key element in creating a transformational flywheel because it brings stakeholders together in a way that goes beyond just a financial transactional relationship. A purpose gives meaning, it guides, and it inspires all stakeholders of the business. Over the years a wealth of research has emerged supporting the positive impact of becoming a purpose-driven organization.[10] It creates higher people engagement, enhances customer loyalty, and delivers higher financial returns.

Without a strong purpose, an organization becomes a group of people without a true north. It becomes transactional and starts lacking a reason for engagement. As Sally Blount and Paul Leinwand put it in their *HBR* piece "Why Are We Here?," "How can [your employees] come to work every day ready to further the business if

---

10   V. Keller, "The Business Case for Purpose," *Harvard Business Review*, 2015.

they don't know what your organization is trying to accomplish and how their jobs support those goals?" Blount and Leinwand go on to state that engaged employees make a big difference in the success of an organization and lead to greater fulfillment in the workplace.[11]

A powerful purpose also strengthens customer satisfaction and loyalty. According to KPMG, many consumers choose purpose-driven brands over their less purpose-oriented competitors, pay premiums to do so, and return again and again as loyal customers.[12] Essentially customers increasingly care about why an organization does the things they do and whether they can identify with that reason.

Part of Apple's appeal is its purpose and what it stands for. Customers also tend to become much more loyal if the employees they engage with are purpose driven and passionate about their organization. Former Harvard Business School professor James Heskett describes this well in his foundational book *The Service Profit Chain*.[13]

Finally, purpose-driven organizations deliver financial returns above their industry standard. In one of the most comprehensive studies on the subject, "Corporate Purpose and Financial Performance," researchers from NYU Stern, Columbia University, and Harvard Business School confirmed the link between financial performance and stock returns.[14] Around 90 percent of purpose-driven companies deliver growth and profitability above their industry average.

So if purpose is so powerful, why aren't more companies guided by it? When organizations are founded, there is usually a clear and compelling reason for being that is driven by the founder's passion. But

---

11 S. Blount et al., "Why Are We Here?," *Harvard Business Review*, 2019.

12 René Vader, KPMG, https://assets.kpmg/content/dam/kpmg/xx/pdf/2019/11/customer-loyalty-report.pdf.

13 J. Heskett et al., *The Service Profit Chain: How Leading Companies Link Profit and Growth to Loyalty, Satisfaction, and Value* (New York: Free Press, 1997).

14 C. Gartenberg et al., "Corporate Purpose and Financial Performance," *SSRN Electronic Journal* (2016).

over time this can fade and eventually be extinguished. Purpose is like fire—you need to attend to it to keep it alive. Many purposes erode due to lack of attention, short-term business optimization decisions, or the arrival of new leaders.

One of the ways to rekindle purpose is to analyze the founding phase of an organization. Lego's transformation provides us with an example of how to keep the flame alive by returning to one's roots. In the early 2000s, the cult children's toy brand was on the brink of bankruptcy. When ex–McKinsey & Company management consultant Vig Knudstorp arrived on the scene as CEO, the company was $800 million in debt.

Lego had been in the red for ten years prior and had invested in everything from a theme park to a decked-out computer games production facility. Yet with no experience in many of their newly founded business lines, they were hemorrhaging money. Within five years Knudstorp managed to pull off what some call the greatest turnaround in corporate history. How? "We had to ask, 'Why does Lego Group exist?' What was its purpose? Lego was born to inspire and develop children to think creatively, reason systematically, and release their potential to shape their own future," not to operate theme parks or create computer games.

This led the brand to remove the fluff, double down on what was already working, and build out again from there. They returned to their core product offering—designs that would help children learn and develop their creative problem-solving abilities—and began to build the Lego empire that we know today. Within five years Lego overtook Ferrari to become the world's most powerful brand.[15] Because Lego went back to their core reason for existence and based

---

15   C. Pash, "Lego Has Overtaken Ferrari as the World's Most Powerful Brand," *Business Insider*, 2015.

the majority of their decisions from this position, they were able to bring their brand back to life.

CASE: THE POWER OF WHY IN EVERY SITUATION

A neighborhood newspaper published an article with the local supermarket's employee of the month. The image accompanying the article showed a high school student who was working his summer job stocking shelves. He was responsible for making sure the fruit and vegetables were fully stocked for the after-work rush.

After congratulating the student, the reporter asked why he was doing such an excellent job. He asked, "Is it so you can make more money or get extra shifts?"

The student replied that he wasn't interested in either of those things.

"Is it because you want to make a career with this company and go on to lead the department?"

Again the student answered in the negative.

"Well, is it because you want to build your CV and get a good reference for later?"

Again the student answered no.

"So what is it then?" the reporter stumbled.

The employee then said something that took the reporter by surprise. "People come into the supermarket after work, and they're tired. Fruit and vegetables are at the entrance of the supermarket, and I believe that well-presented vegetables help people make healthier choices. If the vegetables are fully stocked, there's a better chance customers will choose them for dinner instead of the unhealthier, processed foods at the back of the shop. I want to make sure my community stays healthy."

1.4 How Do You Score on the Purpose Wing?

How strong is the purpose wing of your Transformational Flywheel? Is there room for it to contribute more strength to your transformation? To help you assess where you stand, we have defined four levels. Where do you score your organization? Where will your employees score the organization? What about your customers? Your suppliers? Your investors?

- **Level 1. No or Limited Power: Unclear Purpose.** The organization is focused on economic transactions between customers, employees, and suppliers. Employees could not state the organizational purpose if randomly surveyed. Customers buy the product or service without having a clear understanding of *why* the organization delivers said product or service. Management is focused on and incentivized toward short-term financial targets and KPIs. The organization is characterized as siloed and political.

- **Level 2. Some Power: Purpose on Paper.** There is a purpose statement written down and mentioned in some publications, such as in annual reports. The statement is generic and only somewhat known with employees, but it's not a source of inspiration or motivation. It was developed with the help of some outside marketing agency, perhaps several years ago. Management decisions are still driven by financial incentives, business opportunities, and politics rather than the why.

- **Level 3. Good Power: Living Purpose.** There is a clear, compelling purpose statement developed by the organization. It's widely communicated, and employees can recall it when asked.

It's used to review future strategic direction and innovation decisions. It's used as a check for character fit in recruitment.

- **Level 4. Transformative Power: Passionate Purpose.** Employees are proud and engaged because of the meaning the company's purpose provides. It attracts certain people during recruitment but also repels others who don't feel in tune with the purpose. Investment decisions and innovation directions are fueled by the purpose. The purpose guides long-term decision-making even when it's challenging. The purpose is an active topic in all aspects of the organization. Customers feel the purpose and resonate with your organization's why, and as a result, you've experienced increased loyalty.

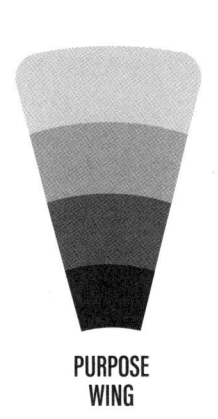

PURPOSE WING

WING-POWER LEVEL		YOUR SCORE?
LEVEL 4	TRANSFORMATIVE POWER	
LEVEL 3	GOOD POWER	
LEVEL 2	SOME POWER	
LEVEL 1	NO POWER	

PETER : EVEN PURPOSE-DRIVEN ORGANIZATIONS CAN LOSE THEIR PURPOSE

For many organizations it's easy for purpose to fade into obscurity during the day-to-day doldrums. I once observed an archetypal example of this when I was asked to help a global sustainability company redefine its reason for being. The organization had a strong focus on helping other companies become more sustainable, but its own sales were rapidly falling. The company was at risk on multiple fronts, both financially and reputationally. They knew their competitive edge was bruised and battered.

What had happened? Instead of focusing on their purpose, they had become incessantly product oriented—an all-too-common story for organizations, both big and small. As a result they had lost their connection with their inner why, which in turn created a disconnect from the external world.

To return to an effective point of flow, they needed to get back to their purpose. This process began with asking their employees about their own whys. Why had they joined the company to begin with? Why were they driven to come to work every day? Their responses painted a story of their employees (and the company) being fighters for a sustainable approach in companies all over the world. Their vision was a world in which companies were transparent about business.

Paying close attention to overlaps, we wrote down the words they said. Because we hadn't started with the product, we were able to reverse engineer the story directly from the employees themselves. As a result it became obvious that, over the years, many of their core products had moved away from their mission of sustainability.

> With too much focus on what and not enough on why, it's easy for companies to lose their way.

The process itself was invigorating. It brought with it creative new ideas, positive energy, and a sense of flow. In the end their purpose needed to be updated to match with the outside markets that were evolving rapidly. Realigning the organization's purpose injected a lot of energy into the organization and resulted in a wealth of positive energy for the path forward.

Focusing on products and services can seem enticing because we all know exactly what we do. It's easy to articulate. But with too much focus on what and not enough on why, it's easy for companies to lose their way.

1.5. How to Strengthen the Purpose Wing

How can you strengthen the purpose wing of the flywheel? Although there is no cookie-cutter approach, as it is both art and a science, there are certain practices that leaders have successfully used, which we have grouped in four practical steps—get in the right mindset, craft the statement, activate it, and live it.

1. **Get in the right mindset.**
   - Getting yourself in the right mindset is absolutely key.
   - Be open to change and don't let yourself be held back by the need for perfection or the fear that it requires hard decisions. Have an open, curious mind.
   - Become aware of potentially limiting subconscious beliefs, like the belief that people only work for an incentive and financial reward. Believing that meaning drives people first is a more empowering starting point.
   - See it as a must and not as a nice-to-have. As the impact is less tangible in the start, a great purpose might be perceived as soft or as merely a nice thing to add.

2. **Craft a compelling purpose statement.** There are several best practices that you can use while drafting a purpose statement:
   - Allocate time to explore, write, and test. Honing in on your purpose may take time, and that's OK.
   - Take the lead. Delegating this task may sound like it's the easiest way forward, but it's the responsibility of the leader in guiding the process of discovery.
   - Find inspirational examples. As we've discussed, a purpose is only tangible when it's expressed in action.
   - Look to the founding period or toward how the company navigated major crisis moments in the organizational history for clues and inspiration.

- Go directly to the source—your employees. Speak with passionate people within your organization and try to understand what makes them tick.

- Avoid "motherhood" and "apple pie." Time and time again, companies avoid being specific in their purpose statement out of fear of offending anyone. A purpose that is generic or blandly sentimental has no purpose.

- Keep it brief. A purpose should be both easily digestible and memorable. So when you're writing a purpose statement, keep it to one sentence.

- Test whether it resonates. Ask the people on your team if they think it represents them and the organization. Does it give clarity or add confusion to their work?

3. **Activate consistently.** When it comes down to it, a purpose is only alive when it's supported by action.
    - Use it in key presentations. Whenever you have an event or a gathering, be sure to communicate your purpose in explicit terms. Say the words that you've written down.

    - Purpose is most powerful when attached to personal experience. When you talk about your organization's purpose, it should be validated by your own lived experiences. And this should be true all the way throughout the organization, from the CEO to the receptionist.

- Write it on the wall. Use your purpose as a criteria lens when considering people, investments, or project decisions.

- Tell the world. Once you truly believe that you are living your purpose, don't be afraid to use it as a part of your external communications.

4. **Identify and celebrate behavior in line with your purpose.** Actively hunt for behaviors that are in line with your organization's purpose. Celebrate these moments and champion those who live by the organization's purpose.
   - Identify key behaviors that demonstrate the purpose. Behavior that is influenced by your purpose may not be easy to see, so highlighting these moments is important. This should not be a job that you do alone. Bring your team in; ask them to be on the lookout as well.
   - Actively communicate the purpose in a celebratory way. When your team reaches milestones or has successes, connect it back to your purpose and celebrate.
   - Find a way to reward your employees. If your culture allows it, you could work with a monthly award system or perhaps with an after-work drink.

References

Isaacson, W. *Steve Jobs*. Simon & Schuster, 2011.

Nicas, J. "Apple Is Worth $1,000,000,000,000. Two Decades Ago, It Was Almost Bankrupt." *NY Times*, 2020. https://www.nytimes.com/2018/08/02/technology/apple-stock-1-trillion-market-cap.html#:~:text=Two%20Decades%20Ago%2C%20It%20Was%20Almost%20Bankrupt.,-Apple%20became%20worth&text=SAN%20FRANCISCO%20%E2%80%94%20In%201997%2C%20Apple%20was%20on%20the%20ropes.&text=On%20Thursday%2C%20Apple%20became%20the,end%20the%20day%20at%20%24207.39.

Jobs, S. "To Me Marketing Is All about Values." California, 1997. https://www.youtube.com/watch?v=22jfMkMXl68.

Satariano, A. "Apple Overtakes Exxon Becoming World's Most Valuable Company." Bloomberg, 2011. https://www.bloomberg.com/news/articles/2011-08-09/apple-rises-from-near-bankruptcy-to-become-most-valuable-company.

Quinn, R., and A. Thakor. "Creating a Purpose-Driven Organization: How to Get Employees to Bring Their Smarts and Energy to Work." *Harvard Business Review*, 2018. https://hbr.org/2018/07/creating-a-purpose-driven-organization.

Gast, A., P. Illanes, N. Probst, B. Schaninger, and B. Simpson. "Purpose: Shifting from Why to How." *McKinsey Quarterly* (2020). https://www.mckinsey.com/business-functions/organization/our-insights/purpose-shifting-from-why-to-how.

Carlisi, C., J. Hemerling, J. Kilmann, D. Meese, and D. Shipman. "Purpose with the Power to Transform Your Organization." Boston Consulting Group, 2017. https://www.bcg.com/publications/2017/transformation-behavior-culture-purpose-power-transform-organization.

Keller, V. "The Business Case for Purpose." *Harvard Business Review*, 2015. https://hbr.org/resources/pdfs/comm/ey/19392HBRReportEY.pdf.

Blount, S., and P. Leinwand. "Why Are We Here?" *Harvard Business Review*, 2019. https://hbr.org/2019/11/why-are-we-here.

Heskett, J., W. E. Sasser Jr., and L. Schlesinger. *The Service Profit Chain: How Leading Companies Link Profit and Growth to Loyalty, Satisfaction, and Value*. New York: Free Press, 1997.

Gartenberg, C., A. Prat, and G. Serafeim. "Corporate Purpose and Financial Performance." *SSRN Electronic Journal* (2016). https://www.researchgate.net/publication/317997813_Corporate_Purpose_and_Financial_Performance.

Pash, C. "Lego Has Overtaken Ferrari as the World's Most Powerful Brand." *Business Insider*, 2015. https://www.businessinsider.com.au/lego-has-overtaken-ferrari-as-the-worlds-most-powerful-brand-2015-2#:~:text=Lego%2C%20following%20the%20huge%20success,leader%2C%20has%20dropped%20to%209th.

INNER GAME POWER

- 1. PURPOSE
- **2. PERSPECTIVE**
- 3. POSITION
- 4. PRIORITIES
- 5. PEOPLE
- 6. PRINCIPLES
- 7. PROMOTION
- 8. PROGRESS
- 9. PASSION
- 10. POLITICAL
- 11. PARTY
- 12. PAY-OFF

CHAPTER 2

PERSPECTIVE

The greatest danger in times of turbulence is not the turbulence; it is to act with yesterday's logic.
—PETER DRUCKER, AUTHOR, EDUCATOR,
AND MANAGEMENT CONSULTANT

2.1 INTRODUCTION: TESLA MOTORS

Around the turn of the twentieth century, the combustion engine was crowned as king of the automotive industry, a paradigm that lasted for well over one hundred years. Then at the start of the twenty-first century, as cleantech was on the rise as the next big thing, two Silicon Valley entrepreneurs, Marc Tarpenning and Martin Eberhard, challenged the traditional beliefs about the practicality of green transportation.

The pair had just sold their battery-powered e-book business, Rocketbook, and started to look for new entrepreneurial opportunities. As a reward to himself for the successful exit, Eberhard was going to buy a sports car. However, he couldn't bring himself to buy a petrol convertible given his concerns over climate change, so he decided to look for an electric vehicle (EV) instead.

However, he soon became frustrated with the EV market. It was a very small, geeky niche market with very unfashionable designs and very restricted range due to old-fashioned battery technology. There had been no innovation for years. As he tested one of the geeky cars, however, he realized the incredible acceleration power an electric car could bring—the thrust sent him back into the seat like a Lamborghini with a floored accelerator. Eberhard wondered to himself if the acceleration power could be combined with a better design to reposition EVs as a cool, sporty car. Could that create a market opportunity? Even then, however, the lack of range still made EVs impractical.

The range of EVs in the era was limited due to the acid type of batteries, which had been in use for decades and had seen very limited innovation and progress. Eberhard's previous projects provided some serendipity in this area and allowed him to connect some dots that others could not. They had used a new battery technology for their e-book business, namely lithium-ion batteries, which were developing very fast with increasingly large capacities. Eberhard and Tarpenning, in a moment of inspiration, realized that these batteries could be used for EVs as well. This would finally make the range for EVs more competitive and eliminate one of the biggest market barriers they'd faced in the past.

The change in their perspective on the EV market was substantial. They saw the potential for the electric vehicle to move from geeky and low end to stylish and high end, from a product positioned only around environment-friendliness to a vehicle that also offered sporty driving, from almost no range to a competitive range. People in the automotive industry didn't see this new perspective, but these two outsiders were able to connect the dots differently and revolutionize their industry.

In 2003 Tarpenning and Eberhard founded Tesla Motors.[16] Their first focus was to build a sports car like the one Eberhard had been looking for only a few months earlier. The Roadster would target the high end of the market, showing that it was possible to make EVs cool while anchoring a whole new futuristic car brand. In 2004 Elon Musk, who had recently sold his stake in PayPal, became one of the start-up's first investors and its chairman. Four years later Tesla Motors successfully launched their first fully electric sports car with a range of 400 km on a single charge. The Roadster's performance was comparable to many gasoline-powered sports cars, and all of this was contained in the sleek chassis of a Lotus Elise convertible.

That year both founders left the company, and Elon Musk took on the role of CEO. After a successful IPO a few years later, they began to break into the next arena—the mass-produced market segment. With their sights set on becoming competitive against the brands that had

---

16   A. Vance, "Elon Musk: Tesla, SpaceX, and the Quest for a Fantastic Future," Ecco, 2015.

dominated the auto industry for the past century, they introduced the Model S, which rapidly expanded their sales. Just seventeen years after its launch, Tesla became the most valuable car company in the world.[17]

Although Tesla's past successes don't guarantee it will be successful in the future, their status-quo-shattering changes do demonstrate that your perspective on your industry and business can make or break you.

2.2 What Is the Perspective Wing on the Flywheel of Transformation?

Perspective is defined as the way you look at something. In the context of the Flywheel of Transformation, we define *perspective* as the leadership team's view on the key trends in the market and how they intend to be successful as a business based on these views. What are the set of assumptions and beliefs a leadership team has, and how accurate are they? When the assumptions are inaccurate, a team can decide to stay put in a situation where a transformation is actually required. It's also possible, of course, that you see things that you think require a change, but you draw the wrong conclusions and instead engage in a flawed transformation approach.

Kodak, for example, spent years dismissing the warning signs that digital photography was on the rise. Since their key business was selling film and printing photos, they couldn't believe there would eventually be an essentially filmless world. "They were convinced that no one would ever want to look at their pictures on a television set,"

---

17 S. Klebnikov, "Tesla Is Now the World's Most Valuable Car Company with a $208 Billion Valuation," Forbes, 2020.

said Steve Sasson, the ex–Kodak employee who invented the technology that eventually enabled digital photography[18]. Instead of incorporating Sasson's technology into their product offerings, the company's management told Sasson he shouldn't discuss his innovation with anyone. Due to this blinded perspective, they were too late to the digital photography space and went from dominating the global film market with over $10 billion in sales in 2007 to bankruptcy in 2012.

What drives people to cling to dated assumptions and beliefs? All humans perceive the world through their senses. Our senses receive literally millions of bits of information every second, and our brains have a limited bandwidth with which to process all this information. To make it possible to process so much information, we create beliefs or, to put it another way, rules about how the world we inhabit works and what things mean. Essentially we create a map of the world that determines our perspective.

Once you have made your assumptions and defined your beliefs on the way things are, you literally start seeing the world with those beliefs. In other words, *as you believe it, so you see it*. As you go on, these beliefs become stronger. You start to ignore evidence that contradicts your beliefs and increasingly believe evidence that supports them. Given the limited nature of such a worldview, to succeed in transforming an organization, the perspective wing of the flywheel almost always has to be strengthened. New, more accurate assumptions have to be developed. What exists that you are not yet seeing?

A strong, adaptable perspective in a transformational situation has two main characteristics:

1. It has a "brutal facts" view on the current situation, brutal in terms of strengths but also in regard to its weaknesses. It respects the past but is not blinded by it.

---

18   J. Estrin, "Kodak's First Digital Moment," *New York Times*, 2015.

2. It has a clear and unclouded view of the different trends that are confronting a business and the industry that it exists in, as well as outside events and their consequences.

> ### MARCO: NEW PERSPECTIVES TO PROPEL TRANSFORMATION
>
> Based on many experiences I had during my ten years at McKinsey, where we looked at the real facts and connected current and future dots differently to unlock transformations, I have become really eager to look for dated beliefs and misconnected dots when I start in a new leadership role. So when I joined the management board of one of the leading listed Dutch companies, TNT Express, one of the first things I did was hunt for the key perspectives insights (alongside, of course, other flywheel wings).
>
> As context this €7B revenues company was in need of a transformation. It was one of the larger global overnight parcel delivery companies. It had a global footprint, but it was competing with substantially larger players like UPS, FedEx, and DHL. A recent merger attempt with UPS had fallen through, and the company's performance had been on a decline.
>
> As I joined the management board, I became responsible for a newly created division that oversaw TNT's large domestic network businesses in Europe, Latin America, and Australia. These were operated by thirty thousand motivated and hardworking employees who helped generate $3 billion in

revenue in a 24-hour, 365-day-a-year complex operation to pick up and deliver millions of packages.

One of my mentors had taught me to always look for vital signs of where beliefs on how to operate the business have become disconnected with reality. So in my first one hundred days, as I traveled literally multiple times around the world to visit all businesses, frontline operations, customers, etc. and worked on fundamentally analyzing the businesses, we discovered several dated perspectives that had to shift.

Let me give you one example. Somehow over the years, the business had adopted the belief that large customers were more important than small to medium enterprises. As a consequence a lot of attention had been focused only on large customers. For example, every presentation was about large customers, every shared customer win was about them, and talented people gravitated to this part of the business. However, this belief had become one of the root causes of putting the business in a negative spiral. When I spoke to employees who had worked at the company for over twenty-five years and asked them when the company was doing very well, they all mentioned the time when the company was focused on SMEs and complemented them with the right large customers. The belief that large customers were the way to go had caused margin pressure but also a lot of operational issues in the complex plane and truck network that connected hundreds of depots and hubs in the 24-hour market cycle where each minute counted. A better balance was needed.

To turn the business around, we had to shift things fast and make SMEs a stronger pillar of the company again. However, how to shift this belief that had become so "unquestioned"? Besides discovering and sharing some brutal facts, we started a series of initiatives to create momentum. For example, we introduced an internal campaign with the slogan "We love SMEs." Also, during every monthly business review, we started with the SME performance first. When visiting each country regularly, we organized events and visits for SMEs instead to role-model their importance. We also started a sales force effectiveness program for the SME salespeople. We even held a competition to see who could get their respective prime minister in a picture first with a "We love SMEs" poster, which Australia won.

Within a year we were able to turn a negative SME growth into positive growth across all our markets. The shift from a belief that SMEs were not important to "We love SMEs" was one of several perspectives that we changed to help transform these businesses around the globe. These changes in perspectives, together with clear value-creation plans, programs to strengthen management teams, large investments in new hubs and depots, rolling out frontline-empowering lean programs around the globe, and our other endeavors, helped turn the spirit and performance of the business around within a year. Several years later TNT was successfully acquired by FedEx to create a global leader.

2.3 Why Is It Important to Have a Strong Perspective Wing?

It's important to have an accurate understanding of the current reality and how the future is possibly unfolding. A vision clouded by cognitive bias can lead to blindness or distortions of reality, misaligned interpretation, inaccurate judgments, and bad decisions.[19] When these factors are applied to an organization, it can spell trouble: taking action based on a limited set of information, overconfidence in the organization's ability to win, or an attachment to the past. As Nobel Prize–winning economist Daniel Kahneman says in *Thinking, Fast and Slow*, "We are prone to overestimate how much we understand about the world."

In a transformational situation, an accurate and compelling perspective is a make-or-break factor for the following three reasons:

1. **Having a brutal fact assessment is a key foundation for starting a transformation.** If you review your current situation and where the world is going with the rose-colored glasses of what worked in the past, there won't be any drive for change. Clinging on to dated beliefs then becomes a too-attractive distortion. The doomed, status quo forces stay in place and win.

2. Creating with an open-minded view on how the world is changing without falling into the new distortions of reality is a key to start crafting the right strategy. If you create the wrong assumptions or quickly become "religious" with new beliefs about how your market is changing, you might understand the need for change but then decide to transform in the wrong direction based on new blind spots and distortions.

---

19   J. Taylor, "Cognitive Biases Are Bad for Business," *Psychology Today*, 2013.

3. **Defining positive and compelling assumptions is an important part of motivating your employees and other stakeholders.** Even if you opened your mind to the brutal facts of the current reality and to new key developments, you can still develop a negatively formulated belief set that jeopardizes your change program. For example, do you define a new technology as a threat or as an opportunity?

> **NETFLIX VS. BLOCKBUSTER**
>
> Serial entrepreneurs Reed Hastings and Marc Randolph were looking to start a new venture after selling their previous company. Hunting for some new perspective on an industry, they began connecting the dots on the state of the video rental market, dots to which established players seemed to be blind. They were intrigued by what Amazon was doing at the time—skipping the store altogether and delivering directly to consumers—so they began applying the same perspective to video rentals.
>
> Hastings had recently had the personal experience of paying a $40 late fee when he returned a copy of *Apollo 13* on VHS to Blockbuster, and this unpleasant fee gave him inspiration that resulted in an opportunity to disrupt a billion-dollar market.[20] A new, compact, and lightweight form of media called DVDs were on the rise, and they decided to try their hand at sending DVDs by regular mail, a business that worked well and at a low cost. As a result they started Netflix in 1998, beginning with a library of around nine hundred titles and a team of only thirty employees.

---

20 A. Ash, "The Rise and Fall of Blockbuster and How It's Surviving with Just One Store Left," *Business Insider*, 2020.

In 2000 as Netflix reached its three hundred thousand subscribers and had around one hundred employees, they needed capital. At only two years old, the DVD rental business was still enduring heavy losses. Hastings thought it would make sense to reach out to the industry leader, Blockbuster, to propose a partnership. At the time, Blockbuster was the dominant leader in the video rental business with $6 billion in revenues, nine thousand rental stores around the world, and sixty thousand employees. This position would have made them the perfect partners for Netflix.

After months of trying to get a meeting with Blockbuster's CEO, they were invited to the twenty-seventh floor of the Blockbuster headquarters in Dallas. Hastings and Randolph proposed that Blockbuster purchase Netflix and that they would then collectively develop and run Blockbuster.com together as an online video rental arm. The idea was flatly rejected by Blockbuster. The industry giant believed that, as they were the biggest and most successful, they didn't need help from a start-up. Their perspective was that their model was so strong that it would continue to work and that an investment in a start-up was unnecessary.

Luckily for Netflix their business continued to grow, and they became profitable several years later. But that wasn't enough. The company wanted to disrupt their own model almost immediately. Hastings realized that online streaming was coming and that it would become big business in the near future.[21] They started to invest in the online space and saw it as a tremendous opportunity because it would fun-

---

21 R. Hastings, "How I Did It: The Founder of Netflix on Developing a Passion Brand, and Sustaining It as Passions Change," *Inc.*, 2005.

> damentally eliminate their mailing costs. They wanted to be ready when the shift to video on demand happened. As video on demand took off over the next six years, Netflix would go on to dominate the market.
>
> Although late, Blockbuster had first tried to counter Netflix by propping up their value proposition via reducing late fees and by investing in their own online service. This, however, was perceived by the supervisory board as cannibalization, and a new CEO undid the changes and restored the company's focus on short-term profit tactics, locking in Blockbuster's outdated perspective paradigm and accelerating its collapse. By 2005 Blockbuster had lost 75 percent of its market value and eventually filed for bankruptcy in 2010.[22]

2.4 How Do You Score on the Perspective Wing?

Where do you currently stand in regard to the quality of your perspective and its power in your Flywheel of Transformation? We have defined four levels for a self-diagnostic to evaluate whether your perspective is accurate and compelling for key stakeholders.

- **Level 1. No or Limited Power: The company has an outdated or misinterpreted perspective (an incorrect map of the territory).** On this level the facts that contradict the current belief about where the market is heading and what it

---

22 F. Olito, "The Rise and Fall of Blockbuster," *Business Insider*, 2020.

takes to be successful in that market are pushed aside. Setbacks are seen as incidents and not as trends. Beliefs about how things are and what made the company successful are almost proudly and religiously held on to, as in the Kodak case, where the company religiously believed that photos taken with film technology would continue to be superior to the then emerging digital technology. There are no active processes to get new insights and pressure test assumptions by, for example, talking to frontline workers or customers or consulting other information sources.

- **Level 2. Some Power: A new perspective has developed but has no traction.** At this level there is actual room and some open-mindedness regarding the brutal facts and possible trends. These elements are also discussed on senior levels. There is, however, a strong debate between believers and deniers. It stays at a standstill and a newer, more accurate set of assumptions and beliefs has not yet emerged. The new beliefs are seen as a threat by many, as their power and influence might be reduced by acting on these new insights.

- **Level 3. Good Power: A new perspective has developed and is propelling the business forward.** The company is proactively developing a fresh perspective on the market and the business by, for example, using third-party consultants, recognizing a crisis of declining market shares and financial performance, courting new investors, or acquiring new leadership. A new perspective based on new facts and insights is created after challenging debates. Although the deniers still have a voice, the status quo paradigm has been broken. Based on the changed perspective, changes are actually put in motion in the organization. However, there is still some question as to the efficacy of the new belief set. Some dated beliefs and ideas still hold sway.

- **Level 4. Transformative Power: A new perspective is fully developed, enacted, and regularly questioned.** Similar to level 3, a new, more accurate perspective has been developed, and a change program has been set in motion. However, at level 4 the new perspective gets regularly pressure-tested and is updated where needed to limit distortions and blind spots. Organizational learning becomes part of the culture of the organization. Netflix, for example, first disrupted video rentals by using mail and then used streaming video to disrupt the movie-by-mail model. They continually explored new avenues on an institutional level.

PERSPECTIVE WING

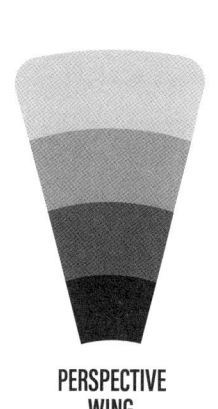

WING-POWER LEVEL		YOUR SCORE?
LEVEL 4	TRANSFORMATIVE POWER	
LEVEL 3	GOOD POWER	
LEVEL 2	SOME POWER	
LEVEL 1	NO POWER	

PETER: CREATING AN EMPOWERING LEADERSHIP PERSPECTIVE WHEN FACING CHANGE RESISTANCE

Our subconscious and our emotions are the biggest influence on our perceptions, which can lead us to override rational thinking. Therefore, it's important to become aware of your perspective limitations by being aware of these factors.

For example, I was once asked to coach a senior leader in a large pharmaceutical company who needed to lead a change program. As he encountered resistance to the changes he wanted to institute, his behavior had become increasingly negative, which had a knock-on effect on the execution of the new business strategy. His perspective was that his team was reluctant to follow his lead and make changes in the business. He started to blame the team and placed himself in a victim role, which shifted his negative emotions onto his subordinates. When you constantly shift responsibility for negative results from yourself to others, it's easy to create a perpetuating cycle of negativity because negativity rewires your brain for more negativity. In this instance the resistant behavior, the team, and his emotional state are all connected.

The biggest problem, however, was that he believed the cause of these negative results was the resistance of his team, which turned his perception into reality. To unlock this dynamic, he had to shift his mindset and his perspective on the situation to a more empowering worldview. When he began to realize that he was 100 percent responsible for all of the results and that nobody was to blame, he gained the ability to challenge this negative narrative and see the situation in a positive light. As a result he began to engage with his team in a constructive way and was able to focus on finding solutions. This not only created an aligned leadership team but also shifted the execution of his strategy into high gear.

To strengthen the perspective wing of the Transformational Flywheel, you need not only to find new perspectives in the market and the business but also to review your own perspective on your emotions, behaviors, and key beliefs. Your perceptions determine your perspective of your own behavior and, in turn, the results you achieve. It's essential to continuously pressure test the way you perceive things, to reframe negativity, and to update perspectives that don't serve the transformational journey.

2.5 How Can You Strengthen Your Perspective Wing?

So how can you strengthen the perspective wing of the Transformational Flywheel? There are several practices you might consider.

1. **Make the pressure-testing of beliefs and assumptions a key part of the management routine.** Have sessions to make this

process explicit. What do we believe is true? How do we know it's true? Where needed, agree to pressure-test these assumptions.

2. Actively and regularly hunt for new insights while striving to get more homogeneous input.
   - Engage with the people in your organization who are closest to the customers—what do they hear and see?
   - Talk to customers and ask how they see the market changing and how they see your business.
   - Ask new employees about their observations—what does and doesn't make sense in their eyes.
   - Visit start-ups in your space and ask what their beliefs are about the market.

3. **Engage in double- and triple-loop learning.** Former Harvard professor Chris Argyris defined the three levels of learning in which a leadership team can engage.
   - On the first level, *single-loop learning*, outcomes that don't fit with the current beliefs are seen as abnormalities and neglected.
   - The next level is *double-loop learning*. At this level unexpected outcomes are used to ask what we can learn and how that might change an assumption. Somewhat negatively these new assumptions then become a strong belief again.
   - The third level is *triple-loop learning*. At this level you create a new perspective and act with conviction but keep an open mind to adapt the belief again when needed. It's being confident but not being too confident.

4. **Use a testing attitude.** Instead of having long debates about beliefs in a boardroom, it can be much more effective to decide

on defining a testing experiment to engage in learning. At Google, for example, rapid experimentation is the way assumptions get quickly tested instead of endlessly debated in abstract.

5. **Become more of an outside-in leader.** The outside-in principle is laid out well in Herminia Ibarra's book, *Act Like a Leader, Think Like a Leader*.[23] She writes that reflection without new actions and insights is not that helpful. Several things you might consider are spending more time with an outside network than with the internal usual suspects with the same belief set. Spend more time away from the day-to-day dance floor and more time on the balcony.

6. **Adapt a growth mindset as an organization.** Carol Dweck, in her book *Mindset*, showed a lot of evidence supporting the benefits of a growth mindset that is focused on learning, sees failures as an opportunity, and likes trying new things. It's an attitude not of knowing it all but of learning it all.

---

23 H. Ibarra, *Act Like a Leader, Think Like a Leader* (Harvard Business School Publishing, 2016).

References

Vance, A. "Elon Musk: Tesla, SpaceX, and the Quest for a Fantastic Future." *Ecco*, 2015.

Klebnikov, S. "Tesla Is Now the World's Most Valuable Car Company with a $208 Billion Valuation," *Forbes* (2020). https://www.forbes.com/sites/sergeiklebnikov/2020/07/01/tesla-is-now-the-worlds-most-valuable-car-company-with-a-valuation-of-208-billion/?sh=407ea7345334.

Estrin, J. "Kodak's First Digital Moment." *New York Times*, 2015. https://lens.blogs.nytimes.com/2015/08/12/kodaks-first-digital-moment/.

Taylor, J. "Cognitive Biases Are Bad for Business." *Psychology Today*, 2013. https://www.psychologytoday.com/us/blog/the-power-prime/201305/cognitive-biases-are-bad-business.

Ash, A. "The Rise and Fall of Blockbuster and How It's Surviving with Just One Store Left." *Business Insider*, 2020. https://www.businessinsider.com/the-rise-and-fall-of-blockbuster-video-streaming-2020-1?international=true&r=US&IR=T.

Hastings, R. "How I Did It: The Founder of Netflix on Developing a Passion Brand, and Sustaining It as Passions Change." *Inc.*, 2005. https://www.inc.com/magazine/20051201/qa-hastings.html.

Olito, F. "The Rise and Fall of Blockbuster." *Business Insider*, 2020. https://www.businessinsider.nl/rise-and-fall-of-blockbuster?international=true&r=US.

Argyris, C. "Teaching Smart People How to Learn." *Harvard Business Review*, 1991. https://hbr.org/1991/05/teaching-smart-people-how-to-learn.

Ibarra, H. *Act Like a Leader, Think Like a Leader*. Harvard Business School Publishing, 2016.

INNER GAME POWER

- 1. PURPOSE
- 2. PERSPECTIVE
- 3. POSITION
- 4. PRIORITIES
- 5. PEOPLE
- 6. PRINCIPLES
- 7. PROMOTION
- 8. PROGRESS
- 9. PASSION
- 10. POLITICAL
- 11. PARTY
- 12. PAY-OFF

CHAPTER 3

POSITION

Price is what you pay. Value is what you get.
—WARREN BUFFETT, CEO OF BERKSHIRE HATHAWAY

3.1 INTRODUCTION: STARBUCKS

Nearly thirty years ago, Starbucks was founded with a new value proposition: bring the Italian coffee experience to America.[24] While on a trip to a coffee conference in Milan, Howard Schultz had experienced the symphony of Italian coffeehouses. He was overwhelmed by the communal feeling of belonging. He reveled in the full-sensory experience. "The Italians had created the theater, romance, art and magic of experiencing espresso," Schultz recalled.[25] In 1970s America, there was nothing romantic about coffee.

---

24 H. Schultz, *Onward: How Starbucks Fought for Its Life without Losing Its Soul* (John Wiley & Sons, 2011).

25 "A Dream Thirty-Three Years in the Making, Starbucks to Open in Italy," Starbucks, 2015.

Styrofoam cups, drive-through queues, and burnt-filter Americanos defined the times. With this new perspective, he saw a new market position in the United States. Just like in Italy, Starbucks could become the "third place" beside home and work. If you infused this emotion and meaning into the ordinary act of getting a coffee, Starbucks could create more value for consumers and consequently build a new market to play in.

Buying into the local Seattle Starbucks coffee shop where he used to work, he started building out his vision. "We began to elevate the romance and theater of the beverage, integrated with the merchandising and storytelling of roasting and selling whole bean coffee."[26] The company's growth increased dramatically, and just ten years later, there were 3,500 Starbucks stores around the globe. By 2000 Schultz stepped down as CEO, and over the next seven years, the company continued to expand at a rapid rate. As they continued to succeed, Starbucks' investors and management became addicted to opening new stores. Their uniquely defined position seemed to work well.

However, in late 2007, when Schultz walked into a Seattle Starbucks store, something hit him. He didn't smell coffee anymore, only burned cheese. To drive sales Starbucks had begun to offer warm bacon and egg sandwiches. Luscious aromas of earth, spice, chocolate, and floral notes were replaced by Monterey Jack, mozzarella, and cheddar. He saw that Starbucks stores had stopped grinding their coffee in store, instead opting for preground beans for cost-sav-

---

26   Ibid.

ing reasons. The original La Marzocco espresso machines had been replaced with push-and-pour machines, removing the sense of craftsmanship the old machines brought. These new machines were also much higher than before, isolating the customer and barista in their own separate worlds. Those daily conversations, which were integral in fostering a sense of community, started to get lost. Shifts in the competitive landscape had also caught Howard's attention. McDonald's and Dunkin' Donuts had begun encroaching from the low end with their own coffee offering. On the high end, hip boutique coffee shops began popping up across urban areas. Based on the drive for new store openings, the rigid location criteria were loosened as well. All of these were smaller, gradual changes, but they combined to weaken Starbucks' market position.

When Schultz raised his concerns that the position of Starbucks was eroding, he was basically ignored by its leadership. The numbers were still strong. Then as the global financial crisis broke, Starbucks' performance began to erode—and fast. Just as Schultz had feared, customers started to come to their Starbucks less often.[27] To regain an air of stability, the board then turned to Howard for guidance, and he was reinstated as CEO in early 2008.

Schultz set in motion not only a turnaround effort but also a transformation focused on strengthening the value proposition that Starbucks was offering its customers. To achieve this he did a range of things. He went back to Starbucks' roots to clarify and communicate the company's purpose: "To inspire

---

27 L. Wayne, "Starbucks Chairman Fears Tradition Is Fading," *New York Times*, 2007, https://www.nytimes.com/2007/02/24/business/24coffee.html.

and nurture the human spirit—one person, one cup and one neighborhood at a time." He began to communicate his perspective on the current economic reality and some brutal facts and related the other challenges the business faced. After establishing the present-day context, he defined the intended future position of substantially strengthening the value proposition offered by Starbucks and pursuing a clear transformation agenda with discrete priorities:

1. Be the undisputed coffee authority.
2. Engage and inspire our partners.
3. Ignite the emotional attachment with our customers.
4. Expand our global presence—while making each store the heart of a local neighborhood.
5. Be a leader in ethical sourcing and environmental impact.
6. Create innovation growth platforms worthy of our coffee.
7. Deliver a sustainable economic model.

Schultz also assembled a new leadership team that included some former leaders who knew what Starbucks and coffee experience was about. To complete the transition, he also hired world-class functional experts. Based on the clarity of the future position and well-defined organizational priorities, he ran an intensive two-year program, then took turnaround measures like closing 600 stores. He and his team set up a transformation agenda focused on improving the value proposition by doing the following:

- Put coffee at the center of the Starbucks experience once again—while also dramatically increasing the quality of their coffee. This measure required a real innovation path that demanded they rediscover the craft of roasting

and experimenting with bean combinations. After many attempts this led to their winning offer of Pike Place Roast and the placement of new beans in store.
- Make an incredible investment by training the entirety of their barista workforce to make the very best espresso by closing all of their stores for a day.
- Modernize the look and feel of the stores with local designers and materials to make them more connected with the community.
- Invest in loyal customers by creating a loyalty program, Mystarbucks.com, and engaging with them on how to improve their experience.
- Empower store managers and their teams by running lean operational programs and providing tools like laptops.
- Bring all baristas together for a big, spirit-lifting celebration and community service event based around the recovery in New Orleans, which had recently been devastated by Hurricane Katrina.
- Continue to invest in healthcare and stock plans for all their partners (as Starbucks employees are called).
- Hire experts to overhaul the entire supply chain, as by 2008 only 30 percent of the orders made by the store managers were delivered incorrectly, creating many out-of-stock situations.

Starbucks' transformation wasn't easy. Schultz had to continuously convince his board, and Wall Street, of his strategy, which had a short-term negative effect on the financials.[28] He warned the shareholders that the stock price would go down before it went up, and there was a lot

---

28   Ibid.

> of pushback. While he was hounded to cut everything from the company's training days to their healthcare benefits, he refused. He felt these benefits were a key part of the principles and culture of Starbucks.
>
> In less than two years, the company had turned around and transformed and was back on a growth path. Customer experience was revived, and Starbucks' employees delivered on the company's new proposition. Schultz's success is partly reflected by the fact that the company's stock price went up by 400 percent over the next decade.

3.2 What Is the Position Wing on the Flywheel of Transformation?

So what do we mean with position in the Flywheel of Transformation? We define it as the future position the organization intends to adopt. Every organization has a future position—the only question is whether it's implicitly or explicitly defined. If it's not clear, your current position is, by default, your future position. In the context of the Flywheel of Transformation, we define the future position as how an organization chooses to change, in which arenas it does business, and what parameters it defines as winning. In *Playing to Win: How Strategy Really Works*, the former CEO of P&G, Alan G. Lafley, and Roger Martin, the former Dean of the Rotman School of Management, claim that the heart of both strategy and posi-

> If it's not clear, your current position is, by default, your future position.

tioning is the answer to these two seemingly simple questions: "where to play?" and "how to win?"[29]

Typical questions that need to be clarified in defining the future position based on "where to play?" are the following:

- What types of customers should be targeted?
- What kinds of products and services should be offered?
- Which geographies should you operate in? In what countries or regions?
- What price tier is the product/service?
- Which distribution channels should be used to reach the customers?
- In what stages of production should you engage? Where along the value chain do you play?

So what then do we mean when we ask, how to win? "How to win?" strategies can be translated to what value proposition you offer to your customers. What are typical questions one must ask to find your value proposition?

- How is the service/product to offer unique compared to that of the competition?
- Are you competing on cost and scale, innovation, service, or customer intimacy?
- What unique capabilities and systems will you have?
- What makes your offering difficult to copy?
- How do you scale and grow your model?

---

29 R. Martin et al., *Playing to Win: How Strategy Really Works* (Harvard Business Review Press, 2013).

- How will you generate profits or cash?

The answer to these two questions creates two fundamental choices in determining your future target position.

- Do you stay in the same playing field or transition to a different one?
- Do you need to fundamentally reinvent your value proposition or "way to win"?

To demonstrate, this matrix illustrates the four fundamental options with practical examples of each:

WHERE TO PLAY?

HOW TO WIN?	Play in the same space	Move to a new or additional place to play
Strengthen current way to win	Starbucks	Amazon
Fundamentally redefine way to win	Netflix Zappos Tesla	Apple Phillips

Play in the same position, strengthening the value proposition. In the Starbucks case, Schultz assessed that the market Starbucks was playing in was still very attractive and that they had a leading position in terms of market share, brand, and other key factors. The focus was, therefore, on strengthening the value proposition and to start winning again.

Add new places to play with a similar way to win. Amazon, after creating a winning model by offering books online, wanted to transform to the next level by leveraging the way they were already winning. They accomplished this by expanding to other product categories and other countries selling online.

Play in an existing space; win with a new value proposition. In the case of Netflix, they were initially competing with a DVD-by-mail service in the already existing home movie market and were modestly successful against the incumbent industry leader. When they decided to innovate and offer direct video streaming, they created a substantially stronger value proposition, forcing Blockbuster out of business.

Play in a new space; win with a new value proposition. When Steve Jobs came back to Apple, he analyzed that Apple's PC market was becoming less attractive and determined that Apple couldn't win there anymore. As a result he changed planets and created a whole new future position with the invention of hardware like the iPod, iPhone, and iPad as well as revolutionary software marketplaces like iTunes and the Apple App Store.

Defining a compelling future position can create a flywheel effect that infuses power into a transformation, and although it's both science and art, there are some common aspects that a strong future position will share:

- It's based on penetrating insights and new perspectives.
- It's decisive, making a clear choice.
- It builds on key strengths the current business possesses.
- It's differentiating and not driven by competitor benchmarks.
- It's ambitious but not overwhelming or just a pipe dream.
- It's not a Don Quixote strategy that involves attacking strong or imaginary competitors head-on.

- It's attractive and positively formulated, creating meaning for the venture.

- It's a real future flag in the ground and not an often moved "new program of the month."

- Some clear stepping-stones are laid down to facilitate progress toward that future position.

- It balances optimizing the current position with investing in a new position.

What current explicit or implicit future position are you navigating toward?

> **MARCO: THE POWER OF PLANTING A CLEAR FUTURE POSITION FLAG IN THE GROUND**
>
> When I was at McKinsey early in my career, I followed my passion and focused on transformational business situations. One of the businesses we had the privilege of supporting was a multibillion-euro global specialized nutrition company that was in trouble. After multiple years of implementing some unfocused strategies, the rise of a stiflingly complex internal bureaucracy, and overreaching acquisitions, the company had become stagnant, and the stock price was on a downward spiral.
>
> The supervisory board appointed a new dynamic CEO. On what was literally his first official day of work, he asked us into his office to help with a transformational program. He immediately applied quite a range of what I would now call

the flywheel wings, such as assembling a new leadership team, conducting a deep-dive analysis of the business and getting accurate perspectives, setting up a transformation program to drive progress, and celebrating milestones in a party-type way.

But maybe the biggest driver of this transformation was that he had put a clear future position on the horizon. The position was about becoming a high-growth and high-margin nutrition company. This new position, in turn, caused a cascade of actions:

- A large portion of the business was sold, including a large US vitamin business that did not fit the new future position, as it had only moderate growth and a moderate margin. This was a bold move in line with the new position, as the business represented more than half the overall business.
- A new leadership team was formed with experienced and younger talents who could deliver on the ambition.
- To drive the high margin and high growth, innovation was needed in the core business. Since the business hadn't innovated for years in their product offerings, it was needed fast. We created cross-functional innovation booster teams. Within two months we had finalized an agenda for concrete innovations and launch dates.
- The high-margin, high-growth position also caused us to review how all sales and marketing investments were done. Budgets were made on a more zero-based budgeting approach and initiatives, and countries with

> high-growth plans could apply every year for funding.
> - It was key to dramatically step up the quality of the products, and the whole supply chain was reviewed step by step and upgraded.

As noted, of course, there were many other things done, but having put this guiding future position on the horizon eventually led to a remarkable turnaround of the business; and five years later, the company was acquired by an eyebrow-raising, high amount by a leading global consumer goods player.

3.3 Why Is It Important to Have a Strong Position Wing?

As mentioned before, every organization has an implicit or explicit future position to where they are heading, even if you choose, by default, to stay in the same space with the same strategy to win; that's a choice. What's important, according to the 2019 *McKinsey Quarterly* article "Why Your Next Transformation Should Be 'All-In,'" is acknowledging change. "The structural attractiveness of markets, and your position in them, can and does change over time. Ignore this and you might be shifting deck chairs on the *Titanic*."[30] Challenging this implied future position and defining an alternative future position that is compelling to key stakeholders is important for three main reasons:

- **A compelling future target gives a reason to leave the current status quo.** Changing organizations is hard, as there is always a substantial gravity toward staying in line with the

---

30 C. Bradley et al., "Why Your Next Transformation Should Be 'All-In,'" *McKinsey Quarterly*, McKinsey & Company.

status quo. It becomes easier to galvanize the transformational change in an organization if you have a compelling future that pulls the organization forward with magnetic power.

- **A precise future target gives direction and allows for making trade-offs along the transformation journey.** Every organization has limited financial resources, human resources/talent, capabilities, and time. Having an enticing target makes it easier to make the necessary trade-offs regarding where or where not to invest resources. The same is true for mergers and acquisitions portfolio decisions in terms of where to divest and what to acquire.

- **Choosing a future position and going on that journey comes at a cost.** In a transformational situation, an organization often has to do two things at once: improve or turn around the existing business while also building a new position, both of which demand a substantial effort from the organization. If the new position is chosen wisely and each change is a stepping-stone toward that better future, confidence grows, commitment grows, and energy gets released. If, however, the new position is chosen poorly (or not at all) and a U-turn has to be made, confidence can erode; time is lost, giving competitors the opportunity to gain ground; and financial resources will have been wasted.

It can all be boiled down to the ancient proverb "Where there is no vision, the people perish."

3.4 How Do You Score on the Position Wing?

How strong is your position wing in your Flywheel of Transformation? To help you assess where you stand, we have defined four simple levels for an initial assessment. How will you score your business? Where will your employees score the organization based on clarity and movement toward a winning future position? Your customers? Your suppliers? Your investors?

- **Level 1. No or Limited Power: All focus on the current position and no real future position defined.** There is no real future position defined. The focus is entirely on optimizing the current position. This is often based on the assumption that the future will be similar to the current situation or that the business faces challenges and opportunities that require no change. The organization is not investing in a future position and is heavily focused on optimizing the current. If management is asked where the company is heading, the answers are conflicting.

- **Level 2. Some Power: Some future defined but regularly changing and no real commitment.** External changes have been analyzed, and some future position is defined on paper—often with help of an external advisor. Some initiatives may be shown; however, there is no significant commitment, and no tough decisions are taken to steer the organization in this new direction. The future position may be regularly changed when there are setbacks or economic headwinds, when momentary opportunities emerge, or when some flavor-of-the-moment programs arise.

- **Level 3. Good Power: Future position defined and rationally driven.** At this level there is a clear and compelling future position defined. There is a road map with tangible milestones and a serious intent to go on the journey to create this new position. The future position is regularly communicated. However, the future position is not unique and may not create real enthusiasm. Also, not all the necessary hard decisions are taken to really let go of the current position and go all in toward the future position.

- **Level 4. Transformative Power: Magnetic future position.** A clear, unique future position has been defined based on a clear perspective on future trends and both current strengths and weaknesses. There is an understanding that there will be setbacks and difficult moments before one reaches the promised land. The new position is communicated consistently, and most stakeholders can see the attractiveness of the new position as well as the potential threat of maintaining the status quo. Energy, time, resources, and management attention are appropriately allocated between the current organization and the new position. Smart bets are made in the direction of the new.

What is the current score of your business? Is there room for improvement? What is your ambition level for this wing of the flywheel?

POSITION WING

	WING-POWER LEVEL	YOUR SCORE?
LEVEL 4	TRANSFORMATIVE POWER	
LEVEL 3	GOOD POWER	
LEVEL 2	SOME POWER	
LEVEL 1	NO POWER	

PETER: RESOLVING THE BUSINESS'S FUTURE POSITION WITH THE LEADER'S DESIRED FUTURE POSITION

It's important not only to define a compelling future position for the organization but also to make sure that, as a leader, this future position is aligned with your personal goals. Where do you want to stand professionally in, say, three years? Is this aligned with the transformation journey? If there is a gap, energy will be lost; and as a result, it will be difficult to be fully committed as the transformation's leader.

For example, I once worked with an energy company that was changing their future position. Like many businesses they were embarking on their digital transformation journey into different market segments with different products. Having grown rapidly, the business was experiencing growing pains, and the leadership style no longer matched the size or desired professionalism of the organization. This challenge stemmed from the two co-owners—one a founder/executive and one a nonexecutive co-owner—who were at odds about their own position within the organization. While both agreed on the direction of the company, their individual notions of their respective future positions did not match.

The executive maintained his founder's mentality while the co-owner saw that this was a problem for the organization. The company was the executive's baby. It was an embodiment of his own purpose and perspective, one that he had set for himself long ago. He felt responsible for everything.

Something had to shift, as this was hampering the transformation of the company toward this new future position. We helped the executive by providing him with the brutal facts on what was needed for the organization to transform. In parallel we provided him as well as the broader leadership team with coaching, as there was a real need to shift the mindset and way of running the business.

By the end of this process, the executive realized that to make his dream of the future of this business real, he had to step away from day-to-day leadership. Both he and the organization would be better off if he took up the role of a shareholder—to influence and lead the transformation from the role that the company needed. As his own position evolved, his relationship with the other co-owner began to mend as well.

When the future position is fully aligned with the capabilities and motivations of leaders, it provides power to the transformation. If, however, there is too much misalignment, roles need to shift. Taking a position of emotional distance and challenging your own personal position as a leader is the first step toward a better overall position.

3.5 How Can You Strengthen Your Position Wing?

Although there is no cookie-cutter approach for the position wing, our experience has revealed that exploring several of the following steps are helpful:

1. Clarify what the current future position is; where is the company heading?
   - Ask the leadership team to separately write it down.
   - Look at recent years' bigger investments, resource shifts, mergers and acquisitions, and other fiscal allocations.
   - Ask customers, employees, and suppliers about where they see the company going.
   - Look at recent strategy documents.
2. Assess if your current future position is the right one and whether it's compelling.
   - Define where you operate in the 2 × 2 matrix (on page 74).
   - Assess where your competitors and new players operate and are heading.
   - Test how excited your team is about this future direction.
   - Define what key technology, customers, and regulatory trends are and how these do or do not fit with the current future position.
   - Answer the question "If you could set up the business from scratch, how would you do it?"
3. Define an improved, compelling future position.
   - Lay out the different options of "where to win?" and "how to win?"
   - Evaluate the options.
   - Make a real decision and create focus.
   - Test if it fits with the purpose and perspective of the organization.

- Test if the choice resonates with key stakeholders.

4. Create momentum behind the future position.
    - Create a road map of future stepping-stones.
    - Create quick-win momentum to build confidence.
    - Allocate the right leaders to the new initiatives.
    - Communicate, communicate, communicate the what, why, and how.

References

Schultz, H. Onward: *How Starbucks Fought for Its Life without Losing Its Soul*. John Wiley & Sons, 2011.

"A Dream Thirty-Three Years in the Making, Starbucks to Open in Italy." Starbucks, 2015. https://stories.starbucks.com/stories/2016/howard-schultz-dream-fulfilled-starbucks-to-open-in-italy/#:~:text=Schultz%20went%20to%20Italy%20to,experiencing%20espresso%2C%E2%80%9D%20Schultz%20recalled.

Schultz, H. "The Commoditization of the Starbucks Experience." Oxford University Press, 2007. https://global.oup.com/us/companion.websites/fdscontent/uscompanion/us/static/companion.websites/9780199379996/pdf/ch7/Starbucks_Memo.pdf.

Wayne, L. "Starbucks Chairman Fears Tradition Is Fading." *New York Times*, 2007. https://www.nytimes.com/2007/02/24/business/24coffee.html.

Martin, R., and A. Lafley. *Playing to Win: How Strategy Really Works*. Harvard Business Review Press, 2013.

Bradley, C., M. de Jong, and W. Walden. "Why Your Next Transformation Should Be 'All-In.'" *McKinsey Quarterly*. McKinsey & Company, 2019. https://www.mckinsey.com/business-functions/strategy-and-corporate-finance/our-insights/why-your-next-transformation-should-be-all-in.

Pooler, M. "Philips Lights on AI to Target Growth in Healthcare." *Financial Times*. https://www.ft.com/content/ce8f3c4a-20bf-11e9-b2f7-97e4dbd3580d.

INNER GAME POWER

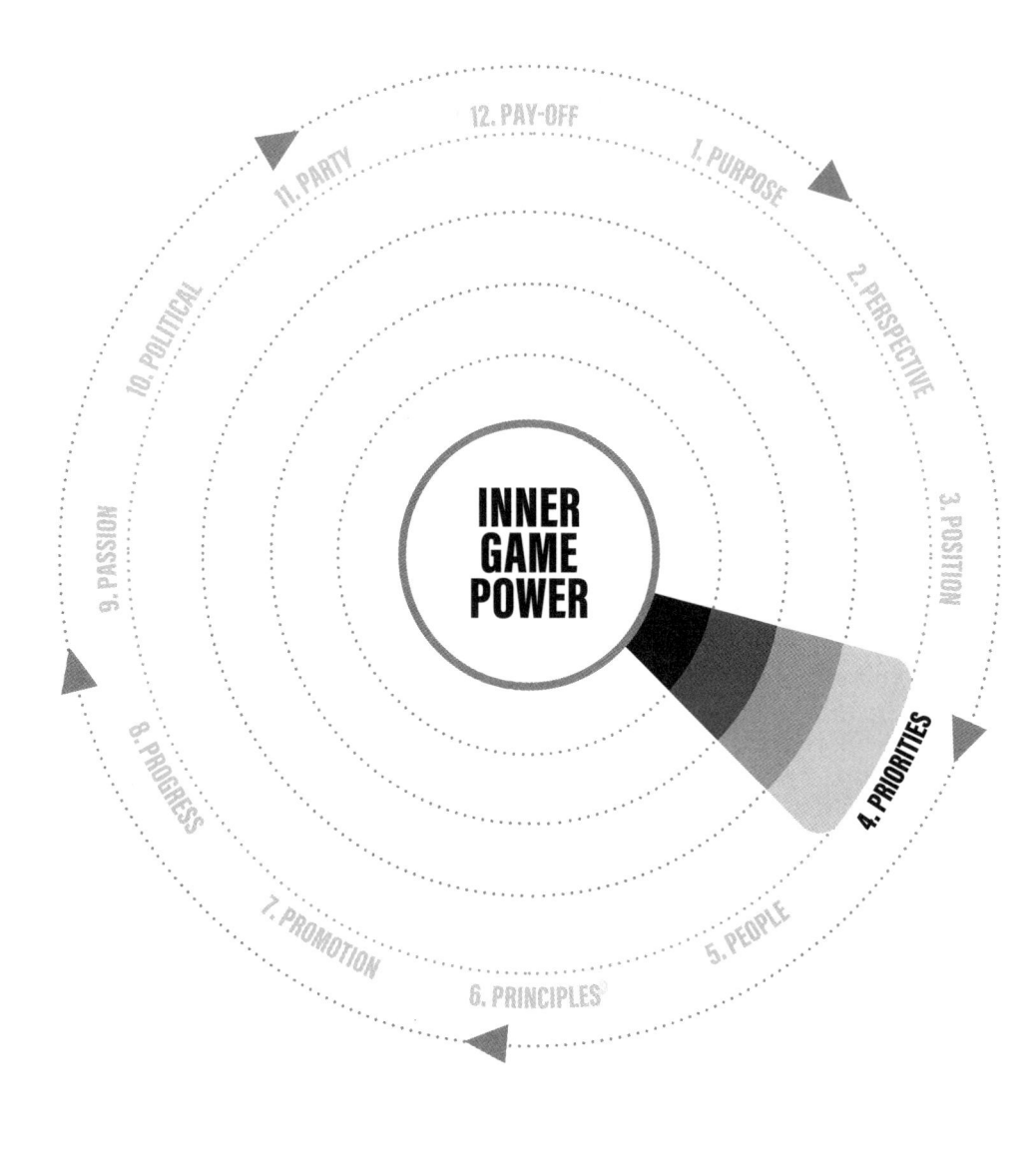

- 1. PURPOSE
- 2. PERSPECTIVE
- 3. POSITION
- **4. PRIORITIES**
- 5. PEOPLE
- 6. PRINCIPLES
- 7. PROMOTION
- 8. PROGRESS
- 9. PASSION
- 10. POLITICAL
- 11. PARTY
- 12. PAY-OFF

CHAPTER 4

PRIORITIES

Lack of time is actually lack of priorities.
—TIMOTHY FERRIS, ENTREPRENEUR
AND BEST-SELLING AUTHOR

4.1 INTRODUCTION: DISNEY

Regardless of where you were born, it's almost inevitable that Disney has had an impact on your childhood, just like those of millions of other children around the globe. From the original *Mary Poppins* to the remake of *The Lion King*, no other entertainment company has had as much of an impact on popular culture as Disney. However, after several decades of success, Disney had begun to lose its magic as it approached the turn of the century.

It was not creating successful new animated features and shorts, the film division was not hitting blockbusters, and their TV channel, ABC, was losing in the ratings. On top of this, a deal with Pixar had collapsed, and they had just barely fought off Comcast Corp., who had tried to take over the company. At the same time, the media landscape was changing quickly. The rise of online distribution was heavily impacting the way content was being developed, and Disney seemed ill equipped to enter this new era. The sentiment that Disney had stagnated was only amplified by Michael Eisner's long-standing position at the helm of the company.

Roy Disney, a major shareholder and then vice-chairman in the supervisory board, publicly came out and said that Disney had lost its way. He accused the company of becoming "rapacious" and "soulless" as he attempted to convince shareholders of the need for change.[31] On September 30, 2005, Eisner's two decades of reign as CEO of Disney came to an end.

The supervisory board embarked on a broad search for a new leader. The general sentiment in the press and from investors was that Disney needed an outsider. A larger-than-life figure who could facilitate a fundamental transformation was needed. There was one "token" insider—potential internal candidate Robert Iger—but few in Hollywood gave him a chance. He was seen as part of the problem, a member of Disney's old guard. Iger had enjoyed an impressive career working his way from the ground up at the American Broadcasting Company (ABC). He had, in fact, worked all the way from being a TV mechanic to the position of president and CEO. ABC Television was bought by Disney in 1996, and in 2000 he was promoted by the supervisory board to the newly created COO role to support Eisner. With this promotion he became the de

---

31 J. Bates et al., "Roy Disney Quits, Urges Eisner to Resign for Good of Company," *Los Angeles Times*, 2003.

facto second-in-command, a move that was not received with a lot of enthusiasm from Eisner.

Iger, who knew he was the dark horse of the succession search at Disney, was asked to join the job interview process alongside external candidates. To prepare he invited a political consultant, with whom he had worked in the past, to his home. From Iger's kitchen table, the consultant bluntly told him, "The only way for you to have a chance is if you aren't seen as the status quo candidate, defend the past but actively position yourself as a real change agent." He told Iger that he would need to display a strong vision for the future.

The consultant then asked Iger what his vision for the future actually was. Iger began to share all kinds of ideas and arguments on how one should change Disney. After five or six, the consultant stopped Iger in his tracks. He said, "Stop talking. Once you have that many of them, they are no longer priorities." His consultant went on to tell him that he could, in fact, only have three.[32]

The consultant explained that to change a global organization and create a focus of resources from its 130,000 employees, you can only have a few clear and simple-to-understand priorities with which they can align. A CEO must provide the company and its senior team with a road map, something that says, "This is where we want to be, and this is how we are going to get there." The longer he thought about it, the more he continued to arrive at the same main priorities for Disney:

---

[32] R. Iger, *The Ride of a Lifetime: Lessons Learned from Fifteen Years as CEO of the Walt Disney Company* (Penguin Random House LLC, 2019).

- Lead with high-quality branded content
- Embrace technology for content creation and distribution
- Become a truly global company

With a clear sense of purpose and a compelling set of priorities for Disney to pursue, he convinced the supervisory board to select him as CEO. However, the decision didn't get a great deal of applause from the external world. Jeffrey Sonnenfeld, an associate dean at the Yale School of Management, described how the Hollywood of the era thought of Iger as "a loyal drone." Sonnenfeld further said, "The expectations were so low for Bob. But no mogul in traditional entertainment has accomplished what he has."[33]

This is not where the story ends. Over the next ten to fifteen years, Iger focused relentlessly on these priorities and on communicating them consistently in order to get buy-in from his management team and stakeholders like Roy Disney. He also made daring moves that challenged Disney's dated beliefs and turned the industry on its head.

In his bid for Disney to lead in high-quality branded content, Iger uncovered a brutal fact almost by accident while at a Disneyland parade in Hong Kong. It struck him that all of the characters involved were over a decade old. What was even more concerning was that the majority were from Disney's former partnership with Pixar and not from their own animation unit. This realization pushed him to undertake further deep-dive analyses, confirming this suspicion. Iger, now armed with this ammunition, began

---

[33] M. James, "How Disney's Bob Iger Went from Underrated CEO to Hollywood Royalty," *Los Angeles Times*, 2020.

to challenge the blinded perspective—that Disney was still the leader in animated content.

Having faced the brutal facts, his first move was to extend an olive branch to Steve Jobs, who was heading Pixar at the time. During his predecessor's tenure, the relationship between the two companies had soured; there had been a clash between Jobs and Eisner. While visiting Pixar, Iger found he was impressed by the team, their dynamic culture, and how they were creating powerful characters and bringing bold stories to life. This, Iger was convinced, was the future. Soon after the relationship was repaired, Iger suggested a bold move to Jobs, a move that was seen as extremely controversial at Disney. Why not join forces? Jobs, intrigued by the audacity, went to the whiteboard and made a list of pros and cons. In 2006 a record $7.4 billion deal was closed, bringing Pixar into Disney and making Steve Jobs one of the largest shareholders of Disney.

Based on this momentum, Iger reached out to the next ambitious target—Marvel Studios. Marvel not only had blockbuster hits including *X-Men*, *Iron Man*, and *The Incredible Hulk* but they also owned the rights to over seven thousand comic book characters. In 2009 Disney purchased Marvel Entertainment for $4 billion. Iger then looked to Lucasfilm, famous for the *Star Wars* movies. This was another deal that was seen as impossible, but Iger and his team succeeded. The acquisition marked the beginning of the new era in the *Star Wars* franchise. This deal is widely regarded as one of the smartest acquisitions in American history.

To achieve his second priority, Iger unflinchingly embraced technology for content creation and distribution. The acquisition of Pixar, with their innovative team and cutting-edge culture, had once again given Disney an advantage in terms of content creation technology. But how could they resolve the distribution model? The traditional model—which saw movies released to theaters first, then to DVD, then to cable, then to TV—was outdated. New digital distribution models like Netflix and iTunes were demonstrating that the system itself was changing. Iger saw that Disney needed to make its way into the streaming market. However, as the company was still making plenty of profit, he faced a horde of internal resistance. To confront this old model, Iger would have to challenge decades-old belief sets. Iger and his team would need to disrupt their own traditional business model.

He knew that building digital distribution capabilities internally would take too long and would be too risky. They needed to find a creative solution—a solution that others did not yet see. Iger had seen ESPN, another Disney business, invest in a technology platform to stream major league baseball games. What if you could use this technology for film and TV streaming? Disney concluded that this technology platform could become a key building block in their streaming strategy. Disney Plus, the company's streaming service, is now going head-to-head with Netflix in an attempt to win the leadership in content streaming. Time will tell if they succeed, but a significant move had been made that was in line with Iger's second priority to invest in technology for creation and distribution.

Regarding his third priority, to create a truly global company, he shifted how Disney had prioritized their international business, giving it more emphasis. He continued to work hard on opening Disney World in Shanghai, expanding its strategic presence in this important growth market. In order to create a truly global presence, Iger pursued another industry-shattering deal. Iger went to visit Rupert Murdoch at his home in LA, seeing if he could create an opening in acquiring key assets from Fox, including 21st Century Fox's movie studio and its library of titles. This not only would help Disney's first priority—to be the branded content leader—but also would substantially increase the company's global footprint. Fox had a number of thriving international businesses including Star India (an Indian direct-to-home television service provider), Fox Deportes (their Spanish-language cable sports network), and FNG Asia. Rupert Murdoch, withstanding internal family pressures, agreed to the deal. This expansion greatly extended Disney's reach into China and India and gave them a foothold in the fastest-growing emerging economies across the globe.

Based on his three guiding priorities, Iger drove the company in a totally new direction that completely transformed Disney. "A CEO must provide the company and its senior team with a roadmap ... This is where we want to be. This is how we're going to get there. Once those things are laid out simply, so many decisions become easier to make."[34] In 2020 as Iger stepped down from a fifteen-year

---

34 Iger, *Ride of a Lifetime*, 101.

> stint at the helm, Disney's share price had grown by 500 percent, and the company had reclaimed its title as one of the world's leading entertainment companies.

4.2 What Is the Priority Wing on the Flywheel of Transformation?

As part of the Flywheel of Transformation, we have defined *priorities* as the top three to five main areas of targeted change in a transformation. These priorities, according to the McKinsey & Company article "Planning in an Agile Organization," should guide planning and budgeting decisions at all levels of the organization.[35] Decisions about what gets funded and what doesn't should thus be based on how each initiative supports that strategic priority.

The force of this wing in the flywheel is determined by the quality of the defined priorities as well as the level of focus, energy, and the commitment an organization puts behind them. As seen in the Disney case, their priorities were clearly defined, and significant action was undertaken to drive each. But how should you define which priorities to choose? Based on research and practice, we have identified multiple characteristics that help to create a powerful priority wing.

> Decisions about what gets funded and what doesn't should thus be based on how each initiative supports that strategic priority.

Let's first identify how to create a quality set of priorities:

---

[35] S. Comella-Dorda et al., "Planning in an Agile Organization," McKinsey & Company, 2019.

- **Select no more than five priorities.** If you exceed this number, organizations become unfocused, and trade-offs become exceedingly difficult to make.

- **Priorities should be clear and memorable.** If a priority is too long or too complex or it can't be recollected easily, it will lose its position at the front and center of people's minds.

- **Align priorities with the other wings of the flywheel.** If the priorities are aligned with the purpose of the organization as well as with its future position, it creates synergy, which in turn empowers a transformation.

- **Address the fundamental leverage points in a transformation.** Great priorities create a ripple effect of change throughout an organization.

- **Formulate positive descriptions for your priorities.** When constructing the wording for a priority, define what you want to achieve in positive terms.

- **Break the status quo.** Priorities should be ambitious enough to overcome the current situation and require real change in order to be achieved.

- **Selected priorities should strengthen each other.** Achieving one priority should help achieve the others. At a minimum priorities shouldn't be in conflict with each other.

- **Give direction to the entire organization.** It's important that everybody in an organization is able to relate to the set priorities and, in some way, contribute to pursuing them.

This brings us to our second factor for strong priorities—the driving force behind defined priorities. What characteristics ensure that a set of well-defined priorities will drive transformative force?

- **Make sure the senior leadership team is aligned behind the priorities.** If an organization senses that there is disagreement from the top, it sends conflicting signals as to what is important.

- **Repetition is everything.** Promote and communicate the priorities consistently and until you become almost sick and tired of doing so.

- **Keep the priorities consistent.** One often sees a loss of power in this area if leaders get tempted to come up with a new set of priorities after only six to twelve months. It requires discipline to stay consistent for several years without being tempted by the latest flavors of the week.

- Link priorities clearly to initiatives, KPIs, responsibilities, and incentives. What gets measured gets managed.

- **Make hard deprioritization decisions.** In many organizations it's often harder to let go of a priority than it is to set one. Only by creating space in terms of time, resources, and attention and by stopping activities can new priorities get a chance.

- **Create and share early wins for each priority.** Early wins are important momentum builders that help set a new direction and give an organization confidence.

- **Walk the talk in where you allocate your time.** Giving priorities prominent time on agendas in key meetings helps give them focus. Leaders must appropriately allocate their time in pursuit of priorities.

- **Assign key talent to priorities**. By assigning your top talents to key priorities, you not only increase the chances of success but also take them out of deprioritized areas and signal to the wider organization that career opportunities have shifted.

MARCO: SETTING PRIORITIES RIGHT OUT OF THE GATE TO SHAPE A TRANSFORMATION

Over the years I have learned the power that priorities have to drive a transformation within an organization as described. So when I stepped in as CEO of DKV Mobility, I wanted to set the organizational priorities as quickly as possible for my first term.

As context DKV Mobility is one of the leading mobility services businesses for transport companies and fleet operators in Europe. At the time, it had around €10 billion in transaction volumes on its platform, was active in over forty-five countries, and headquartered in Germany. It offered services including fuel cards, toll payment solutions, and access to the largest EV-charging network in Europe, etc. with more than 250,000 customers and 5 million users. I was asked by the shareholders to step in as a new outsider CEO to accelerate growth and lead both a digital and sustainability transformation.

In terms of priorities, I decided to do something unconventional as I had several weeks before I would officially start. I wanted the company's priorities to be clear in my first weeks and not wait until six months after my start. So I began with full immersion. I very literally read anything I could get my hands on. I spoke informally with senior leaders and then to all shareholder representatives in depth, reviewed analyst reports and competitor reports, and did additional analysis based on what I'd found. After this I tasked myself with defining the top five priorities for the next three years and considering what success might look like during that time. It was not so easy, as my lists were ending up with as many as seven or eight priorities. After several interactions and productive sparring sessions with selected stakeholders, I was able to narrow it down to five.

Based on this, I shared my priorities on the agenda of the first supervisory board meeting after I'd officially started. I convinced them to go with these priorities immediately by offering a caveat that if after nine months I saw the need to change one or two priorities, we could always change them. But if the priorities were right, we would gain nine months in the transformation by not continuing to debate them for almost a year.

To make sure everybody in leadership and the organization was aligned behind the priorities we

- conducted sessions with all senior leaders to align visions and leadership;
- started to communicate intensively the who, what, where, why, and how of the priorities;
- repeated the priorities in every presentation meeting and put large posters of the priorities in each meeting room;
- made "CEO talk" videos on each of the priorities for all employees to watch and held regular sessions with all new employees on our priorities;
- put a standard on my desk with the top five priorities for the company for the next three years and that year's related key objective;

- rolled out the overall priorities to the top fifty leaders, who were each tasked with creating their own top five priorities and each having their own standard on their desk;
- defined a whole program of initiatives behind each of the five priorities with specific responsibilities, deliverables, and a separate program office;
- started every supervisory board, management board, or broader company meeting with the top five priorities and our progress toward these endeavors;
- aligned our reporting and KPIs to the priorities;
- allocated key talents to the priorities; and
- focused our M&A agenda to the priorities.

After six months everybody understood the priorities and their role in them, and we had already created a feeling of momentum as we shared our first quick wins. We also, of course, spent time strengthening all of the other flywheel wings, but the igniter of the flywheel in this situation was setting the appropriate priorities right at front and center.

4.3 Why Is It Important to Have a Strong Priority Wing?

Why is it crucial to set priorities during a transformation? It all comes down to creating focus. Focus on where to expend energy and spend resources so that one is able to defy the inertia of the status quo and create the new—where focus goes, energy grows.

Priorities give a sense of direction and urgency. Setting clear priorities inspires an organization to change. It sets an ambitious direction toward a future destination while inviting people to join on the journey.

Priorities give guidance in resource trade-offs. Every organization has a limited number of resources when it comes to the time and focus of their employees. This is also true of financial resources and other operational realities. Strategic resource trade-offs have to be made all the time. Having clear, universally well-understood priorities gives guidance across the organization as to where to spend precious resources and where to abstain.

Priorities can spark creativity and innovation. If priorities are set correctly and require real change, they unlock the need to be creative and try different approaches. Creativity comes from rising to meet a challenge.

Priorities allow for the ability to track progress, celebrate successes, or course correctly. Having clear priorities allows us to measure progress toward the transformative future. For each priority you can measure activities, successes, and progress but also setbacks and ways to correct.

Priorities can attract the right external opportunities. When an organization has clear priorities as to its development, it often starts to attract external opportunities. For example, customers can become attracted to an organization that has a certain clarity of direction on where to go and where not. Talent can also be attracted by those priorities, which makes recruitment and hiring easier. The same is true for M&A opportunities, specific suppliers, and advisors—human beings, like an organization, that have a mission and a clear path to achieving that mission.

In an article by Chris Cancialosi in *Forbes* magazine, he interviews CEOs about their priorities. Cancialosi concludes that "those leaders who are able to identify their options and carefully select two or three key areas of focus tend to be those who make the largest sustainable gains."[36]

---

[36] C. Cancialosi, "What Are the Greatest Priorities for Rapidly Growing Companies?," *Forbes*, 2016.

4.4 How Do You Score on the Priority Wing?

How strong is the priority wing of your transformational flywheel? Is there bandwidth to give it more strength in your transformation? To help you define your current strength, we have defined four levels of strength in the flywheel. Where would you score your business, function, or team? Where would your employees score the organization on clarity and movement propelled by clear priorities? Your customers? Your suppliers? Your investors?

- **Level 1. No or Limited Power.** There are no, too many, or vaguely defined priorities. Each of the different parts of the business is optimizing their own areas due to a lack of overall priorities. Trade-offs of resources are driven by historical allocations and political games rather than analysis and need.

- **Level 2. Some Power.** Some priorities are defined, but they are regularly changed. In principle the company attempts to allocate resources based on priority, but difficult decisions are avoided. Priorities are somewhat better communicated than a business at level 1, but not all employees can recite the priorities when prompted.

- **Level 3. Good Power.** A clear set of priorities has been set and is intensively communicated. Resources are allocated based on these priorities, and progress is measured toward these priorities and is tracked and analyzed. The leadership team is aligned with the priorities and is committed. At level 3, however, not every nonessential priority has been dismissed, and those that have ceased have not been rigorously evaluated. The number of still remaining priorities may be causing initiative overload.

The priorities in place appeal to logic but not to the heart. The priority wing is not yet creating a "going through walls" level of drive.

- **Level 4. Transformative Power.** Powerful priorities have been defined, and they are communicated consistently and relentlessly. Resources are allocated to priorities in a disciplined way, and hard cuts have been made in nonpriority areas. Progress against priorities is measured and celebrated. The priorities are not only understood by everyone but they also live in the mind and heart of those involved, giving a sense of mission. Everybody is raising their game to achieve these priorities, and distractions are avoided. In level 4, priorities are aligned with the other wings of the flywheel.

What is the current score of your business, function, or team?

WING-POWER LEVEL		YOUR SCORE?
LEVEL 4	TRANSFORMATIVE POWER	
LEVEL 3	GOOD POWER	
LEVEL 2	SOME POWER	
LEVEL 1	NO POWER	

PRIORITY WING

PETER: PRIORITIZE FOCUS ON PRIORITIES

It's one thing to have defined priorities for the organization but a very different thing for leaders to keep their focus and attention on them. Being emotionally able to focus while not allowing distractions to take over is key in a change program.

Let me share an example. Once I was facilitating an off-site strategy workshop where the management team wanted to define their top three priorities. The business had a global scope based on appealing to different cultures, but their business model was being challenged by large consultancy firms. It was obvious that a transformation was needed to answer this challenge. As part of this process, they agreed that the organization's top three priorities were:

1. improving cooperation and rapport,
2. innovation, and
3. improved sales and marketing.

During a leadership meeting, I briefly stepped out of the room as their leadership went to work on detailing these priorities, and I briefly stepped out of the room. When I returned, only a short twenty minutes later, they had become completely sidetracked. The discussion had devolved into operational challenges such as creating new IT systems, which processes did not currently work, and the challenges they faced with their supply chain. What's worse, the discussion had not only moved away from the three priorities but had also taken a distinctly negative turn.

> Talking about these operational topics in an argumentative emotional state had become a pattern for the leadership. For this team it was very easy to slip back into this anchored behavior. It's so common to get caught up in details—like focusing on day-to-day problems, arguing about where things usually go wrong, or where they regularly argued—that they didn't even notice it anymore.
>
> The team had become their own anchor. Their lack of focus didn't stem from a lack of priorities but rather from their inability to focus on them. They continually kept coming together and discussing irrelevant things. Their meetings lacked structure, and this was, in turn, preventing them from focusing on the priorities.
>
> To make the team more effective, we had to shift this team dynamic. By reworking their governance and meeting structure, it was possible to restore their focus so that they could find their true priorities.

4.5 How to Strengthen the Priority Wing

How did you score? There are many things you could do to strengthen the priority wing of your Transformational Flywheel. We have listed five steps that might help you.

STEP 1. DEFINE THE PRIORITIES

- Take time to define the core priorities of your business, which will often take several iterations.

- Draft a sentence for each priority. Limit them to around five.
- Organize them in order of importance.
- Test them with several trusted people to check if they resonate.
- Check if each priority is actionable.
- Define which current priorities need to be deprioritized.
- It's also critical to have clear reasoning behind each decision on these priorities.

STEP 2. GET BUY-IN ON THE PRIORITIES

It's essential that your team (as well as key stakeholders) can see and support the priorities.

- Have one-on-ones, share these priorities, get feedback, and calibrate where necessary.
- Use some team time to review the top five priorities. Do they make sense? Are they clear? Are they compelling? Do they motivate you? Do they fit with your future target? Can you make it actionable?
- After some final input, hard-freeze the priorities and don't make more changes.

STEP 3. COMMUNICATE AND EVANGELIZE PRIORITIES

Once the priorities are landed, make sure they are extensively communicated.

- Share in one-on-ones.
- Use at team meetings, off-sites, and top one hundred meetings.
- Use internal communication tools like videos, posters, screensavers, etc.

STEP 4. OPERATIONALIZE PRIORITIES

Once priorities are communicated, it becomes key to making things happen and creating momentum.

- Align key budget and investment decisions.
- Align the M&A agenda and make portfolio moves where needed.
- Cascade the priorities into the organization. How does every leader see their personal top five priorities, and how are they aligned with the company priorities?
- Make people allocations by shifting key talent to the priority areas.
- Allocate your time to key priorities and away from nonpriorities.
- Align KPIs and measure progress toward priorities.
- Align incentives to priorities.

STEP 5: KEEP MOMENTUM AND STAY CONSISTENT

It's absolutely key to keep momentum.

- Continuously communicate the priorities (ad nauseum).
- Celebrate progress openly.
- Further sharpen the resource allocation toward priorities.
- Make priorities key agenda items for business reviews.
- Take symbolic actions that demonstrate priorities.

References

Bates, J., and R. Verrier. "Roy Disney Quits, Urges Eisner to Resign for Good of Company." *Los Angeles Times*, 2003. https://www.latimes.com/archives/la-xpm-2003-dec-01-fi-disney1-story.html.

Iger, R. *The Ride of a Lifetime: Lessons Learned from Fifteen Years as CEO of the Walt Disney Company*. Penguin Random House LLC, 2019.

James, M. "How Disney's Bob Iger Went from Underrated CEO to Hollywood Royalty." *Los Angeles Times*, 2020. https://www.latimes.com/entertainment-arts/business/story/2020-03-01/bob-iger-transformed-disney-and-hollywood.

Comella-Dorda, S., K. Kaur, and A. Zaidi. "Planning in an Agile Organization." McKinsey & Company. McKinsey Digital, 2019. https://www.mckinsey.com/business-functions/mckinsey-digital/our-insights/planning-in-an-agile-organization.

Cancialosi, C. "What Are the Greatest Priorities for Rapidly Growing Companies?" *Forbes*, 2016. https://www.forbes.com/sites/chriscancialosi/2016/03/07/what-are-the-greatest-priorities-for-rapidly-growing-companies/?sh=447c22da50c7.

INNER GAME POWER

- 1. PURPOSE
- 2. PERSPECTIVE
- 3. POSITION
- 4. PRIORITIES
- **5. PEOPLE**
- 6. PRINCIPLES
- 7. PROMOTION
- 8. PROGRESS
- 9. PASSION
- 10. POLITICAL
- 11. PARTY
- 12. PAY-OFF

CHAPTER 5

PEOPLE

People are not your most important asset. The right people are.
—**JIM COLLINS, AUTHOR OF** *GOOD TO GREAT*

5.1 INTRODUCTION: MICROSOFT

Despite its early domination of the operating system market, by 2014 Microsoft had lost its innovative edge. The company had become internally focused and siloed. It also was under threat of not adapting fast enough to new technologies like the cloud, mobile, and AI. The Microsoft of 2014 saw other technology players as enemies instead of as parts of the broader market ecosystem. As a consequence of all this, the stock price was going sideways. A transformation was clearly needed.

After a careful search, the board of directors nominated an internal candidate, Satya Nadella, to succeed Steve Ballmer and become the third CEO in Microsoft history. Satya was a native of India, and he had already been with Microsoft for over twenty years, forging a career in different roles. Most recently he was heading up the company's avant-garde cloud services, demonstrating where Microsoft needed to go.

Although he was an insider, Satya wasn't naive to the fact that Microsoft had to dramatically transform because the company was losing its way. To get what he called the "flywheel of change" spinning,[37] he formulated five *priorities*:

1. To communicate the company's mission and innovative business ambitions clearly once again
2. To drive cultural change from the bottom of the organization to the top
3. To build new and surprising partnerships that would "grow the pie" and delight customers
4. To be ready to catch the next wave of digital innovation and platform shifts with urgency
5. To put the right team in place to make the other four priorities happen

It was clear that their founding purpose, "to put a computer on every desk and in every home," had become outdated. PCs had become commonplace, and new technologies were taking over. After a period of reflection and testing with his colleagues, Microsoft announced its new mission statement: "To empower every person and every organization on the planet to achieve more."

Satya made some fundamental shifts in Microsoft's future position and made some bold choices. Although Microsoft had just spent billions acquiring Nokia, he assessed that the

---

37   S. Nadella et al., *Hit Refresh: The Quest to Rediscover Microsoft's Soul and Imagine a Better Future for Everyone* (HarperCollins, 2017).

mobile phone war was already lost. It was not possible to win there anymore. This led to the company writing off the Nokia acquisition. Instead, he defined a different view of mobile technology. It was less about creating a winning mobile offer but more about actively enabling people who were on mobile platforms—to create a seamless experience across different devices for the services Microsoft was providing.

He made a difficult decision to shift from the company's historical software distribution model and pricing and move to a cloud-first approach. They shifted the focus from software development to solutions that enabled businesses and individuals to achieve more. This decision also meant that they had to end a range of products and initiatives that did not fit this future position.

Another key factor to the flywheel of change was to create a shift in culture—what we call principles in our transformational flywheel model. Satya went on a quest to consistently communicate and act as a role model of the new culture. The following are three examples on how he approached this.

The first was to shift its internal focus and reorient it toward its customers. Everywhere he went Satya met with customers, large and small. At the new leadership's first off-site retreat, where he gathered the company's top one hundred leadership team, he revealed that teams would meet with Microsoft customers. They would consult with a wide array of customers, ranging from hospitals and retailers to small mom-and-pop stores. Microsoft's leaders were now connected to their customers, gaining insight into where their products and services needed to be changed. Second, he also changed the incentive systems to break through the silos and increase interdepartmental cooperation. Third, one of the larger initiatives Microsoft embraced, and one that cascaded across the organization, was growth mindset work from Carol Dweck. This set of ideas focused on shifting the organization from a mindset of "knowing it all" to one of "learning it all."

Satya set his sights on breaking down another long-held belief—that all innovation was better done in-house. Microsoft had always been hostile to other technology companies and saw both emerging players and major competitors as enemies. Shortly after his appointment, Satya controversially began reaching out to other technology players including Apple, Google, IBM, and Facebook to explore possible collaborations. He wanted to learn and collaborate, even if they competed in certain areas. This move sent shock waves throughout the organization.

Although Satya had defined his priorities immediately, he knew that success lay in the hands of the leadership team he was to assemble. He not only wanted to assemble the right people but also wanted to dramatically shift how the top team worked together. As was described previously, one of the major issues in Microsoft was that each department had become siloed, focusing only on defending their own specific interests and competing for resources. If the company was to truly transform, this had to change. His first steps were to begin personally inviting potential leadership talents to the newly formed top team. He also had to make some tough decisions—who to let go. Satya's dream team would be a diverse team of both insiders and outsiders who were passionate about unleashing Microsoft's potential to make a positive difference in the world. The people he assembled in his leadership team were composed of a diverse array of insiders, outsiders, and internal promotions and had a high level of diversity:

- To make a shift in Microsoft's stance on alliances, Satya personally reached out to Peggy Johnson, who had spent more than two decades at Qualcomm. Peggy, who knew Silicon Valley inside out, was the ideal candidate to help build out Microsoft's partnership strategy, becoming the EVP of business development.
- To change Microsoft's culture, he promoted growth mindset evangelist Kathleen Hogan to head up the human resources department. Hogan was a former Oracle developer and McKinsey consultant turned Microsoft veteran.
- For the corporate strategy role, Satya reached out to an outsider who could also serve as insider—Kurt DelBene, a veteran Microsoft leader who had left the company to serve the Obama administration as an advisor to the US secretary of health and human services.
- For the CFO position, he promoted Amy Hood, who had joined Microsoft a decade earlier from Goldman Sachs and had critical capital market experience.
- Next came Qi Lu, who had been recruited by Steve Ballmer from Yahoo. Lu was a computer science engineer who had over twenty patents to his name.

Qi was tasked with leading Microsoft's technological transformation game plan.
- Brad Smith, an ex–Covington and Burling partner, continued as chief legal officer and was the longest-serving Microsoft executive in the new management board.
- Former Walmart executive Kevin Turner, who had joined Microsoft as COO in 2006, continued in the COO position.
- Satya promoted Microsoft loyalist Scott Guthrie, with whom he had worked closely. Guthrie took over the company's fast-growing cloud and enterprise business, a division where he had previously worked closely with Satya.
- Former software entrepreneur Terry Myerson was promoted as windows and devices chief.
- Chris Capossela, who'd joined Microsoft out of university, took over as chief marketing officer.
- Harry Shum, who had earned his PhD in robotics from Carnegie Mellon, headed up Microsoft's AI and research group.

To build the high-performance team that he desired, Satya would need to change the historical leadership dynamics at Microsoft. He reached out to performance psychologist Dr. Michael Gervais, who was an expert in bringing high-performing teams together. Gervais was well known in Seattle due to the fact that he had helped the Seattle Seahawks win the Super Bowl the year prior.[38] Wanting to bring some of the same team-building magic to Microsoft, Satya asked Gervais to organize an admittedly less athletic leadership meeting at an off-site location.

38 Modern Workplace, "The Psychology of High-Performing Teams," Microsoft.

At the start of this off-site, Gervais asked for a volunteer who would stand up for an exercise. For a moment it was awkward when nobody volunteered, until the CFO, Amy Hood, jumped up. He asked her to recite the alphabet, interspersing every letter with a number—A1, B2, C3, and so forth. As Hood began to speak and eventually struggle, Gervais intervened and turned to the entire crowd—he asked why they weren't all jumping up to help her. Shouldn't this be a high-performing team? He suggested that beneath the reserved surface of the crowd, there was a fear of being ridiculed, of not looking like the smartest person in the room. There was a sense of arrogance, the attitude that they were too smart for these games. His intervention, and his bluntness, broke the ice.

As the retreat went on, each of the group began sharing their passions, life stories, personal philosophies, and spirituality. This was an opportunity to see everybody in a different light. It was the start of the process of really becoming a team. They talked about their struggles as parents and their desire to empower others. From that day on, they would be each other's first team and beholden to their respective departments as only a secondary focus.

Six years after Satya started, Microsoft had fundamentally transformed and again became one of the most valuable companies in the world, achieving a market cap of over $1 trillion.

5.2 What Is the People Wing on the Flywheel of Transformation?

How do we define the people wing in the Flywheel of Transformation? As the Microsoft case demonstrates, when the right leadership team comes together—at both the top team level and in the layers below—and performs at a high level, transformations come to life. The people wing represents the need to bring the best possible team together to achieve a transformation. We have identified two key elements that can either hamper or strengthen the people wing of the Flywheel of Transformation—the quality of the team members and the team's dynamics.

> When the right leadership team comes together—at both the top team level and in the layers below—and performs at a high level, transformations come to life.

THE TEAM MEMBERS

As you can see by the Microsoft example, Satya spent significant time and energy deciding who should be part of the leadership team that would help the company transform. These decisions were informed by the company's new purpose, the desired future position, and the priorities he had set. In *Good to Great*, Jim Collins describes the team-building process with an apt metaphor: great teams are built by "getting the right people on the bus in the right seat, and the wrong people off the bus."

So what do the right team members look like? There is no magical formula, but some aspects you might consider are the following:

- **Which roles should be in the top team?** In a transformational effort, key roles that drive the transformation forward should be part of the top team, determining who is given a key seat at the table. Are the key future functions that will drive the transformation represented?

- **How large should the team be?** We have seen different sizes work. The most effective teams of Navy SEALs are around five people. While that might be too small for a business team, any team with more than ten people in the top team becomes more of a group than a team. Do you have the right-sized team?

- **How many roles on the current top team need to change?** Here the right balance is needed. Often to shift a transformation to the next gear, some new impulses, experiences, views, and energy are required. However, if too many people are changed out, there might be a loss of understanding and experience.

- **Should one choose insiders or outsiders?** The mix between people who have worked outside the organization and those who have already had a long career in the organization needs to be right. A team of only insiders may lead to blinded perspectives, yet a team composed entirely of outsiders might not understand an organization's history and culture.

- **Does your team have enough diversity?** Practice and research show that in a transformation, creating a constructive dynamic of diversity in a team is key.[39] What is the diversity of your team in terms of gender, religion, nationality, age?

- **How should you mix personality types?** For example, a team full of extroverts is vulnerable, as is a team made of only introverts. A team full of alpha males is a recipe for conflict. There are many different ways to look at personalities, but finding the right balance is key.

---

39   V. Hunt et al., "Diversity Wins: How Inclusion Matters," McKinsey & Company, 2020.

HIGH-PERFORMING TEAM DYNAMIC

Putting the right team members in place is not solely about creating a high-performing team, says leadership expert Patrick Lencioni in his book *The Five Dysfunctions of a Team*.[40] He describes that excellent top teams will have the following characteristics:

- They have a high level of trust and the ability to share openly and to reveal vulnerability. The team members feel that it's a safe environment to speak up and that they have the desire to help each other.

- They deal constructively with conflicts. They confront problems and issues quickly and head-on. They focus on developing practical solutions. Input is given by all team members, and politics is reduced to a minimum.

- They feel very committed to the team and the transformation mission. The team has buy-in and alignment on common objectives. The team also has clarity on direction and priorities. Team members feel very engaged and as if their careers and endeavors are a mission.

- Excellent teams take responsibility and accountability. Standards are set for everyone. Poor performance is addressed by the team, and poor performers are held accountable.

- A top team focuses on results. There is a relentless focus on recurring, extraordinary performance. There are also clear, team-based results. The team is highly motivated to achieve these outcomes.

Bringing together the right team members and developing a high-performing team dynamic are the basis for team success.

---

40   P. Lencioni, *The Five Dysfunctions of a Team* (Jossey-Bass, 2002).

Another element to consider is where the top team's allegiance lies. A high-performing top team sees the top team as "team one" and their functional business teams as "team two." In weaker teams people usually regard team one as their own functional and business teams and see the top team as team two. In this situation the top team operates more like the United Nations, where each person feels as if they are representing their own area in a fight for resources and attention. In a transformation difficult decisions need to be made, and certain team members are asked to execute difficult decisions that can be unpopular in their own functions or business areas. As a result when a top team member sees their business team as team one, it inevitably creates tension with these difficult decisions.

> ### MARCO: ONLY WITH TRANSFORMATIVE LEADERSHIP TEAMS CAN YOU TRANSFORM
>
> In all the transformations I have been part of, a key element was to get the right leaders on the bus and in the right seat. To begin this process, in the first ninety days leading a transformation, I always make what I have now defined as "the transformational leadership grid."
>
> **Get the right leaders on the bus and in the right seat.**
>
> To get a good overview of, say, the top fifty leaders, I have learned that, in most cases, you cannot always depend on an HR evaluation system or on an open debate. For example, when I arrived as a new management board member to lead a particular transformation,

I found that all of the leaders had been rated outstanding in the official HR reports even though the business was in a downward spiral. I have also found that open debates around people can often become anecdotal, be swayed by the loudest voices in the room, or be bogged down by one team defending or promoting their own people.

Here's how I practically approached this problem in one situation; after traveling extensively through a company in my first ninety days and visiting key countries and functions to get personal exposure to the company's leaders, I called an unexpected meeting with a few of the trusted senior leaders who have had good exposure to the top fifty leaders of the organization. As they walked into a conference room, all the chairs and tables were put aside. On the wall there were posters with different countries/functions with the names, titles, and years in position of the various leaders. I invited everyone to do an initial exercise by putting a range of colored dot stickers next to the names on the posters, red indicating that they should have been replaced (no power), yellow that they are not performing well (some power), green meaning they are performing well (strong power), and blue marking a transformer (transformative power). Then to deter people from being able to track who put which sticker where, I ask everybody to start at once while also limiting the time to ten minutes, which created a bit of a frantic feeling, and nobody could follow anymore who had put what dot to which person on the poster.

After ten minutes I asked everybody to stand back and take a look at the outcome. There were clear patterns, a sort of collective wisdom and a concentration on leaders with red and with blue dots. Then we saw clear greens and yellows, as well as mixes between the two. Before discussing individuals we simply looked at the color mix of the different functional/country/business teams to see which ones have more blue, green, yellow, or red. We then also looked at the level of diversity in each team in terms of people with different backgrounds and duration of tenure in the teams. Only then did we start to discuss individuals to calibrate. The picture on the wall always created a collective aha moment and group alignment.

We then defined an initial action plan by shifting blue leaders to the key priorities, recruiting new blue leaders internally or externally for key positions, letting the red leaders go, and providing coaching to yellow leaders with a clearly communicated expectation of the need to step up, etc. Once the new teams were in place, we invested in offering the teams effectiveness off-sites, coaching, facilitators, etc. Once we saw more green/blue leadership teams in the different positions, we saw these areas accelerate in transformation and performance.

Making sure the right people are on the bus and in the right seat is a prerequisite for any transformation.

5.3 Why Is It Important to Have a Strong People Wing?

An effective people wing is key in creating a flywheel effect for your transformation. Without a high-performing top team at the helm—with a team that lags perhaps due to fear, stagnation, or denial of the need to change—an organization can drift, miss opportunities, and lose sight of unaddressed threats.[41]

Of course, it's essential that the team is aligned with the purpose of the organization,[42] the future position, and the priorities that will allow them to get there. These are what Harvard University professor of social and organizational psychology J. Richard Hackman identified as "enabling conditions." In over forty years of research, Hackman found that a compelling direction, a strong structure, and a supportive context are as important as (if not more important) than the sum performance of the individual team members.[43] If a high-performing team executes the wrong strategy, the speed of decline in an organization may actually increase—a boat with a hole in it will take on more water as it accelerates after all. So assuming the direction is right, why is a strong leadership team so important?

- A transformation requires a real team dynamic where one plus one is three. The challenge at hand often requires a great team performance.

- Decisions on direction, priorities, resource allocation, and similar matters often come together in the leadership team.

---

41   D. Dean, "A CEO's Guide to Reenergizing the Senior Team," McKinsey & Company, *McKinsey Quarterly*, 2009.

42   G. Satell et al., "High-Performing Teams Start with a Culture of Shared Values," *Harvard Business Review*, 2021.

43   M. Haas et al., "The Secrets of Great Teamwork," *Harvard Business Review*, 2016.

If this team is not operating effectively, then suboptimal decisions are made. (Or no decisions are made at all.)

- The leadership team is a role model to the rest of the organization. If a leadership team amplifies the behaviors that are required for a transformation, many will follow. However, if the leadership's behaviors are dysfunctional, it also sets an example that might become a detriment.

- In any transformation there will be challenges and setbacks. A great team can absorb these, give each other strength, and focus on a path forward. In less effective teams, these moments often lead to a loss of momentum.

- Any transformation is also a creative process, and people only become creative in a trustworthy, positive environment. A toxic environment leads to defensive behavior, which actively enhances the status quo.

5.4 How Do You Score on the People Wing?

How strong is the people wing of your Flywheel of Transformation? Is there bandwidth to give this wing more power? To help you assess where you stand, we have again defined four simple levels of assessment. Where would you score your team? Where would your employees score your team?

- **Level 1: No or Limited Power: Dysfunctional Team.** At this level the leadership team does not have the right composition to help lead a transformation. Typically there are several people who have been there a long time and are (consciously or unconsciously) defending the past. Team dynamics and levels of cooperation are low. People defend their own departments first. There are a lot of old wounds and bad blood between team members that hinder relationships. Some critical functions needed for the future are not represented on the team.

- **Level 2. Some Power: Functional Team.** Several positions have the right people, but there are also several that do not—this is often for legacy reasons. The team is able to work functionally together, but everybody is focused only on delivering their own function/part of the business. There is little collaboration between teams. People don't really challenge each other as they also don't want to be challenged by others.

- **Level 3. Good Power: Well-Performing Team.** Most people are correctly selected for the right positions. Despite this, there are a few imbalances. The team enjoys working together, and there are a common agenda and objectives. Investments are made to strengthen team dynamics. Some difficult (but necessary) issues are still avoided, as they might hurt the team spirit. The team might also lack some level of diversity. Not all the decisions of the team are supported by those outside the team, but overall the team works well.

- **Level 4. Transformative Power: High-Performing, Purpose-Driven Team.** All positions are filled with the right people with a good mix of diversity, personalities, and capabilities. The team is clearly purpose driven and on mission. The standards are set high, and each of the team members is held accountable when results are not achieved. The team celebrates progress. The team feels that they are part of something special, that they are raising their game. The leadership team is clearly team one. Issues are resolved head-on, and difficult trade-offs are made. Difficult decisions are debated, but once they've been made, the team closes ranks and speaks as one outside the team.

	WING-POWER LEVEL	YOUR SCORE?
LEVEL 4	TRANSFORMATIVE POWER	
LEVEL 3	GOOD POWER	
LEVEL 2	SOME POWER	
LEVEL 1	NO POWER	

PEOPLE WING

PETER: BRINGING A DIVERSE TEAM TOGETHER

One of the key elements for successful teams in a transformation is when a team can work well together even if there are diverse or conflicting values. Awareness of the similar and differing values of a team is key for constructively managing tensions that might arise.

For example, I was once working with a management team from a large IT company where a team leader was new and had obviously been put in place in order to drive forward a bold change agenda. The team was composed of seasoned professionals with many years of experience, but they often struggled to understand each other.

Within the team there were two subcultures: one that was like a big family that took care of each other and another that was much more business oriented. They had a direct approach in their communications and a professional attitude. Because these two groups were so different, there was little overlap between the two, and it was holding the transformation back.

As a result I was brought in to help the family subculture adopt a more businesslike approach. To facilitate this change, we organized transformation days to align the team and prepare them for huge changes in the company. On these days we talked not only business but also why we wanted the different groups to understand and appreciate each other's values more—to find ways to cooperate better.

We ran a few outside-of-the-box activities (including an escape room in the wilderness) and held competitions with unexpected changes of rules that required the teams to adapt on the spot and work cooperatively together. The afternoon was fun, and in combination with other exercises and activities, both sides really got to know each other.

This transformation day helped the team respect the differences and overlaps in their values and was the first step in finding common ground. Once they had started to discover which values were hindering their cooperation, they could see which were helping and worked toward enhancing these. This understanding helped shift the way the team came together and align their transformational forces.

5.5 How to Strengthen Your People Wing

How can you strengthen the people wing of your Transformational Flywheel? Based on our best practices, you can use four key steps to strengthen your senior leadership team.

1. Design what team setup is required to deliver the transformation priorities.
   - Use a blank-slate, tabula rasa approach based on the future position target and priorities and don't use the current team organization as a starting point.
   - Define key roles, responsibilities, and transformational priorities by function.
   - Play around with different alternatives and evaluate their respective pros and cons.
   - Once team roles are set up, decide what types of profile leaders are ideally required for each position and for the whole of the organization. It's helpful to use lenses like diversity, insiders versus outsiders, seasoned leaders versus up-and-coming talent, and industry experience versus experience in other industries.

2. Assess the current team members.
   - Collect input from others and own input of current leaders and leadership talents.
   - Decide who to bring in the team and who to transition out.
   - Identify any gaps that will need to be filled with external talent.

3. Make the required changes.

- Move relatively quickly and provide clarity as to who is in and who is out.
- When you do let people go, do it gracefully and with respect.
- Define search profiles for recruitment.
- Look for candidates from outside-the-box channels, platforms, and companies. Transformative people are often attracted to more dynamic places on the periphery of an organization and can consequently have less linear career paths.

4. Align and motivate the changed team.
   - Once the team is in place, invest in aligning roles and responsibilities to reduce any unnecessary ambiguity and friction.
   - Set clear objectives and priorities for both teams and each team member.
   - Invest in getting to know each other with off-site retreats or events where you create an environment for sharing motivating personal matters like life goals, passions, worries, and desires so that your team sees each other as the complex, driven people they are.
   - Define explicitly how the team makes decisions.
   - Decide what stays in the team and what can be shared outside the team.
   - Lay out a constructive process for conflict resolution. Outline the kinds of conflicts that might arise and how they might be solved before you embark on your journey together.
   - Celebrate progress together regularly.

References

Nadella, S., T. Nichols, and G. Shaw. *Hit Refresh: The Quest to Rediscover Microsoft's Soul and Imagine a Better Future for Everyone.* HarperCollins, 2017.

Microsoft. "The Psychology of High-Performing Teams." https://info.microsoft.com/ww-thankyou-The-science-of-high-performing-teams-video.html.

Hunt, V., S. Dixon-Fyle, S. Prince, and K. Dolan. "Diversity Wins: How Inclusion Matters." McKinsey & Company, 2020. https://www.mckinsey.com/~/media/McKinsey/Featured%20Insights/Diversity%20and%20Inclusion/Diversity%20wins%20How%20inclusion%20matters/Diversity-wins-How-inclusion-matters-vF.pdf.

Lencioni, P. *The Five Dysfunctions of a Team.* Jossey-Bass, 2002.

Dean, D. "A CEO's Guide to Reenergizing the Senior Team." McKinsey & Company. *McKinsey Quarterly*, 2009. https://www.mckinsey.com/business-functions/organization/our-insights/a-ceos-guide-to-reenergizing-the-senior-team?cid=soc-web.

Satell, G., and C. Windschitl. "High-Performing Teams Start with a Culture of Shared Values." *Harvard Business Review*, 2021. https://hbr-org.cdn.ampproject.org/c/s/hbr.org/amp/2021/05/high-performing-teams-start-with-a-culture-of-shared-values.

Haas, M., and M. Mortensen. "The Secrets of Great Teamwork." *Harvard Business Review*, 2016. https://hbr.org/2016/06/the-secrets-of-great-teamwork.

Schultz, H. *Onward: How Starbucks Fought for Its Life without Losing Its Soul.* John Wiley & Sons, 2011.

INNER GAME POWER

- 1. PURPOSE
- 2. PERSPECTIVE
- 3. POSITION
- 4. PRIORITIES
- 5. PEOPLE
- 6. PRINCIPLES
- 7. PROMOTION
- 8. PROGRESS
- 9. PASSION
- 10. POLITICAL
- 11. PARTY
- 12. PAY-OFF

CHAPTER 6

PRINCIPLES

*When your values are clear to you,
making decisions becomes easier.*
—ROY E. DISNEY

6.1 INTRODUCTION: ZAPPOS

Sometimes life-changing ideas happen when you least expect them. For Tony Hsieh, CEO of Zappos, that moment was during lunch at a Mexican restaurant with one of his executives. "Have you read *Good to Great* by Jim Collins?" he asked his compatriot. The two had been discussing which direction the five-year-old online shoe retailer should take to win in the future. Since their founding in 1999, Zappos had experienced constant growing pains. Hsieh felt they were not yet on a trajectory to meet their bold ambition to become a $1 billion company before the end of the decade.

"Great companies have a greater purpose and bigger vision beyond just making money," Tony said. Yet many "fall into the trap of just focusing on making money and they'll never become a great company."[44]

Zappos, Hsieh believed, needed to become bigger than shoes. As an active poker player, Hsieh said the most important factor determining whether you were going to win a hand or not was which table you chose to sit at in the first place.[45] At that point his lunch partner began to suggest other markets the company could enter. Handbags? Apparel? Perhaps they could become the leading retailer outfitting people head to toe.[46] But Hsieh was thinking bigger. He was thinking Virgin big, but rather than focusing on building a brand around the image of being hip and cool, Zappos should be about providing the best customer service known to man.

To provide the best customer service experience possible, however, the company would need to fundamentally transform. When Nick Swinmurn, inspired by Amazon, started with the business idea of selling shoes online in 1999, he found an investor in Tony Hsieh. Hsieh had just sold his first start-up and was looking to invest his money in innovative dot-com projects with high growth potential. They changed the name from ShoeSite to Zappos, a play on the Spanish word *zapatos*. Not much later, as Hsieh had

---

44 T. Hsieh, *Delivering Happiness: A Path to Profits, Passion, and Purpose* (Hachette Book Group, 2010).
45 T. Hsieh, "'Delivering Happiness': What Poker Taught Me about Business," *Huffington Post*, 2010.
46 Ibid.

started to put more and more of his own capital in, he recognized that he should step in as CEO, excited about the opportunity he saw ahead. As a kid Tony had always been enthralled when he received a package in the mail. He saw Zappos as an opportunity to help people relive this feeling and deliver happiness.

However, the last years had been a constant operational and financial struggle. They were still not profitable and had difficulty raising funds. They were in fraught negotiations with Wells Fargo to get some additional loans.

So after reading Jim Collins's best seller on why some companies make the leap and others didn't, Tony knew he had to do something to make Zappos great. He began to reexamine what it was that made Zappos a customer's first choice. Sure, they sold shoes, but you could buy shoes anywhere. No, shoes didn't make Zappos stand out. There were other sites online where you could even buy shoes for cheaper or had a bigger selection, so it wasn't price or portfolio either. What made Zappos great was their customer service. "Zappos is a service company that just happens to sell all the nifty shoes, clothing, and accessories and whatnot found on Zappos.com," Tony famously said. With this realization and that lunchtime epiphany, Zappos began to focus on building the world's greatest customer service experience.

They started to reset the foundation of the business in a transformative way, driven by this vision to become the world's greatest service company:

- They focused relentlessly on providing outstanding customer service and decided to challenge some conventional perspectives/beliefs in the industry. Customers could now order as many pairs of shoes and freely send them back as necessary. Customer service people were free to talk as long as they wanted to help customers—and there was no forced script. If customers were looking for a shoe that Zappos didn't have in stock or didn't sell at all, the customer service people would recommend them to specific competitor sites that offered the product. Everything was focused on customer service.
- Overnight they decided to stop drop-shipping, which made up 25 percent of their total business. Drop-shipping involves attracting customers to your site for a sale but then fulfilling that order via another retailer or shoe manufacturer. Zappos realized that, although it was financially attractive for them, they couldn't provide the same level of service when they were acting as a middleman. Drop-shipping orders were only delivered on time 95 percent of the time, ultimately leaving 5 percent of their customers upset with the service. If they were serious about their purpose, it had to be stopped. They had to refocus their energy on carrying their own inventory.
- They moved the headquarters from the Bay Area to Las Vegas, uprooting the lives of all key employees, convincing seventy of their ninety to join them on this journey. In the Bay Area, it was very difficult to attract, train, and retain great customer service talent. Also,

the cost of living was too high in the Bay Area for their service employees. Rather than outsourcing customer service to India, they wanted to make it a core part of the business, and Las Vegas was a rapidly growing service economy. It was a much more natural home.
- They took charge of their own warehouse operations in full since reliable overnight delivery was key. To make this happen, they moved away from a third-party provider and moved their main distribution center close to one of the main UPS airline hubs. Orders from the evening could now be shipped and received the next day, surprising and delighting customers.
- They decided to begin treating their vendors the way that they would treat their customers. Shifting the traditional paradigm, which saw vendors treated harshly and transactionally, they began extending a hand of respect. Not only did they ensure that payments would be paid on time but Zappos also gave them access to their own sales data to make vendors' jobs easier. As an amicable gesture, Zappos also began inviting vendors to meetings at their head offices.
- They stopped all marketing spend and instead used that budget to make their current customers happy by investing in excellent service that would create customer loyalty and word-of-mouth promotion.

They realized, however, that the most foundational aspects of their customer service success were their company culture and their values—what we call "principles" in the Transformational Flywheel. Their core goal was to make customers extremely happy, and Zappos believed that this was achieved by providing incredible customer service. As Zappos went deeper into creating this service, they realized that the way employees interact with customers is influenced by how employees themselves experience happiness in their work—and that experience was driven by Zappos's culture and their operating principles. If you get your culture right, then all the other stuff—from customer service to building a long-term brand—will fall into place naturally.[47]

> If you get your culture right, then all the other stuff—from customer service to building a long-term brand—will fall into place naturally.

Hsieh and his team went on a relentless path to create this unique culture. Together, the entire company codified ten core principles and detailed what each means in terms of mindset and behavior. The list included the following:

1. Deliver wow through service.
2. Embrace and drive change.
3. Create fun and a little weirdness.
4. Be adventurous, creative, and open minded.
5. Pursue growth and learning.
6. Build open and honest relationships with communications.
7. Build a positive team and family spirit.
8. Do more with less.
9. Be passionate and determined.
10. Be humble.

---

47 T. Hsieh, "Your Culture Is Your Brand," *Huffington Post*, 2017.

Defining the principles was one thing, but Hsieh wanted these values to become the backbone of the company, worth hiring and firing over, guiding decisions that aligned the organization. To live up to this standard, Hsieh sent out an email to all employees with one question: how does Zappos itself (and everything that happens within the company) live up to these values? From the website's copy to their job application forms, they began to examine how to make the online retailer better reflect these core values.

One of the fundamental areas for strengthening the company culture and reality of their principles was the key HR processes of hiring, training, and promotion that they developed. In the beginning Hsieh had interviewed each candidate himself, basing if a candidate was going to fit the culture's feeling. However, as they grew they needed to find a way to solidify cultural fit without Hsieh present. To achieve this they focused 50 percent of the weight of the first hiring interview on cultural fit with Zappos—if they didn't pass this first interview, they couldn't go on to meet the hiring manager.[48] Once a candidate accepts a position at Zappos, a rigorous onboarding process begins.

Since a core value at Zappos is creating wow moments, new hires must learn the main challenges Zappos's customers have. The first four weeks are spent manning the phones in the customer service center—regardless of the job. This process immerses new hires into the Zappos culture, what their core values mean, how Zappos lives

---

48 D. Wisenberg-Brin, "Zappos' New Recruiting Strategy Seen as Innovative, Risky," Society for Human Resource Management, 2014.

them, and what their expectations are of each employee to help maintain and grow their culture. Once they've finished these initial four weeks, all employees are reimbursed for their time; plus they're offered a lump sum of $3,000 to leave the company—an offer that says, "Don't stay just for the money if you don't think you'll thrive here." Zappos provided a serious career, constant training, and development steps for those truly committed to customer service. As a final touch, there were constant parties and activities to make Zappos a fun place to work.

That single lunch in 2003 set Zappos on a trailblazing trajectory that would transform them into a company that provided world-class customer service while driven by their unique culture. "We hadn't expected to make a life-changing choice over a plate of fajitas, but when you're part of a fast-growing company, a lot of decisions arise at unlikely moments." Empowered by this newfound direction and the set of principles that underpinned it, Zappos crossed the $1 billion mark in 2009. Zappos has consistently ranked among the best places to work in the United States, as well as one of the best customer service companies of all time. By applying these principles consistently and vigorously to every aspect of their operations, Zappos has become a cult brand.

As a final example of just how seriously Zappos takes customer service, consider this story. At some point after he'd transformed Zappos, Hsieh once visited the Skechers sales conference in Santa Monica, California. After a long night of barhopping, a small group of conference goers headed up to someone's hotel room to order some food. His friend from Skechers wanted to order a pepperoni pizza from the room service menu but was disappointed to hear that the kitchen was closed and that no hot food could be delivered after 11:00 p.m. As a dare the group challenged the friend to call Zappos instead to try to order a pizza. She called Zappos's customer service while on speakerphone and explained the dire situation to a patient Zappos—that they were in a Santa Monica hotel and craving pepperoni pizza and that the hotel kitchen was closed. They asked whether she could help. The rep was initially a bit confused and put them on hold. When she returned a few minutes later, she had a list of the five closest places in the Santa Monica area that were still open and delivering pizzas at that time.

Every time one of these events occurred, Zappos always pointed to their core values as the driving principles behind it. Just as Zappos reached the unicorn milestone in 2009, the company was acquired by Amazon for $1.2 billion.

6.2 What Is the Principle Wing in the Flywheel of Transformation?

We define *principles* in the Flywheel of Transformation as the key values that shape a company's culture and behaviors. The ten principles defined in the Zappos case are an example of what we mean by this. These principles impact how people act and relate to one another not only within the company but also with customers, suppliers, and other stakeholders. As a consequence a change in principles will lead to different behaviors and decision-making. These principles, therefore, can make or break the success of a leader, team, or company. Because success depends on how employees, clients, and other stakeholders experience the company, they all will notice when a culture has changed for the better.

Principles differentiate an organization from what could otherwise be just a group of people working together. They give guidance on how the people in an organization look at the world and how that group wants to operate in it. They're the "invisible threads" of what people describe as the culture—or the heart—of the business.[49] When there is a good alignment between organizational and individual values, it creates more positive employee attitudes such as organizational commitment and job satisfaction. According to a McKinsey study on why culture matters, organizations with clear company values have a significant competitive advantage in three key areas: performance, authenticity, and adaptability.[50]

But what exactly underpins a strong culture? Principles. Here are some more examples of the key principles held by some well-known organizations:

---

[49] C. Branson, "Achieving Organizational Change through Values Alignment," *Journal of Educational Administration* (2008).

[50] McKinsey & Company, "Culture: Four Keys to Why It Matters," https://www.mckinsey.com/business-functions/organization/our-insights/the-organization-blog/culture-4-keys-to-why-it-matters.

Ikea's key principles

- Humility and willpower
- Leadership by example
- Daring to be different
- Togetherness and enthusiasm
- Cost consciousness
- Constant desire for renewal
- Accepting and delegating responsibility

Nike's key principles

- It's our nature to innovate.
- Nike is a company.
- Nike is a brand.
- Simplify and go.
- The consumer decides.
- Be a sponge.
- Evolve immediately.
- Do the right thing.
- We are on the offense—always.
- Remember the man—the late Bill Bowerman.

Google's key principles

- Focus on the user, and all else will follow.
- It is better to do one thing really, really well.
- Fast is better than slow.

- Democracy on the web works.
- You don't need to be at your desk to need an answer.
- You can make money without doing evil.
- There's always more information out there.
- The need for information crosses all borders.
- You can be serious without a suit.
- Great just isn't good enough.

Every organization has either some implicit or explicitly defined principles. The importance of principles in relation to the flywheel is about how powerful these ideas are in supporting or hindering the transformational direction of the business. In almost all transformational situations, more power is needed in the principle wing to let a transformation fly. Peter Drucker said it well in his famous quote. "Culture eats strategy for breakfast."

So what creates strong power in the principle wing? There are two drivers: how well the values are defined and whether the values are lived by an organization. Often if there are problems, one of the two or both have eroded; and as a result, the organization requires a shift. Before Satya Nadella took over as CEO at Microsoft, as laid out in chapter 5, it had a very strong and well-lived culture, but it was not fit for the future position, and he went on a large-scale transformational culture change journey. When Tony Hsieh at Zappos wanted to shift the company from good to great, he felt that they already had the good elements of the culture but could still make these a stronger force if they were truly lived. When Howard Schultz stepped back in as CEO at Starbucks (as discussed in chapter 3), he realized that the once powerful culture had eroded and that he needed to once again bring it front and center.

But how do you know that there is room to increase the power in this wing? There are no absolutely correct values or values that fit every organization. It's an art to define and live them, so it powers an organization in line with its purpose and position. There are, however, several best practices for well-designed and well-lived principles. Powerfully designed and crafted principles

- are short and memorable;
- guide a way of perceiving the world, of connecting with others, or of doing things;
- support the transformational direction;
- are authentic, differentiating, and unique to the organization;
- have an opposite value that might be viable for other organizations;
- are often not longer than a list of seven to ten items;
- create a sense of passion and meaning;
- are detailed below the catchphrase in sample behaviors; and
- are ordered in a hierarchy.
- Powerfully lived principles
- are lived all the time and intensively communicated,
- are consistently used to make decisions,
- ensure that the recruitment process selects people who fit the values,
- require leaders who exemplify the principles and act in accordance with them, and

- provide recognition for those who set the example of acting in accordance with the principles.

One of the challenges with working on the principle wing is that you need to be able to live them with conviction and passion in order to succeed—they also need to be reflected upon regularly so that an organization can determine if they're still providing the culture a business needs in order to thrive.

> ### MARCO: SHIFTS IN PRINCIPLE ARE THE KEY TO DRIVING DIFFERENT BEHAVIORS
>
> I strongly believe in the power of using principles and values as a transformation lever. This belief developed during the early years of my career. After my MBA at Harvard Business School, I was recruited by McKinsey, where I would work for over a decade across the firm's Chicago and later San Francisco and Amsterdam offices. It was an incredibly rewarding experience to not only serve clients across the globe, from Silicon Valley start-ups to *Fortune* 500 companies, with their transformations but also work with incredibly smart and driven colleagues.
>
> One of the drivers of McKinsey's ongoing success is its values, which are used daily in all key decisions, from recruiting to promotions, which projects to accept, etc. Values like putting client interest first, observing high ethical standards, pursuing holistic impact, being nonhierarchical and inclusive, and upholding the obligation to engage and dissent are put front and center by all employees.

Based on my formative experience at McKinsey, I quickly developed a sense that when I step into a new situation as a leader, I should observe the explicit and implicit principles an organization applies to their operations and culture. I observe how decisions are made, how people interact with their colleagues, how customers are treated, how people respond to opportunities and challenges. I also ask key leaders, frontline people, customers, etc. how they describe the culture. Once I have a hypothesis assessment, I share it with the leadership team to discuss and calibrate. The next step (which is as much an art as it is a science) is to define the five to ten key principle shifts needed to support the transformation. Once we have defined these recalibrated values and tested them, we begin to very actively communicate and exemplify these ideas in the organization to make a shift happen.

Let me share an example. At one of the recent businesses I was responsible for, I observed a dysfunctional behavior where the global head office and the different country head offices had become ivory towers. Leaders in the head offices asked for ever-increasing reports from the different countries, creating a sprawling bureaucracy. There was an implicit principle that the different businesses were there to serve the HQ and not the other way around. When I asked leaders in the HQ about the last time they had visited one of the businesses and customers, I got mostly mumbling answers.

So one of the new principles we designed was "From reporting up to supporting down." The head office was meant to help the businesses in the different countries and not the other way around. We then started to activate this principle by exemplifying this behavior as leaders who "supported down"—we did this by stopping reports; role-modeling weekly visited countries, customers, and frontline operations by tracking how many days out of the month each of the senior leaders had spent in the field; and renaming the regional head offices from "headquarters" to "support centers." We also had local leaders assign a monthly score (from 1 to 10) evaluating how well the different central functions were helping them succeed.

Let me share one more example. In another transformational situation, I observed during my first weeks in the job that there were a lot of meetings that were attended by a lot of people. I also received very long emails. I also assessed that a lot of key projects were stalled or progressing too slowly. Something had to change on this front to empower the flywheel's principle wing more, and one of the new principles we defined was "We get things done." We stopped, shortened, and reduced the required attendance of many meetings. I role-modeled by spending less than five minutes a day on email, basically answering "yes," "no," or "call me." We allocated clear responsibilities and milestones. We celebrated people and teams who "got things done," and soon the cycle time of getting things done went up and became a competitive advantage.

6.3 Why Is It Important to Have a Strong Principle Wing?

Having clear and powerful principles helps ensure that an organization is able to drive toward a future and goals that are shared across the company. Values that are not supportive might derail a transformation completely. This importance is due to several factors:

- Strong principles/values are a means to attract, select, and retain the right talent. Good principles are differentiating. Some people feel a strong connection with them, and others might not—which is OK. As was demonstrated in the Zappos case, having a clear set of values allows you to better select people who you want in the team and in key positions.

- Powerful principles can have a very positive impact on employee engagement and motivation. They give clear guidance on how people can do well in the organization and what mindset and behaviors are appreciated. If these values then also partially overlap with your personal values (which can be more likely, thanks to intensive recruiting screening), it can create a powerful internal motivational drive and sense of meaning.

- Strong principles/values help guide decision-making at all levels of the organization. They guide everybody in the organization to make the right decisions. For example, at Zappos a customer service person feels supported by the values in their quest to provide a wow experience. Strong principles guide their unlimited call time and emphasis on customer service above volume.

- Strong principles/values help improve communication and problem-solving among teams. If you bring a group together with all kinds of different principles, it's often a recipe for conflict, as everybody judges each situation according to different values. If you are aligned on the key values, then communication and decision-making flow much easier.

- Powerful principles help customers better understand how the company is different and what customer experience to expect from them. If your customers share the same values or if they aspire to the same principles you stand for, it can substantially strengthen the relationship you have with customers. For example, Apple's "Think different" campaign created a much stronger bond with customers than those of their competitors. The same you can say of Tesla.

6.4 How Do You Score on the Principle Wing?

How strong is the principle wing of your Flywheel of Transformation? Where do you stand now, and is there room for improvement? To help you define your current strength, we have described four levels of strength in the flywheel. Where would you score your business, function, or team? Where would your employees score the organization on its principles? What about your customers? Your suppliers? Your investors?

- **Level 1. No or Limited Power:** The principles might be dated, too vaguely defined, or not fit for the purpose of the organization. They are not lived. In the case of dated values, it might be that they are a powerful force but one that works in the opposite direction of the flywheel, bringing the transformation backward. Vaguely defined values and values that aren't lived can cause conflicts, a lack of clear decision-making, misalignment, and cynicism.

- **Level 2. Some Power:** The principles are defined in a way that supports the transformational direction. There is some communication done around values. There are still incongruencies between living the values and merely having them. Several leaders and key people do not behave in line with the values, and there are no consequences. When difficult decisions are being made, especially in terms of how to deal with customers, short-term profit targets frequently overrule the principles.

- **Level 3. Good Power:** The principles are well defined, aligned with the transformation, and usually known and followed. Only in times of difficulty do they struggle with living them, but generally they are lived and translated clearly into rules and into behaviors. In some parts of the business, these rules and behaviors are strict and universal, but in others they are not equally applied. The leader lives them and tries to get the team to do so as well, but they do not always succeed in that.

- **Level 4. Transformative Power:** The principles are lived by everyone in the organization from the leader to all levels and functions in the organization and transformative force. The principles are clear as is the hierarchy of the principles. Even in the case of setbacks, obstacles, or problems, the values are still lived. People have a high investment and belief in the principles from a personal and professional point of view. The principles guide in key processes, especially in people processes, such as recruiting, training, and promotion. Customers, suppliers, and other stakeholders feel attracted and connected to the principles the organization is living. The principles are a real competitive advantage.

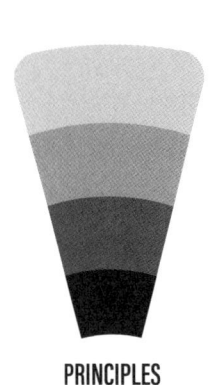

	WING-POWER LEVEL	YOUR SCORE?
LEVEL 4	TRANSFORMATIVE POWER	
LEVEL 3	GOOD POWER	
LEVEL 2	SOME POWER	
LEVEL 1	NO POWER	

PRINCIPLES WING

PETER: EMPOWERING YOUR PRINCIPLES

Many leaders underestimate how much the example set by their behavior determines how values and principles will be treated in an organization. Being aware of how well your personal values and behavior are aligned with the principles of a transformation is vital. If you are fully aligned, then there is a strong alignment of your inner game. If not, the power of your principle wing gets diluted.

For example, we once worked with a leader from an international transport company. They were in the middle of a transformation, and this CEO was attending our international leadership training to aid in the process. He thought that he connected well with his team, but he was wondering if there was any potential for improvement.

During one of our role-playing sessions, he realized he was not actually leading his company. Playing out scenarios made him realize that his assistant was continuously telling him what to do. She would hear something from within the organization and tell him what action he should take on the matter, and this had become a pattern.

To get back to the root cause of the issue, it became obvious that the CEO held a deep-seated principle: to bring and keep people together. This meant that he placed a heavy emphasis on avoiding conflict. He realized that he should have been saying no much more, deciding for himself, telling people, "This is my decision," rather than apologizing. Instead, he lost a lot of time and energy; and in the end, he was never actually doing what he wanted. Despite feeling that he was being responsible by avoiding conflict, saying no was, in fact, a form of taking responsibility for himself.

Once he realized that this value of avoiding conflict was negatively affecting his leadership abilities, he began to shift. From that moment the organization became more mature because this communication style rippled down to the lowest levels of the organization. Saying no, expressing emotions clearly, and taking responsibility became part of the new culture, which was badly needed for the transformation of the company.

6.5 How to Strengthen Your Principle Wing

So how does one strengthen their principle wing? To change the values and, in turn, the culture of an organization is not an easy task. It takes time, and there's no quick fix. To change an organization's set of beliefs is an interesting challenge, and it can be done. In our minds it's something that should be high up on every transformational leader's priority list. So what are typical good practices you can do to strengthen the principle wing? We have defined seven steps; the importance of each step depends on your starting position and how you need to leverage principles in your transformation.

1. **Step 1: Make the Company's Current Principles Explicit.** First, it's key to clarify what key implicit and explicit values currently drive people's behaviors, communication, and decisions in the organization. It can help to write the most important ones down based on some of the following actions:
   - Nonjudgmentally observe meetings and one-on-ones and be aware of what principles seem to be at work.
   - Ask people, "What are values that are important in this organization?"
   - Interview new recruits or former employees about how they perceive the values of the company.
   - Interview former leaders and founders to see what they stood for.
   - Get different views from people in different parts and roles in the business.

2. **Step 2: Assess What Values Work and Which Ones Do Not.** Once you have more clarity on the top ten driving values, assess the strengths and weaknesses of the current values.
   - Assess the benefits and consequences of the current values and how they affect the results of what you try to achieve. It's important to think through the broader consequences of each value.
   - Assess how well there is a clear value hierarchy and how these values coexist. If, for example, your value is "wow customer service" and another one is to reduce costs, it might create tension.
   - Review how well the values are lived by the whole organization. How are they reflected in recruiting, decision-making, and internal and external communication?
3. **Step 3: Examine What Values Would Make Your Transformation a Success.** This is a clean sheet exercise, not to be hampered by existing values.
   - What culture would propel the transformation?
   - How would the culture stand out?
   - What would be the most important values in such a culture? Which beliefs are related to these values?
   - What other business could be a role model in terms of values?
4. **Step 4: Define the Future Target Principles/Values for the Business.** Create a new set of values based on both your assessment of the current principles and your ideal clean-sheet new values. The questions to consider are as follows:

- Which of the existing values should be nurtured and enhanced?
- Which of the existing values should be abolished?
- What is the must-win new value to develop?
- What is the right order of the values? What's the best hierarchy?
- Do these values fit with the other flywheel wings?

5. **Step 5: Get Buy-in from Senior Leadership and Key Stakeholders.** Check with key senior leaders and stakeholders about their feedback and reaction to the key values and adapt where needed.

6. **Step 6: Launch an Active Change Process to Make the New Values Come Alive.** This is where the hard part starts since historical values can be very sticky and resilient. Businesses that are able to change their historical values do several of the following things:
   - Use principles in making key decisions and use their values in communicating why decisions are made. This is a big signal to the organization.
   - Create new rituals supporting the principles. For example, if one of your values is kindness, then a company might implement a ritual like a Random Act of Workplace Kindness (RAWK) week.
   - Use it as a clear screening criterion in hiring new people. People will be hired only when there is a value fit. They should not be hired if there is no strong cultural fit—even if they have outstanding capabilities and experiences.

- Make values and behaving according to the principles a key part of deciding who receives internal promotions. Promote only people who demonstrate that they live by the values and principles of the company.

- Communicate the values intensively and create stories around them.

- Celebrate the behavior of people who demonstrate the values, creating new heroes.

7. **Step 7: Regularly Review and Discuss How Well the Principles Are Lived and How Well They Are Aiding the Transformation.** On the one hand, it's key to drive the values with conviction and attention all the time. On the other hand, when the world changes or the future position target changes, don't forget to calibrate in response.

References

Hsieh, T. "How I Did It: Zappos's CEO on Going to Extremes for Customers." *Harvard Business Review*, 2010. https://hbr.org/2010/07/how-i-did-it-zapposs-ceo-on-going-to-extremes-for-customers.

Hsieh, T. *Delivering Happiness: A Path to Profits, Passion, and Purpose.* Hachette Book Group, 2010.

Hsieh, T. "'Delivering Happiness': What Poker Taught Me about Business." *Huffington Post*, 2010. https://www.huffpost.com/entry/tony-hsieh-zappos-ceo-del_b_589543?guccounter=1&guce_referrer=aHR0cHM6Ly9lbi53a WtpcGVkaWEub3JnLw&guce_referrer_sig=AQAAAL7KoHdS5-WSEZ-tAG9xY_UzAZR_3wBELDxIJF5kz9E-Dh2swfJtwhlHNCHzRE9QhjqiVTU-6I1to3krN2J8nWq2raLJZPxjq1mwVPSx0GdB7OZ0WJUxXSTcQkvZp3rf-1brI84EoOyuAYXT0xS2Vit8g3YSMKlV1tO6JzwG7IOmNYv.

Hsieh, T. "Your Culture Is Your Brand." *Huffington Post*, 2017. https://www.huffpost.com/entry/tony-hsieh-zappos-ceo-del_b_589543?guccounter=1&guce_referrer=aHR 0cHM6Ly9lbi53aWtpcGVkaWEub3JnLw&guce_referrer_sig=AQAAAL7KoHdS5-WSEZtAG9xY_UzAZR_3wBELDxIJF5kz9E-Dh2swfJtwhlHNCHzRE9QhjqiV-TU6I1to3krN2J8nWq2raLJZPxjq1mwVPSx0GdB7OZ0WJUxXSTcQkvZp3rf-1brI84EoOyuAYXT0xS2Vit8g3YSMKlV1tO6JzwG7IOmNYv.

Wisenberg-Brin, D. "Zappos' New Recruiting Strategy Seen as Innovative, Risky." Society for Human Resource Management, 2014. https://www.shrm.org/resourcesandtools/hr-topics/talent-acquisition/pages/zappos-job-posts.aspx]

Branson, C. "Achieving Organizational Change through Values Alignment." *Journal of Educational Administration* (2008). https://www.researchgate.net/publication/243463540_Achieving_organisational_change_through_values_alignment.

Doucette., R, and C. Dewar. "Culture: Four Keys to Why It Matters." McKinsey & Company, 2018. https://www.mckinsey.com/business-functions/organization/our-insights/the-organization-blog/culture-4-keys-to-why-it-matters.

Obama, B. *A Promised Land*. Penguin Books, 2020.

INNER GAME POWER

- 1. PURPOSE
- 2. PERSPECTIVE
- 3. POSITION
- 4. PRIORITIES
- 5. PEOPLE
- 6. PRINCIPLES
- **7. PROMOTION**
- 8. PROGRESS
- 9. PASSION
- 10. POLITICAL
- 11. PARTY
- 12. PAY-OFF

CHAPTER 7

PROMOTION

The art of communication is the language of leadership.

—JAMES HUMES

7.1 INTRODUCTION: SALESFORCE.COM

Marc Benioff was the youngest ever person to be promoted to vice president at Oracle, but despite his youth, he has always been a challenger. After thirteen years with the company, he was looking to pave his own way. While on a sabbatical in Hawaii and India, Marc began to develop a new perspective on the way in which the software business was conducted.[51] Inspired by the rapid growth of Amazon, he began to ask the question Why are we still loading and upgrading software on physical media when we can now do it over the internet?[52] The way business

---

51 M. Benioff et al., *Behind the Cloud: The Untold Story of How Salesforce.com Went from Idea to Billion-Dollar Company—and Revolutionized an Industry* (Wiley-Blackwell, 2009).

52 J. Dyer et al., "The Innovator's DNA," *Harvard Business Review*, 2009.

software was sold and installed was thoroughly outdated. Benioff believed that it should be easier to install, more democratic, and more flexible. Armed with this new perspective, he saw an opportunity and decided to challenge this outdated global norm by selling software via the cloud.

Marc saw cloud computing as a solution to software's inefficiencies. Focusing on building a customer relationship management (CRM) program—something he'd had experience with while still working at Oracle—Marc began to build a new cloud-based CRM software to show proof of concept for software as a service (SaaS) and bring this idea to life. Setting up an office in a one-bedroom apartment next to his house in Telegraph Hill, San Francisco, he hired a few software developers from his network, and Salesforce was born.

In July of 1999, Marc took the plunge and left Oracle. Heavily influenced by Apple's "Think different" campaign as well as by Oracle's lavish marketing efforts, Benioff knew that to succeed, they would need to be bold. They wanted to improve the lives of software users, but they also wanted to challenge the outdated software industry itself, which they saw as obsolete, a behemoth ill-suited for the task at hand and ready to be disrupted.

What followed was a true David vs. Goliath story. Salesforce knew they had two options: be the market leader or go head-to-head against them. At the time, Siebel and Oracle dominated the CRM market and left very little room for competition. Salesforce only had one position left, the underdog. To take on Siebel, Salesforce created a marketing-obsessed culture. Everything became a calculated effort to promote Salesforce's brand and position itself as the antithesis of the outdated software behemoths. And so began the legendary software war in external communications, which Benioff dubbed "the end of software."

Marc had an advert drawn up that depicted a modern fighter jet shooting down a hopelessly outdated biplane fighter, a concept he stole directly from the Oracle founder. The modern jet represented the more advanced technology of Salesforce's SaaS solutions. The other plane, a relic of a bygone era, represented the software industry. Logos were drawn up with the word *software* in the middle of a big red circle—the symbol you'd expect to see on a No Smoking sign or in the *Ghostbusters* logo. Badges and banners were made, and the logo would appear on all promotional material from that day forth. He even changed the company's phone number to 1-800-NO-SOFTWARE.

Although it broke most of the conventional rules of PR, marketing, and communications, Benioff didn't care. His number one rule in marketing overruled all of this reasoning: you have to differentiate your brand. "If the company's facts (speed, price, quality) are superior to the competition, any good competitor will duplicate them, or worse, improve upon them. What a company can own, however, is a personality.

> You have to differentiate your brand.

We own NO SOFTWARE—not because we are the only one doing it, but because we were the first to think it was important to customers."[53] By consistently delivering an attitude that is future focused and pioneering, Benioff could deliver a fresh, new attitude in the industry.

To launch their first product, Salesforce threw an unforgettable event at Regency Theater to tell the story of "the end of software." On the first floor, actors were dressed as salespeople who had been trapped in cages and were pulling their hair out. Actors dressed as software executives were demanding that guests sign million-dollar contracts. The whole place was meant to represent a standard experience with enterprise software ... or what Salesforce simply described as "hell." On the second floor, however, heaven was waiting—the end of software. Benioff himself, decked out in army fatigues, was waiting to escort guests to safety and lead the battle against the established software industry. Right in the middle of the burgeoning dot-com software boom, Salesforce—with its two-page website and its ten employees—exploded.

Within months, as the burgeoning team began to fill up their new office, Salesforce began to experience immense growing pains. Did these newcomers really live up to the brand? When Salesforce's marketing director overheard three different responses to the question "What exactly does Salesforce do?" they immediately knew that something had to be done to unify their message. To successfully communicate, everyone in the company had to be on the same page. Benioff asked the company's PR firm to craft a consistent message to ensure "that everyone is

---

53 Benioff et al., *Behind the Cloud*, p. 32.

on message with the precision of a sophisticated political campaign." The firm produced a two-sided laminated cheat sheet that stated in one sentence exactly what the company did. This essentially turned everyone at the company into a key player on their marketing team.[54]

Salesforce's promotional tactics exploded in 2003 with the launch of their first major industry event, Dreamforce. Drawing everyone from tech entrepreneurs to enterprise executives and celebrities, Dreamforce quickly became the year's most acclaimed technology event—a cult phenomenon. At each event Salesforce would unveil a new product, but Benioff was sure not to make it solely about Salesforce. There would be a host of keynote addresses from some of the most influential figures in the industry. Other companies unveiled or launched their own products. High-profile bands including Neil Young, Metallica, and the Red Hot Chili Peppers would play concerts. The events acted as another mechanism to position the company as an alternative to the traditional software companies and establish Salesforce as the leader in cloud computing.

Next, they set their crosshairs on Siebel. The goal? That whenever anyone thought of Siebel, they would automatically think of Salesforce. The upstart company missed no opportunity to be, as Benioff describes it, "a gnat on the back of an elephant."[55] They knew that as the new kids on the block, penetrating the industry narrative wouldn't be easy. What they could do, however, was hijack the

---

54   Ibid, p. 33.
55   Ibid., p. 38.

coverage that their competitors were already getting. Over the next few years, there are many examples of Salesforce stealing Siebel's thunder. They organized a mock protest outside Siebel's annual industry event, demanding an end to software; and as a coup de grâce, when Siebel's executives called the police, they arrived to help the protestors. At another Siebel conference in Cannes, Salesforce hired all the taxis in the region and replaced them with their own cars, filling them with information about the benefits of Salesforce over Siebel.

The story of Salesforce and the birth of SaaS contains many elements that are embedded in a successful transformation. Benioff and his team began with a strong purpose, a new perspective, and a well-defined future position. They employed a progressive pay-off logic from the beginning, making "giving back to society" part of their DNA from the outset of the company. They had a defined set of principles. Despite all these strong elements, Benioff considers Salesforce's success to be directly attributable to its ability to leverage promotion. Their aggressive clarity in communicating their "end of software" narrative allowed them to become front of mind in their industry. Salesforce's resolute positioning, belligerent guerrilla marketing tactics, and staunch belief in being different from their core created the fastest-growing enterprise software company of all time.

7.2 What Is the Promotion Wing on the Flywheel of Transformation?

Strengthening the promotion wing of the Flywheel of Transformation can be a key lever for your transformational takeoff. We have defined *promotion* in this context as the power of encouraging a transformation through internal and external communication. The internal communication component is focused on communication to employees while external communications focus on customers, suppliers, the labor market, the industry, and investors. There is, of course, some overlap, as external communication can also be seen by the employees. To illustrate this, below is a diagram of the typical communication tools that are used for both internal and external communications as well as where they overlap.

INTERNAL COMMUNICATIONS
- MEETINGS
- TRAINING
- INTRANET
- EMAIL
- NEWSLETTER
- VIDEO CONFERENCING
- SLACK
- ETC.

(Overlap)
- EVENTS
- VIDEO
- WEBINAR
- SOCIAL MEDIA
- WEBSITES
- INTERNAL CONTENT
- JOB REVIEW SITES
- EMPLOYEE ADVOCACY
- ETC.

EXTERNAL COMMUNICATIONS
- PRESS RELEASES
- PUBLIC SPEAKING
- CONTENT MARKETING
- THOUGHT LEADERSHIP
- CONFERENCE ATTENDANCE
- ADVERTISING
- EMAIL MARKETING
- ETC.

What are the elements that make communication transformative? There are certain practices that make communication more effective—the strategy, the message itself, and the different manners of distribution all contribute to the effectiveness of the content.

For internal communication these are practices you might consider:

- Behind each individual piece of content, there is an overall strategy and a messaging calendar that provides the desired rhythm.
- The messages are clear on why the status quo is no longer an option, where the organization needs to go, and what it will do—and not do—to get there.
- Messages are both intellectually compelling and emotionally appealing.
- Consistent messaging doesn't constantly change.
- Next to digital content, personal communication from the leaders is key.
- There needs to be room for dialogue and feedback rather than a one-way monologue from management.
- The leadership shares examples of progress and behaviors that are in accordance with the transformation.
- The communication is authentic—like a conversation with a coworker—and not too glossy and produced like a top-down brochure.
- A broad range of communication tools are employed to get a consistent message across.

For external communication we have seen the following best practices utilized in successful transformations:

- There is an overall strategy and messaging calendar with a deliberate rhythm.
- Messages are clearly targeted to target audience segments.
- The communication is creative and demonstrates the direction in which the company is heading.
- It claims a unique position in the future.
- There is real progress to be shared.
- Creative ways are used to communicate with key stakeholders both inside and outside the organization.
- There is consistency and recognizability.
- These external messages are aligned with the internal messages.

MARCO: COMMUNICATE, COMMUNICATE, COMMUNICATE

I strongly believe in the power of intensive and consistent communication as part of a transformation. When I stepped in as COO at LeasePlan, the largest global car-leasing company, which had just been bought by a private equity consortium, I became P&L responsible for the €6 billion European business with offices in twenty-five countries.

To immediately drive the transformation, we gained new perspectives, defined a future position, set our priorities, assembled a new leadership team, defined new principles, and set up a full-scale transformation program across all markets tracked by a PMO and started to celebrate (party) progress.

However, internal promotion was a key wing to strengthen to give the whole Flywheel of Transformation further momentum. Once we knew the direction in which we were headed, we began to intensely communicate about the nature of our transformation. Here are some examples of what we did in the first year:

- After traveling exhaustively to the key markets in the first sixty days, we brought together the top one hundred people to an off-site to share and discuss the case for change, the future direction we proposed, and our priorities. We then agreed that we would meet again in six weeks and that everybody should have developed a detailed plan for execution that we could review. We then followed that up with off-site meetings every two to three months. These meetings created alignment, a sense of camaraderie, and feelings of momentum and urgency.
- Next, I made a goal to visit all twenty-five countries, walk through all their offices, and shake hands with all of the more than six thousand employees at each of their desks. We conducted town halls, sharing and dis-

cussing the case for change, our strategy, the key initiatives, the expected principle shifts, and initial results.
- Every presentation started with the key elements of the transformation: priorities, principles, initiatives, etc.
- We had posters made, changed the intranet, and changed all coffee mugs so that they sported our priorities.
- We launched fun competitions between each country on the key KPIs for each priority and had massive champion league cups that could be won by the best-performing regions.
- We made regular videos on strategy, priorities, principles, and progress that all employees watched.
- Every Friday afternoon we organized drinks in the lobby of our new head office for everybody to join where we would give updates and share customer wins and projects completed. We made a really fun event with music, snacks, and drinks, and it became a moment a lot of people looked forward to in wrapping up the week.

I learned early on that consistency, level of engagement, and frequency of communication are all key.

7.3 Why Is It Important to Have a Strong Promotion Wing?

Strong internal and external communications are important levers to drive the Transformational Flywheel. When a leader communicates their future position, their priorities, and their values effectively, clarity cascades through the organization. And with clarity comes unity—specifically unity in the direction of the organization and alignment in the path taken to that goal. When leaders neglect communication, however, they tend to experience a weak promotional flywheel, which undercuts the momentum gained from the other wings. Recent research published in MIT Sloan indicated that there is a dramatic drop of understanding a company's strategy and priorities once people are further removed from the senior leadership team. It also indicated that leaders structurally overestimate how well their communication is understood in the organization.[56]

Strong internal communication helps a transformation in several ways:

- **Gives clarity of direction.** If there is a clear messaging about where to go and what the priorities are in this direction, it provides guidance and makes it easier for employees, teams, and departments to set their own priorities.

- **Coordinates.** If employees understand the future direction, it makes it simpler for individuals to direct their own activities and makes cross-departmental decision-making easier.

- **Motivates employees.** Being informed with effective promotion increases the level of engagement employees experience. When a compelling future is communicated effectively

---

56 D. Sull et al., "No One Knows Your Strategy—Not Even Your Top Leaders." *MIT Sloan Management Review*, 2018.

and progress toward this target is documented and shared, it gives a sense of meaning and accomplishment.

- **Creates trust.** Sincere and regular two-way communication helps establish more trust in an organization. If people are not informed, they often create negative explanations. This is not out of inherent malice but rather because of a lack of context.

- **Sets a cadence and progress milestones.** Internal communication moments like town hall meetings, global video conferences, and newsletters can create a drive to meet progress milestones so that they can be shared in real time.

- **Creates opportunities for feedback and exchange.** Asking employees for feedback about what does or does not go well or about how clearly defined they find defined priorities can be incredibly valuable input when it comes to having an open perspective.

- **Sets the culture.** By bringing clarity to which behaviors, which people, which achievements are celebrated—and which are not—can impact the culture and principles of an organization.

Just like internal communications, powerful external communication—like in the Salesforce example—can be an accelerator of a transformation. There are several reasons as to why this is so:

- It can signal the future position of the company to both stakeholders and those external to the company. Great external communication can set the expected path of the future position and set, for example, the purpose. This is, for example, what Steve Jobs did with the "Think different" advertising campaign when he returned to Apple.

- It can create awareness and interest in an improved (or unique) value proposition to customers. When Scandinavian Airlines moved from a general airline to a business traveler airline, they didn't just stop all consumer advertising but they also invested in targeting the business traveler with their newly created value proposition.

- It can have a positive impact on motivating employees. External PR and advertising can have a positive effect on employees. Several years ago Accenture had a large wall covering advertisement at several major airports, which was partially directed to their employees who traveled frequently. Many described how they became proud after seeing the advertisement.

- It can set the pace of a transformation rhythm. Using external conferences, PR event deadlines, and other elements that publicly pace the company can help set the internal progress pace. At Salesforce they held monthly press conferences where something new always needed to be announced in order to set the fast pace of advancement needed at the aggressive company.

- It can create investor awareness. The billboards along Highway 101, which goes from Los Angeles to San Francisco, are famous ad spaces known for the fact that start-ups use them to get the attention of venture capital investors.

CASE: SCANDINAVIAN AIRLINES

In the mid-1980s Scandinavian Airlines (SAS) was plagued by pricing wars, increased competition due to industry deregulation, and rising operational costs.[57] To survive in

---

[57] J. Carlzon, *Moments of Truth* (Harper Business, 1989).

this new context, they had to transform, and Jan Carlzon was brought in to do just that.

While Carlzon followed many of the wings, which we outlined in our transformation framework—he started with purpose and perspective when he repositioned the airlines to court the growing business-class traveler segment and laid out his priorities with clear promotion—his continuous focus on communication was crucial in turning the organization around. In his memoir, *Moments of Truth*, Jan Carlzon describes how, from his first day as CEO, he made communication a top priority, investing half of his working hours in it.

The word going around was that any time three employees gathered, Carlzon would materialize and begin talking with them. In his view a leader tasked with communicating a strategy to thousands of decentralized decision makers must go further than just issuing corporate messages; his employees, after all, were the ones who must then go and apply a general strategy to specific situations. Communication and storytelling were key in shifting the perspectives and mindsets of both the public and the employees of SAS.

Using plain and straightforward language was essential. According to Carlzon there was no such thing as an "oversimplified" phrase. Clear and simple messages issued from a leader helped establish targets that everyone could work toward. For example, he issued a famous, red-covered booklet entitled *Let's Get in There and Fight*. Many thought it was too simple as it only had a few words and a big font

> type, and each page was filled with cartoon drawings of an airplane smiling, frowning, and even covering its eyes with its wings as it went into a nosedive. He wanted to convey his vision for the airline in a way everybody could understand and engage with.
>
> In a larger internal speech, he felt it was key to engage in some showmanship as well as to communicate some vulnerability. In his eyes the same applied to external communication through advertising, PR, and other public communication. Under Carlzon's leadership, SAS went from near bankruptcy to profitability within 365 days. Only a few years later, *Air Transport World* named SAS Airline of the Year.

7.4 How Do You Score on Your Promotion Wing?

How strong is the promotion wing of your Flywheel of Transformation? Is it already a transformational force, or can it be improved? To help you calibrate your current position, we have defined four levels of strength for this wing in the flywheel. Where would you score your business, function, or team? If you asked your leadership team, your employees, and your external stakeholders, how would they say the organization scored?

- **Level 1. No or Limited Power.** On this level, only a few tools are used internally and externally, and there are no clear or compelling messages aligned with setting the direction of the transformation. Communication does not stand out in comparison to the competition, and it feels like doing obligatory does not have a clear agenda.

- **Level 2. Some Power.** A broader set of tools is used both internally and externally. Most of the communication is delegated to the communication department. There is an intent to use the communication to help the transformation, but there is no overarching strategic communication road map for internal and external communication.

- **Level 3. Good Power.** A broad array of tools is utilized to promote innovative ideas. There is an overall communication strategy and road map aligned with the transformation. However, the internal and external communication is not yet fully in sync with the various business initiatives.

- **Level 4. Transformative Power.** At this level internal and external communication forms an agenda-setting rhythm of expected deliverables. Senior leadership is actively involved in defining and driving the communication, which is supported by a professional comms team. The communication is innovative and synergistic, balanced between internal and external. It's part of creating a movement. The messaging itself is a differentiating factor for the company and the transformation.

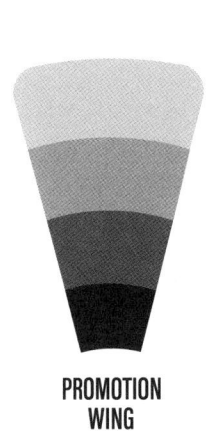

	WING-POWER LEVEL	YOUR SCORE?
LEVEL 4	TRANSFORMATIVE POWER	
LEVEL 3	GOOD POWER	
LEVEL 2	SOME POWER	
LEVEL 1	NO POWER	

PROMOTION WING

How do you score at the moment? Could you improve internal, external, or the synergetic affect most?

PETER: FROM PARENT-CHILD TO ADULTLIKE COMMUNICATION: UNLOCKING RESPONSIBILITY IN THE TEAM

Often leaders are not aware that their communication style has an enormous influence on what the rest of the organization does. For example, I once worked with the director of a company in the automotive industry who needed help with his communication. His communication style was a challenge for many of his peers. Few in the organization—including those in the head office—believed he could change.

The challenge was that he always adopted a style of communication similar to that of a parent speaking to their child. However, many of the organization's younger peers did not appreciate the apparently demeaning style of interaction. The organization knew they needed to address this challenge, and five years from his retirement, they decided to give it one last try.

In this situation we decided to use the "transactional analysis framework."[58] This theory explains that every communication between two people, regardless of age, can be either parentlike, adultlike, or childlike. Each dynamic changes how people express their emotions and how they take responsibility.

- **Parentlike.** A parent is a role where emotions are expressed in one way and are often not fully expressed. This communication is often without any vulnerability and without considering what this communication means for others. There is implicit judgment when the parent role is that of the normative parent, and there is too much caring, which takes away the responsibility (and agency) of the "child" party in this model.
- **Adultlike.** The adult role takes responsibility for themselves and expresses emotions with subtext that matches how they actually feel. They intend to have an equal exchange, which creates a two-way relationship.
- **Childlike.** A childlike role is when people don't take responsibility and also express their emotions in a way that tends toward complaining and blaming others and harbors a particular resentment toward leaders.

---

58 E. Berne, *Transactional Analysis in Psychotherapy* (Grove Press Inc., 1961).

We worked together with this leader to boost his awareness of this dynamic. He wanted to discover why he was sometimes angered by his interactions with his employees. To get started we trained him to express himself and his anger in a more adult way. After six months of intensive coaching and my joining him in key meetings, he became aware of his own behavior and realized he wanted to change. At the same time, we were training his team so that they could provide him with valuable feedback.

Afterward I received a call from the head office that was filled with praise and amazement about the journey of change this individual had undertaken. In the end he stayed in the company for the remainder of his career, shedding his paternalistic style of communications in exchange for a more respectful mode of interaction.

Often when teams don't take sufficient responsibility, a leader has not created the right atmosphere. The attention, time, and energy that employees will put toward following the personal principles of the leader depend highly on the example the leader sets for the team.

7.5 How to Strengthen the Promotion Wing

So how does one strengthen the promotion wing of the flywheel? There are several best practices that are helpful for increasing the power of this wing of the Transformation Flywheel.

1. **Make promotion a strategic priority as a leader.** It's something a communication team can help with, deciding on the key messages and allotted time for the different communication activities that need to be leader led. How much time have you carved out for communications?

2. **Define the communication team and way of working.** Define and select/recruit a team who have not only the skills and experiences needed but also a transformative mindset in their use of communications.

3. **Set clear strategic objectives for internal and external communications.** Can you and your team articulate the three most important outcomes or shifts that you want to achieve in the next one to two years?

4. **Assess existing communication approaches and consider new ones.** Often an organization is stuck in historically defined events and approaches. We have found that it is helpful to look at things with a clean slate.

5. **Define a clear strategic road map of communication milestones, events, and key messages that are aligned with your transformation plan.** It's good to look at least twelve months ahead.

6. **Choose the right communication channels and approaches, including the newer digital channels.**

7. **Have a regular planning and review process examining the progress of communication.** You should review how well recent communication moments went and what can be done better. You must also look ahead at upcoming events to enhance preparedness.

References

Benioff, M., and C. Adler. *Behind the Cloud: The Untold Story of How Salesforce.com Went from Idea to Billion-Dollar Company—and Revolutionized an Industry*. Wiley-Blackwell, 2009.

Dyer, J., H. Gregersen, and C. Christensen. "The Innovator's DNA." *Harvard Business Review*, 2009. https://hbr.org/2009/12/the-innovators-dna.

Sull, D., C. Sull, and J. Yoder. "No One Knows Your Strategy—Not Even Your Top Leaders." *MIT Sloan Management Review*, 2018. https://sloanreview.mit.edu/article/no-one-knows-your-strategy-not-even-your-top-leaders/.

Carlzon, J. *Moments of Truth*. Harper Business, 1989.

Berne, E. *Transactional Analysis in Psychotherapy*. Grove Press Inc., 1961.

INNER GAME POWER

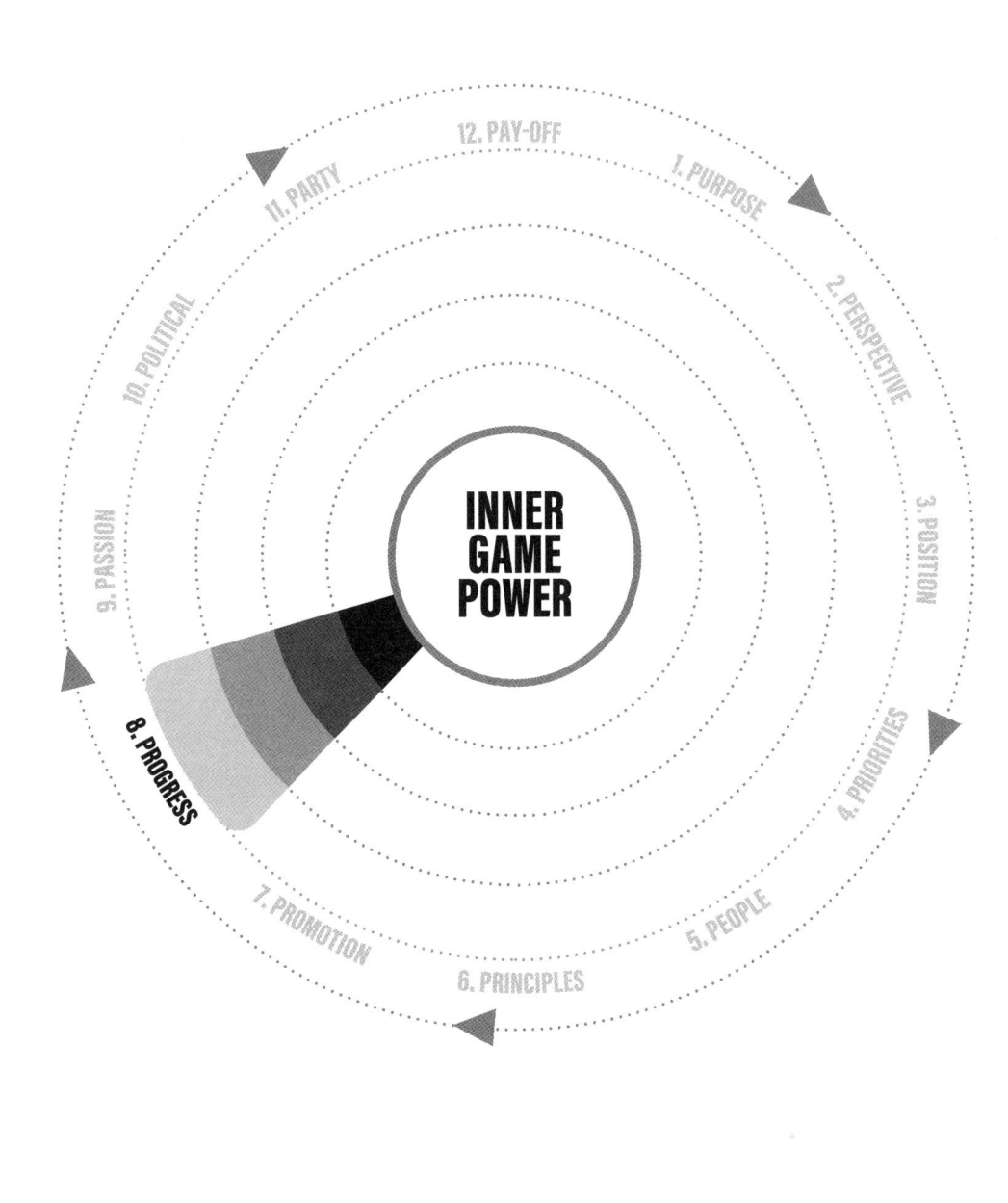

- 1. PURPOSE
- 2. PERSPECTIVE
- 3. POSITION
- 4. PRIORITIES
- 5. PEOPLE
- 6. PRINCIPLES
- 7. PROMOTION
- 8. PROGRESS
- 9. PASSION
- 10. POLITICAL
- 11. PARTY
- 12. PAY-OFF

CHAPTER 8

PROGRESS

Planning is everything; the plan is nothing.
—DWIGHT D. EISENHOWER, THIRTY-FOURTH
PRESIDENT OF THE UNITED STATES

8.1 INTRODUCTION: 3G CAPITAL

In early 2017 Alex Behring, a founding partner of 3G Capital and the chairman of Kraft Heinz, reached out to Unilever CEO Paul Polman as the first step of a $143 billion takeover bid. The deal would have created the second-largest consumer goods company in the world. Unilever fought tooth and nail to prevent the takeover and, in the end, succeeded. But how did this investment firm, which today owns multiple globally recognized brands, nearly pull off one of the largest corporate takeovers in history?

To answer that question, we have to go back to the early '70s, when a few young Rio de Janeiro locals bought into their first business. A recent Harvard graduate and national tennis champion Jorge Paulo Lemann saw an opportunity in the emerging stock trading business in Brazil and wanted to start something where he would have an equity stake. After putting an ad in the newspaper, he bought a small brokerage company, bringing in two partners, Sicupira and Telles. Garantia was born.[59]

Impressed with what Goldman Sachs was doing at the time, they wanted to create a similar performance-driven culture and partnership setup. They wanted to create a true performance-driven meritocracy—a structure governed by people selected according to merit. Dubbed the "Garantia model," this philosophy gave high-performing employees the opportunity to become company partners and shareholders and to make a fortune in the process.

It was about modest salaries supplemented by high bonuses for top performers. It was about hiring young eager talents: they looked for PSDs—poor, smart people with a deep desire to get rich. It was about giving people a growth path to become an equity partner. However, underperforming was not tolerated: Garantia would also let the bottom ten percent go every year. Rather than pay excessive compensation, the money the company earned was invested back into its own growth, so partners could not spend it and instead stayed eager. Garantia's new model was about hard, dedicated work, low costs, and having no frills. They had an informal dress code, there were no corner offices,

---

[59] C. Correa, *Dream Big: How the Brazilian Trio behind 3G Capital Acquired Anheuser-Busch, Burger King and Heinz* (Primeira Pessoa, 2014).

and management sat alongside the rest of the team. Within a decade this logic fueled Garantia's growth to become the leading investment bank in Brazil.

And this was just the beginning. Rather than paying dividend profits out, they wanted to continue growing the firm, so they began looking for opportunities outside the investment business. After an initial phase of some minority investments, they concluded that if they wanted to make a difference, they needed control—at least 51 percent ownership. They needed to be the majority owners of the business and transform from bankers into businessmen. This decision set in motion a series of high-stakes acquisitions.

In 1982 they bought a majority stake in Lojas Americanas—a struggling Brazilian retailer that had lost its sparkle. One of the three founding partners of Garantia, Sicupira, stepped in as CEO at Lojas, bringing with him a small team of Garantia talent. Although Sicupira had no experience in retail whatsoever, he was determined to turn the business around. They tried to assess the situation by deep analyses via commonsense observations of the operations and by looking for best-practice models from around the globe. Before they stepped into the business, they began reaching out to a handful of leading retailers worldwide. They asked whether they could visit so they could learn from them. Sam Walton, founder of Walmart, who was intrigued by the letter, invited them to Walmart's headquarters in Bentonville, Arkansas, leading to a long-term friendship. While at Walmart, Sicupira also learned lots of best practices that would go on to help him transform an organization in an unfamiliar industry.

Once Sicupira and his team of Garantia talents stepped in and had a sense of what to do, they ruthlessly applied Garantia's meritocracy playbook. They broke down the walls between the board offices and put all the executives at one table rather than in the classic corner office. They put strict goals in place for the leaders, stopped giving outrageous perks, and reduced the number of employees. To set an example, Sicupira started coming to work in jeans and sneakers, forgoing the briefcase for a backpack. His actions showed that this was going to be a very different work environment.

They also set their sights on the executive remuneration system, implementing the classic Garantia bonus model. No longer would there be guaranteed bonuses paid since the company's position had been weakening in previous years. Low base salaries would become the norm, but the goals became tougher, and the bonuses, which could be as much as ten times the annual salaries for high performers, became much more aggressive.

Building on this success at Lojas, the head office back at Garantia started to look for the next opportunity, which led them to buy a majority stake in the Brazilian beer brewer Brahma in 1989. This time it would be Telles who stepped in as CEO. Brahma was a traditional, family-owned Brazilian company that also had developed some serious negative character traits driven by a bureaucratic structure: inefficiencies, high salaries, and extreme levels of red tape. Again, before they hit the ground running, they analyzed the business, made commonsense observations, and reached out to the best industry players in the world.

They then began to immediately implement the classic Garantia playbook. In their first year, they swapped out ten of the seventeen plant managers at the local breweries and filled them with young, ambitious people who might have had limited experience but had a high drive to deliver. These signature meritocratic measures saw Brahma turn around, and in 1991, only two years later, Brahma was selected as Company of the Year by *Exame* magazine. Their revenues had expanded by 7.5 percent in one year, and profits had tripled. Furthermore, 35 percent of the highest-performing employees received a bonus of somewhere between three and nine times their salary—roughly equating to 10 percent of the company's total earnings in 1990.

The Garantia model was working, but Telles and his team wanted to evolve their model to achieve the next level of value creation. They started to develop several new approaches:

- To create a pipeline of talent, they started to actively recruit yearly forty to fifty talents for a trainee program each year and intended to give young people big opportunities early in their career—which quickly became one of the most sought-after programs in the country.
- To measure and standardize the processes in the

different breweries, they asked professor and specialist in Japanese efficiency Vicente Falconi of the Christiano Ottoni Foundation to develop a new approach. He set targets for everyone who worked in the brewery—from the shop floor to the directors—and bonuses were linked to meeting those targets.
- To create and implement a novel cost-cutting program, after Falconi's method became common practice, Telles asked Falconi to develop another method to control costs. Falconi looked for inspiration in well-known cost-cutting programs and created a simplified version for Brahma's situation, which became the renowned zero-based budget. This radical cost-control program prescribes a complete annual revision of all capital allocation based not on historical budgeting but rather on necessity.

In 1999, armed with these new approaches, they were able to buy Brahma's Brazilian competitor Antarctica, creating one of the larger breweries in Latin America, calling the umbrella organization Ambev. They then began to implement their signature turnaround logic on the acquired company. Following this, in 2004 they bought a large stake in Interbrew, one of the large global yet very traditional Belgium brewers. They again used their execution approach to transform this business. After the successful transformation of Interbrew, they made the bold move to acquire the iconic US brewer Anheuser-Busch, also adding Miller beer to the brewing empire, creating AB InBev, the world's biggest brewer.

> During this journey of consolidating the brewery market and transforming it based on their performance playbook and meritocratic culture, they created 3G as an ownership and investment vehicle and began to set their sights on other markets. Their next target included Heinz and Kraft in a consolidating consumer goods play and ultimately Burger King, which led them to then eye Unilever as a target.
>
> The 3G method has created admirers as well as critics—their ruthless ability to execute and progress at scale has been a big engine in their Transformational Flywheels.

8.2 What Is the Progress Wing of the Flywheel of Transformation?

We define the progress wing of the flywheel as the power an organization has to execute its priorities and achieve a better future position. How much force is behind your plans? Change must always work against the inertia that keeps the status quo in place. To get past this, it's about making plans of execution, creating clear tasks and responsibilities, and delivering on these actions to make smaller changes that cascade into a larger transformation. It's where the rubber meets the road. You can have a great purpose, smart

> It's about making plans of execution, creating clear tasks and responsibilities, and delivering on these actions to make smaller changes that cascade into a larger transformation.

perspectives, a clear future position, powerful priorities, great people, and intensive promotion—but only execution makes change happen. That being said, execution by itself, without having the other steps in place, also leads to limited transformative power, as execution has limited direction.

Transformative execution power is different from the execution of the ongoing daily, routine tasks. Many organizations have their daily operational activity processes like planning, budgeting, or monthly reviews based on a yearly cycle. However, a transformation requires going beyond this. It's often not about operating something better but operating this while also transforming/changing the business. A McKinsey & Company research shows that companies who successfully transform[60] not only step up in terms of execution and performance of the current business but do so while driving forward a transformative agenda in parallel. Both execution powers are needed at the same time. It's therefore integral that a strong plan for maximizing the existing business is defined around sales, cost, and other fundamentals as well as taking into account a longer three-year transformative agenda.

What are some of the approaches successful companies have put in place to secure the execution of the transformation agenda? We have seen and experienced that a mix of the following approaches create power behind the execution of the transformation:

- **Transformation Agenda.** A clear three-year transformation agenda and plan is developed, communicated, and implemented by the key stakeholders. The plan has clear, measurable outcomes, is chunked into yearly actions, and divides the current year by quarters. The plan has clear responsibilities and KPIs. Although the three-year outcome can be aspira-

---

[60] Bradley et al., "Why Your Next Transformation Should Be 'All-In.'"

tional and ambitious, the concrete steps ahead are tangible and manageable. As the famous proverb from Lao-tzu says, "The journey of a thousand miles begins with one step."

- **Senior Sponsors.** Targets and activities are allocated to departments and managers. Clear responsibilities are assigned. Every major initiative has clear senior leaders.

- **Program Management Office.** Almost always a separate program management office is set up to oversee and track the program. This team is often small, but it is the voice of truth that tracks, reports, and coordinates the progress to senior leadership. In the article from McKinsey, a chief transformation officer (CTO) is defined as someone who has to question, push, and praise. The leadership is aligned with a longer-term transformational journey, as it might require short-term investments and might cause a temporary drop in profits. The job of the CTO is to cajole (and otherwise irritate) an organization that needs to think and act differently. For example, when Howard Schultz started his transformation at Starbucks (as described in the "Position" chapter), he spoke with Michael Dell, who had recently returned to Dell and successfully transformed the business. Michael recommended for Howard to put in place a transformational program office, which he did.

- **Organizational Incentives.** Incentives are put in place for management who are aligned with the transformation. If management's incentives are just focused on making short-term budget targets, it can create a hand brake effect on the entire organization's transformation effort. For example, one of the things private equity players do is to put a management equity program in place to make sure leaders have a focused long-term incentive for the transformation.

- **Zero-Based Budgeting.** Budget decisions and capital investments are done on a zero-based-budgeting basis and should reflect the organization's transformational priorities. Rather than simply following on from last year, this budget is about making deliberate decisions about where to put the resources to make the transformation happen. Research published in *McKinsey Quarterly* shows that companies with higher levels of efficiency in their capital reallocation experienced higher average shareholder returns.[61] Taking a measured approach as to where to deliberately save and where to invest is a must when it comes to creating power in the transformation.

- **Focus on Progress.** There is a relentless focus on creating progress, clarity, and transparency—a company should not operate with a focus on blaming others when things fall behind. Focus on creating early signals if something is offtrack and then quickly learning how to resolve any difficulties. Similarly it's important to celebrate and highlight the progress, of course.

MARCO: MAKING PROGRESS CAN BE ADDICTIVE

In all the transformations I have led, shifting gears, relentlessly executing, and getting the right things done was a key driver to create the necessary progress momentum.

---

[61] S. Hall et al., "How to Put Your Money Where Your Strategy Is," McKinsey & Company, McKinsey Quarterly, 2012.

Although all situations are, of course, different, certain approaches can be effective in many situations. Let me share some practical examples of practices.

- In the first one hundred days of a transformation, I always invest in creating a three-year transformation road map based on the future position and priorities. This plan defines key initiatives, deliverables, milestones, and responsibilities. The plan should also be linked to financials (P&L) lines.
- I always create a clear summary navigation map as a one-pager. This features a chart that lists our corporate priorities with measurable objectives, the main initiative areas by priority, and the titles and initials of those who are responsible. We color the priorities and initiatives like a traffic light. I use this page in all key meetings.
- I also always set up a small transformation program office (TPO) and appoint a chief transformation officer (CTO) who reports directly to myself on progress and challenges as they resolve issues related to the transformation. I normally place that office very near mine. Most of the time, we also set up a transformation room as the symbolic engine room of the transformation with big posters of key work streams, goals, and progress milestones; progress on KPIs; financials; and reminders of other important concepts.
- To make sure that resources are shifted to priority areas and that nonpriority areas are getting fewer resources, I also like to force substantial choices via the yearly budget and capital expenditure cycle to shift resources

toward transformative priorities—what will be funded, and how will that cause progress?
- Perhaps the most important lever is to put the right transformative leadership talent in charge of key transformative priorities. Identifying the transformational talent and giving them opportunities to make a difference on the most critical functions and initiatives for the transformation is key.
- To keep momentum and attention on the progress, I typically carve out two hours a week to rotationally do deep-dive sessions on a few of the most critical initiatives—M&A projects, countries, functions, and other structural programs. We get the responsible team in the room, as well as any key stakeholders who can help solve the key challenges, and decide upon the next steps. The attitude of "challenge and build" naturally leads to progress. The sessions are focused on finding solutions to problems and not creating further problems that inhibit solutions.
- On a quarterly basis, all the senior leaders should carve out and take a step back to review the transformational journey. What have we achieved? What has gone well? What needs to go better? What have we learned? What do we need to figure out better? These are key questions that need to be addressed, but they are also opportunities to reflect on key successes. Celebrating microwins is important in these sessions. Nothing drives progress better than a sense of success and clear goals for even more future triumph.

> In my experience, at some point, an organization gets an "execution momentum"—a joy derived from progressing instead of the malaise of clinging to the status quo, and as a result, the different initiatives start positively affecting each other. Making progress can be addictive.

8.3 Why Is It Important to Have a Strong Progress Wing?

In business just as in nature, you either grow and develop or stagnate and decline. There is no stable status quo point. As we've previously said, execution is where the rubber meets the road in terms of achieving meaningful progress. During a transformation it's key to create meaningful momentum quickly and to share this momentum so that the organization becomes convinced that change is indeed possible and that stasis is unacceptable.

Progress keeps key stakeholders involved in the change journey. At the start there is quite often a smaller internal change coalition who are thoroughly convinced of the need for change. But these are often juxtaposed with large groups of potential early adopters, late adopters, and laggards among the ranks of the leaders and employees in an organization. Creating execution momentum will convince the early adopters to join the transformation journey first. Then when the late adopters see the early adopters embracing change and acting to make the transformation a success, they will get social proof and be convinced that they need to follow along. Progress will also convince other critical stakeholders like investors, customers, and suppliers that the transformation is not just talking but also really happening. At some point this momentum leads to a point of no return with no way back to the old status quo.

If there is, however, a lack of tangible progress, then doubt, or perhaps even cynicism, can take root and rob all the momentum from the change effort. Winning the game of transformation is all about getting points on the board.

> ### CASE: SALESFORCE.COM AND V2MOM
>
> One of the success drivers behind Salesforce.com's incredible growth and their transformation of an industry is the use of the V2MOM approach, which Marc Benioff used from day one.[62] But what is V2MOM beyond a weird-sounding acronym? V2MOM is a single page that is given to all the leaders in an organization from the CEO down to all managers and leaders. This document succinctly clarifies what the targets are each year. This approach to company alignment is used religiously at Salesforce.com. The acronym stands for the following:
>
> - **Vision:** What do you want; what are you trying to achieve? This part of the acronym refers to getting crystal clear on where you want to go rather than not what is traditionally seen as a vision.
> - **Values:** What's important to you? This establishes the most important reasons for achieving an outcome. What is the set of principles and beliefs that allows for achieving the vision?
> - **Methods:** How will you get results? This part of the framework outlines what actions are needed to get the job done.

---

62 Benioff et al., *Behind the Cloud*.

- **Obstacles:** What might stand in the way? What are the impediments blocking you from achieving your goal? This could be, for instance, a lack of information, time, or some other obstacle.
- **Measures:** How will you know when you have it? By defining what data or metrics are attributed to success, you can objectively say when you have arrived at your goal.

As an example we have attached the first V2MOM that Marc Benioff created when he started Salesforce.com:

Salesforce.com's First V2MOM, 4/12/1999

Vision

Rapidly create a world-class Internet company/site for sales Force Automation.

Values

1. World-class organization
2. Time to market
3. Functional
4. Usability (Amazon quality)
5. Value-added partnerships

Methods

1. Hire the team
2. Finalize product specification and technical architecture
3. Rapidly develop the product specification to beta and production stages
4. Build partnerships with big e-commerce, content, and hosting companies
5. Build a launch plan
6. Develop exit strategy: IPO/acquisition

Obstacles

1. Developers
2. Product manager/business development person

Measures

1. Prototype is state-of-the-art
2. High-quality functional system
3. Partnerships are online and integrated
4. Salesforce.com is regarded as leader and visionary
5. We are all rich

8.4 How Do You Score on the Progress Wing?

How strong is the progress wing of your Transformational Flywheel? Is it in full force, or is there room to find the next gear? How would management and your employees rate the strength of getting things done in the business? To what extent is your execution power a competitive advantage (as it is for 3G and Salesforce.com, for example)?

- **Level 1. No or limited power.** At this level there is limited execution power available to deliver the execution of the transformation. The focus is only (and continuously) on day-to-day current operations and on achieving short-term budgetary goals. No new approaches such as program management office (PMO), V2MOM, or another system are put in place. People are cynical about the transformation, and efforts toward transformation are seen as one of the frequently changing "flavors of the month" company programs. Incentives are not aligned with progress goals.

- **Level 2. Some power.** At this level some efforts are made to launch certain initiatives to make the transformation happen. The topics are regularly discussed on the management level, but many people are still on the fence and unwilling to make the hard choices about reallocating budget, talent management, etc. The company culture still finds problems to solutions and not solutions to problems. Some incentives are aligned with progress goals, but many are not.

- **Level 3. Good power.** A clear transformation program has been put in place with a program management office. There is a three-year plan, and targets are set. KPIs are tracked.

Progress is celebrated, and bottlenecks are quickly identified and resolved. Most people are behind the transformation, but some are still taking a "wait and see" approach before wholeheartedly joining the journey. Incentives are aligned with the transformation goals.

- **Level 4. Transformative power.** The organization has set up a strong, nonnegotiable approach to executing the transformation with a clear senior sponsor, a transformation program, a program office, and incentives that are aligned with the transformation. Furthermore, powerful tools like V2MOM run through the DNA of the company. There is pride from making change happen, and it has become a real competitive advantage. The company can outperform its competitors when it comes to executing change.

PROGRESS WING

WING-POWER LEVEL		YOUR SCORE?
LEVEL 4	TRANSFORMATIVE POWER	
LEVEL 3	GOOD POWER	
LEVEL 2	SOME POWER	
LEVEL 1	NO POWER	

PETER: DEFINING DIFFERENT EXECUTION SPEEDS IN PARALLEL TO ACCELERATE CHANGE

I was once brought in as an organizational change advisor for a global software company to transform their personnel and systems divisions. Due to the political environment, the organizational culture, the structure, and the history of the company, many of their internal processes were slow. The organization had a slow rhythm when it came to getting things done. One small example is that the identification pass I needed to enter the building only arrived on my last day at the company—a full nine months after I applied.

Although we had a good plan, from the start we had to deal with the slow execution speed and shifting priorities. To achieve a better execution speed, we needed to shift our mindset and become much more flexible in our approach. We identified several activities we could do much faster if we somewhat detached from the larger, slower project dynamic.

In my last month with the organization, everything seemed suddenly urgent. After months of seemingly waiting and waiting, everything needed to be finished yesterday. However, moving fast contradicted the culture of the company. There's a lot you can do when you ramp up the pressure and imagine you only have a day or a week to finish something that usually would normally take a month in your mind. The ability to shift gears for part (or the entirety) of the change programs when possible is often key to making change happen.

8.5 How Can You Strengthen Your Progress Wing?

In section 8.2 we described the key building blocks that can create a stronger progress and increase the execution power behind your Transformational Flywheel. Execution is all about creating a disciplined focus on transforming the business, alongside the day to day, toward which the majority of an institution's energy tends to gravitate.[63] The following are several concepts that are helpful in strengthening this transformational wing:

- Create a clear three-year transformation plan with explicit objectives, deliverables, responsibilities, milestones, and financials.

- Set up a program management office (PMO) for the transformation and appoint a strong transformation officer who has the focus on cross-functionally overseeing the transformation program and acts as the voice of truth to motivate the organization.

- Align incentives. Make it clear how key stakeholders will benefit from the proposed progress.

- Have clear senior sponsors who engage in deep dives into the key initiatives.

- Set up transformation review meetings that are separate from the day-to-day operational meetings.

- Have simple and clear monthly reporting on the company-wide progress.

---

63 M. Bucy et al., "Transformation with a Capital T," *McKinsey Quarterly*, 2016.

- Begin with a focus on quick wins and catalytic initiatives. These will scaffold into larger initiatives.

- Celebrate progress to demonstrate momentum.

- Put execution tools in place like V2MOM that build across the organization execution capabilities for the long run.

- Remind yourself that progress beats process.

References

Correa, C. *Dream Big: How the Brazilian Trio behind 3G Capital Acquired Anheuser-Busch, Burger King and Heinz*. Primeira Pessoa, 2014.

Benioff, M., and C. Adler. *Behind the Cloud: The Untold Story of How Salesforce.com Went from Idea to Billion-Dollar Company—and Revolutionized an Industry*. Wiley-Blackwell, 2009.

Hall, S., D. Lovallo, and R. Musters. "How to Put Your Money Where Your Strategy Is." *McKinsey Quarterly*, 2012. https://www.mckinsey.com/business-functions/strategy-and-corporate-finance/our-insights/how-to-put-your-money-where-your-strategy-is.

Angevine, C., and D. Bates. "The Transformation Office: Key Success Factors." McKinsey & Company, 2019. https://www.mckinsey.com/~/media/McKinsey/Business%20Functions/Transformation/Our%20Insights/The%20transformation%20office%20Key%20success%20factors/The-transformation-office-Key-success-factors-vF.ashx.

Bucy, M., S. Hall, and D. Yakola. "Transformation with a Capital T." *McKinsey Quarterly*, 2016. https://www.mckinsey.com/business-functions/rts/our-insights/transformation-with-a-capital-t?cid=eml-web#.

INNER GAME POWER

- 1. PURPOSE
- 2. PERSPECTIVE
- 3. POSITION
- 4. PRIORITIES
- 5. PEOPLE
- 6. PRINCIPLES
- 7. PROMOTION
- 8. PROGRESS
- 9. PASSION
- 10. POLITICAL
- 11. PARTY
- 12. PAY-OFF

CHAPTER 9

PASSION

I would rather die of passion than of boredom.
—VINCENT VAN GOGH

9.1 INTRODUCTION: NIKE

In his early twenties, Phil Knight had just finished his studies at Stanford and had a decision to make: would he choose the corporate life or pursue his passion? Although he was equipped with an MBA from a great business school and had many opportunities ahead of him, there was something standing in his way. Knight was a keen track runner. He was entranced by the feeling of freedom that running brought with it, and he wanted to win. But although he was a good athlete, he admitted that, unfortunately, he wasn't great. That, however, did not diminish his desire for a life full of his passion.

Then one morning back in 1962, while blazing down a misty Oregon track at dawn, he had an epiphany. "What if there is a way, without being an athlete, to feel what athletes feel?"[64] He wanted to experience the focus, the determination, the playfulness, the pain, the single-minded dedication, and the purpose that athletes felt each and every day—and he knew that he wouldn't be able to find that in the corporate world.

The alternative was what he called his "crazy idea."[65] A few months earlier, he'd written a paper for his final class on entrepreneurship at Stanford outlining the market opportunity of importing Japanese running shoes to the United States. The paper showed how Japan was advanced in technologies—producing everything from cameras to cars at a high quality—and that they must also be advanced in shoe technology. While his professor was impressed, no one else found the idea quite so enticing as Knight. However, that morning Knight's crazy idea stopped seeming so crazy. That morning he told himself, "Let everyone else call your idea crazy ... just keep going"—a philosophy he'd borrowed from the runners of the day.

Driven by this passion and armed with this unique perspective on the market opportunity of selling low-cost running shoes from Japan, Knight decided to make a bold step and visit Japan while on a world trip that he'd convinced his father to pay for. Once he arrived in Japan, Phil was blown away by the majesty and spirit of the country. Everything about it was interesting, even musical. Soon after he

---

64   P. Knight, *Shoe Dog: A Memoir by the Creator of Nike* (Simon & Schuster Ltd, 2019), pp. 3–4.
65   Ibid., p. 4.

arrived, Knight reached out to a Japanese shoe manufacturer, Onitsuka, and asked if he could come and visit. When he arrived at that first meeting, he was confronted by a handful of Japanese executives in suits. Understandably he was anxious and felt out of his depth.

When one of the Japanese executives asked the recent graduate which company he represented, he wasn't prepared for the question. His mind took him back to his childhood home and the prized first-place ribbons displayed in his bedroom. Almost without thinking, he blurted out, "Blue Ribbon Sports, Portland, Oregon." And then he began to recite his Stanford research paper. He bluffed that the market opportunity for these imports could be as big as $1 billion, a number that intrigued the Japanese executives. Having survived this first hiccup in business, the two parties began discussing an initial sample shipment of the manufacturer's premier running shoes, the Onitsuka Tigers.

After that daunting experience, his curiosity to see the world won over flying back home to the United States, and he continued his trip around the world. However, it certainly wasn't the only experience that would leave an impression. During his stay in the Greek capital, he saw the still proud remains of the temple of the winged goddess of victory at the Acropolis of Athens, the Temple of Athena Nike, a name that would stay with him for years to come.

Back in Portland he took a job at one of the "big eight" national accounting firms and worked in their Portland office. After nearly a year of uncertainty, the sample of twelve pairs of Tigers finally arrived. Knight immediately sent two pairs down to his former track coach, Bill Bowerman. Bowerman was a top-level coach and an obsessed "shoe dog" (someone who intensely devoted themselves to the making, selling, buying, or designing of shoes). He considered shoes the one piece of gear critical to an athlete's development. He was always stealing athletes' footwear and pulling them apart and stitching them back together. Bowerman would spend days tinkering with running shoes and making modifications so that his athletes could increase their performance on the track. Bowerman would go to any lengths in his quest to shed weight from the materials of his athlete's shoes. He was willing to try any mineral or material—he'd even used kangaroo leather and cod—to increase an athlete's performance.

Upon receiving the shoes, Bowerman immediately organized a lunch with Knight. Bowerman wanted in. The two entered into a fifty-fifty partnership, and Blue Ribbon was officially born. Phil immediately ordered three hundred pairs of Tigers and asked Onitsuka for exclusive dealerships for the Western United States.

Looking back, the duo's sales strategy was simple—but this was by necessity. After being rejected by a couple of sporting goods stores, they decided to sell their Tigers out of Phil's car trunk. All other doors were closed. Phil would go to various track events across the Pacific Northwest and catch up with coaches, runners, and the fans between races and show them the shoes. Phil knew he wasn't the best salesman, but because he was so passionate about the product and the benefits they could bring to athletes, he didn't really feel like he was selling anything. Rather, he believed that sport would make the world a better place, and people sensed that belief. Belief is irresistible! As a result of this honest passion, word of mouth began to spread. They couldn't write orders fast enough. Prospective customers even began showing up at his parents' house to buy the shoes.

This passion attracted Blue Ribbon's first employee, Jeff Johnson, another distance runner and avid shoe dog. Johnson was offered a commission-based salesman position, which he accepted, whereafter he immediately began to drive Knight nuts. To Knight it seemed like he never stopped writing. Every time Johnson had an idea for the business, Jeff would write it down and send it to Knight by mail. Johnson was totally fanatical—fanatic about the product, fanatic about the customer, and fanatic about running. He would obsess over his customer's success and even sent them their own index cards that stated their personal shoe size. Johnson even sent them birthday and Christmas cards. He truly believed that runners are God's chosen ones and that if running was done right, it could lead to nirvana. Although Knight questioned whether he had hired the right guy, he loved the energy. Johnson was so passionate that it was only natural that he represented the company.

As Blue Ribbon continued to grow, Knight was continuously fighting with local banks to extend his credit lines. In those days capital was scarce, and funding business growth was difficult. But Knight was so passionate about their vision that he rented an apartment in downtown Portland, and Johnson opened their first retail space in Santa Monica with the intention of making the store a mecca for runners. Despite this growth Blue Ribbon still couldn't afford a salary for its founder. Consequently Knight took a job with Price Waterhouse and spent every other waking hour running Blue Ribbon—early mornings, late nights, and every weekend and vacation.

But it wasn't enough. He needed another job that would require fewer hours and give him more time for the company. Eventually he was able to quit the accounting firm and accepted an assistant professor job at Portland State University. Simultaneously Blue Ribbon's growth allowed him to continue to hire more people—"most were ex-runners and eccentrics, as only ex-runners could be"[66]—and by the end of 1969, just as Blue Ribbon was on track to hit $300,000 in sales, Phil quit his teaching job and began to fully concentrate on his now not-so-crazy idea.

That year after the Olympics in Mexico, the leader of Onitsuka (the Japanese company he was sourcing the shoes from) decided to visit Blue Ribbon's Portland office as a detour from a trip to see the games. Worried that he had oversold his "worldwide HQ"—which was actually a

---

66   Ibid., p. 137.

tiny downtown apartment—to the suppliers, Knight quickly put up a map of the United States on the wall and covered it in red pins. Each represented a location where Blue Ribbon had sold a pair of Tigers. Later that year Phil flew to Japan again and secured another three-year contract. However, despite the fact that the business was growing, he continuously had to deal with cash flow challenges. He, therefore, had to make the deal with another Japanese trading company to secure a loan.

He then heard that Onitsuka was trying to get new distributors on the East Coast behind his back—even though they had earlier signed a new contract. A representative of the company came to visit Knight and offered to buy him out. He faced an existential crisis. His dream looked to be crushed. Knight decided to make a bold move and start his own sports shoe brand. He found a soccer shoe manufacturer in Mexico and believed it might hold the answers to his problems. He convinced the supplier to produce shoes for him. Designing and branding their own shoes was a big leap from selling imported shoes. What should the logo be? An artist made some very cheap sketches, and Knight settled on the now famous "swoosh" logo. Soon the factory manager in Mexico was calling to tell Knight that they needed a name immediately. Without a brand to stitch, they could not start the manufacturing machines. They had played with all kinds of planets, animals, and other options, but they ultimately couldn't decide.

> The next morning Jeff Johnson called, saying that the new name had come to him in a dream—Nike. As soon as he heard it, Phil thought back to his round-the-world trip and to the Temple of Athena Nike, the goddess of victory, and he made a snap decision. Victory was, after all, what the company was all about.
>
> However, as one issue was resolved, another presented itself. The next challenge was whether any retailer would actually buy Nike's shoes. Although their first batch of shoes to come out of Mexico were only so-so, people gave Nike the benefit of the doubt based on the passion they had radiated over the past decade. Given all the goodwill and reputation they had built up, many people decided to give Phil and his team a shot. From that moment on, Nike's growth began to explode and, in the process, transformed an industry.

9.2 What Is the Passion Wing in the Flywheel of Transformation?

Passion can be a powerful wing in the Transformational Flywheel. In almost every case study we have shared, passion has been one of the major factors that have contributed to success. Without passion, change at large scale misses the drive and the conviction to overcome the inertia of the status quo. Passion comes from the heart. It's fuel to go beyond the comfort zone.

The etymology of passion arises from the Latin word *pati*, which literally means "to suffer." It's a feeling of intense enthusiasm toward a compelling desire with the implication of accepting that one must endure suffering to attain that desire. When human beings are passionate about something or someone, this burning desire is what keeps them focused on achieving their goal.

We all recognize when people are passionate about what they set out to accomplish. It radiates in how they communicate and how they engage with the challenges ahead. When people live with their passion, people speak more enthusiastically. They see solutions where others see problems. They focus on pursuing their goals, which become front and center for them. This passion fuels them to go the additional mile and not stop at a setback or an unforeseen challenge. Was there a time when you were truly passionate about the professional challenge ahead?

Every leader, leadership team, and organization has a certain level of passion to realize a transformation to get toward a better future. The question is not whether you have passion or not—the question is the degree of this passion, how strong that passion is. At the low end, a lack of passion can result in low levels of engagement and in obstacles that act as roadblocks that block progress or prevent accomplishing an objective. At the high end, passion can cause high levels of engagement and drive, lending the affected party the ability to tackle problems head-on.

One note of caution, however—without moderation, passion tends to make one blind since it comes from the heart and can cloud intelligent thinking and rationality. A person running east to see the sun set will never succeed no matter how strong their passion, just as Kodak's passion for analogue photography was not helpful when the world shifted rapidly toward digital photography. Therefore, having other flywheel wings strongly in place (such as a smart perspective, a clear future position, the right people, empowering principles, and a good progress plan) will help direct a strong passion wing so that all that energy is put to good use.

MARCO: WITHOUT PASSION A TRANSFORMATION CAN'T GAIN MOMENTUM

I strongly believe that you need heart and mind together to make change happen. In most transformations I have been part of, the level of passion needs to be enhanced, or the team needs to become more focused on the priorities of the transformation. I also believe that passion is contagious, so it's important that your own passion for the transformation at hand stays high. We say more about this in the "Inner Game" chapter. I also strongly believe that any team or organization's level of passion can be influenced. As a habit, when I walk into any meeting, department, or part of an organization, I check the level of passion I sense, and then I rate it on a scale of one to ten and gauge whether or not that passion is directed to the right priorities. Let me share two short cases, one where passion needed redirection and another where it needed to be unleashed to empower the Flywheel of Transformation.

When I was a manager at McKinsey, I became part of a team that had been created to help transform one of the leading global fashion brands. I quickly realized that the business had an incredibly high passion for the brand and designing new collections. On my first day, before I even started, they took me to one of their stores to make sure that I wore their clothing line. One of the challenges was that this passion for fashion and new collections had led to a sprawling range of SKUs, which led to a high level of markdowns and suppressed profitability.

To demonstrate the problem, we had drawn white lines on the floor of part of the room where the board met, representing the typical size of the floor space in a store. During the board meeting, we wheeled in the full collection of the coming season, which had been heaped into a big pile in the limited space. Then we picked out ten items that were actually responsible for 100 percent of the profits. It was eye opening.

The next challenge was not to have the brand ruled by numbers while also keeping the passion and creating more focus. We worked with the design teams to let them design a wide range of ideas, which were then narrowed down by customer and retailer panels' feedback. However, we also allowed for around 10 percent of the SKUs to give designers full experimental freedom. At the end we were able to redirect the passion without losing it.

Let me share another case of unlocking passion. When I led a global division for TNT Express, we had to rapidly transform hundreds of depots around the world. While visiting a lot of these depots in my first few months and speaking to the frontline workers, I noticed that they wanted to do well but that they were often frustrated with a lack of support from the organization, not having the room to make changes, with the lack of proper equipment; and as a consequence, their passion had become low. To prove that we could turn this around, I asked which of the depots was the worst performing. The depot had very low morale, which only compounded the challenges. We quickly developed a four-week program where a support team

> would work with the current employees, with the ambition of making it one of the best-performing depots within a few weeks. Most of the people thought it was impossible, but we launched a test program that was based on a mix of lean and total quality management techniques.
>
> In this highly engaging pilot program, the local depot team defined their metrics of success, listed which problems to tackle first, and then brainstormed ideas and implemented them right away. These changes range from having runs start fifteen minutes earlier to painting white lines on the floor, creating stand-up meetings with the different shift teams, investing in some new equipment, and engaging with customers to better understand their needs. Within weeks the depot team went from a demotivated crew to a team that was once again highly passionate. This depot catapulted to the top of many internal rankings—and stayed there. It became an example of what was possible. After this initial success, we rolled out this program around the world.

9.3 Why Is It Important to Have a Strong Passion Wing?

Why is passion such a critical ingredient to achieving change? For change to succeed, new beliefs, new ways of working, and new relationships have to be created. A new way has to be trailblazed, and learning always, at least initially, feels awkward and uncomfortable. To let go of the familiar while the new future is not yet fully secure requires positive energy, resourcefulness, determination, and conviction. A strong passion not only fuels your own path to the future but also has a positive ripple effect on the people around you. Passion can, therefore, positively impact a transformation because of the following:

- It creates a higher level of conviction about what achievements are possible.

- It increases a high level of drive and resourcefulness for making things happen and overcoming roadblocks.

- It keeps more focus on the targeted future outcome and pushes distractions and the "pain of change" aside.

- It stimulates a growth mindset, which allows for the creation of new solutions that fuel constructive ideas.

- It is infectious for your current team and stakeholders including employees, customers, and investors.

- Passion is attractive. It draws in opportunities in the form of new talent, new customers, and new M&A targets who can feel if the organization and its leaders are passionate about what they do and what they're trying to achieve.

On the opposite end of the spectrum, a lack of passion can be damaging. If leaders and their employees are not passionate about what they are doing, it can be felt immediately. Roadblocks look bigger, decisions take longer, and the comfort of the known starts to look more attractive than the uncertainty or the better new future.

9.4 How Do You Score on the Passion Wing?

How would you rate your personal passion for organizational change? What about your team's passion for the transformation? The passion within the organization as a whole? Is this wing of the Transformational Flywheel at maximum power, or can it be strengthened? How would customers and investors rate your organization's passion? As with the other wings, we have defined four levels to allow you to do a quick assessment:

- **Level 1. No or Limited Power: Dispassionate and Unenthusiastic.** At this level there is a limited passion to deliver the execution of the transformation. There is limited enthusiasm to make change happen beyond some lip service and token initiatives. You don't see sparks in the eyes of the leaders. Change is seen as an unattractive, hard climb, and there is a certain level of cynicism. People who are passionate about the need for change are seen as unrealistic outliers.

- **Level 2. Some Power: Pockets of Passion.** At this level some passion exists in small pockets of the organization. There is some conviction in some areas, and some leaders are passionate. However, many people are still on the fence and say they like the change but are not willing to lead it. Several lighthouse initiatives have some amount of traction. Next to the innovators in the organization, the early majority is still unsure about getting behind the change agenda.

- **Level 3. Good Power: Passion Drives Progress.** At this level there is a sincere passion within the leaders and the organization to make a better future. Progress is celebrated, and setbacks are used as opportunities for learning. People increasingly focus on finding new ways forward instead of merely finding solutions to immediate problems. Meetings are more than just going through the motions, and there is a real spark to try and learn new things. The passion radiates outside the organization. Customers, suppliers, and new recruits get the sense that something exciting is happening.

- **Level 4. Transformative Power: Passion Is a Driving Force.** There is a very high level of passion in the organization, and it's contagious. Leaders and employees share a real passion for the purpose of the organization, its perspective, and the target future position. This passion gives a sense of meaning and fulfillment and an acceptance of the suffering that change brings. People who don't share this passion don't feel at home in the organization and leave. On the other hand, it attracts different people who share that passion. Meetings are lively, conversations are engaging, and progress is celebrated. Roadblocks are seen as opportunities to find a new solution and show creativity and resourcefulness.

How passionate are you about your transformation?

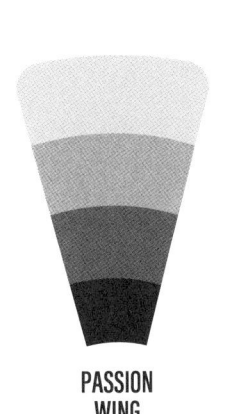

PASSION WING

	WING-POWER LEVEL	YOUR SCORE?
LEVEL 4	TRANSFORMATIVE POWER	
LEVEL 3	GOOD POWER	
LEVEL 2	SOME POWER	
LEVEL 1	NO POWER	

PETER: WITH PASSION IT'S EASIER NOT TO GIVE UP

I have found several things that help fuel passion—even when the going gets tough. First, it is important to continuously appreciate. Appreciation starts with what you appreciate about yourself and about the transformation you are undertaking. Second, you want to encourage passion with others by focusing on what goes well and by rewarding people who are showing passion and openly communicating. Last, passion is best maintained by asking yourself this—what is your intention as a leader in transformation and for your actions? This question is different from what goals need to be achieved.

> Passion is best maintained by asking yourself this—what is your intention as a leader in transformation and for your actions?

For instance, when I started my own company, I began doing too many activities at once in order to get the business going. This ranged from interim positions and consulting work to cultural training courses and offering international training courses on neurolinguistic programming (NLP).

I had a lot of passion for the NLP training courses. However, they were not that profitable. My passion, however, kept me convinced that there was a way to make this a healthy business in the long run, and I kept investing time and resources. My conviction was that it would take time to build a reputation, which was needed to succeed in the long run. I was also convinced that after we get students in for these training sessions, they would start using other services and ultimately become profitable customers. I also felt that this expertise was critical for the mindset and other coaching programs we were developing to help others.

In the end my strong belief came true. After many ups and downs, our persistence paid off, and our vision became reality beyond all my expectations. We had fought our way into a market that was crowded and created our own niche. I was able to persist because of my belief, mindset, and passion for the NLP toolbox. It not only brought a lot of fulfillment but it also was planting a seed that was going to bring a lot of benefits in the long term. Without the fuel of passion and the resulting convictions, developing this business would have been impossible, and I would have missed the joy I experience when I use NLP to help others personally and professionally transform.

Ultimately passion is about unleashing the potential of yourself and others.

9.5 How to Strengthen Your Passion Wing

Passion is not something an organization has by some random luck. In many of the case studies that we have provided at the start of each chapter, leaders were able to dramatically raise the level of passion on the organizational level to fuel the transformation and manage it actively. So what are some of the levers that leaders can use to increase the passion and drive the level of passion in the organization? We have identified seven practical attributes for passionate leaders to harness:

- As a leader, take responsibility for the level of passion in the organization and make it a management agenda item. How often do you measure your teams' level of passion? For that matter what about your own? Remember, what gets measured gets managed.

- Position the transformation as part of a higher purpose focused on helping others (as is discussed in the "Purpose" chapter). There is a wealth of research that demonstrates how finding purpose beyond personal gain fuels the levels of passion in an organization.

- Have a clear, compelling vision and future target picture. Without a clear, compelling future, it's difficult to feel passion. What is the promised land that is motivating you to trek through the desert?

- Select, promote, and recruit people who share a high level of passion for the company's purpose and transformation agenda. Phil Knight, in the early days of Blue Ribbon, attracted and selected fellow runners, athletes, and "passionados."

- Be a role model for the infectious passion at every meeting and touchpoint. Create a continuous ripple effect. "Fake it until you make it" is a famous expression that holds true in this context. Be passionate even if you don't feel like it, and you might begin feeling like it.

- Keep the focus on progress by celebrating and reflecting on key milestones. When you climb a mountain, the top continues to look far away. It's only when you pause and look back that you can see the distance you've already covered. In team meetings you can always ask for people to share the last week's or month's progress with each other, for example.

- Shift the conversations to what is wanted, not what is unwanted. Stay focused on what you can influence.

References

Knight, P. *Shoe Dog: A Memoir by the Creator of Nike*. Simon & Schuster Ltd, 2019.

Duckworth, A. *Grit: The Power of Passion and Perseverance*. Scribner Book Company, 2016.

Hagel, John, III, and John Seely Brown. "How to Create a Workplace That Actually Inspires Passion." *HBR*, July 2020.

INNER GAME POWER

- 1. PURPOSE
- 2. PERSPECTIVE
- 3. POSITION
- 4. PRIORITIES
- 5. PEOPLE
- 6. PRINCIPLES
- 7. PROMOTION
- 8. PROGRESS
- 9. PASSION
- 10. POLITICAL
- 11. PARTY
- 12. PAY-OFF

CHAPTER 10

POLITICS

The purpose of getting power is to be able to give it away.

—ANEURIN BEVAN

10.1 INTRODUCTION: INSTAGRAM

In 2005 Kevin Systrom was introduced to Mark Zuckerberg through a few of his Stanford University friends. Zuckerberg was just becoming the tech industry wunderkind for his work at TheFacebook.com, a simple site, which he had started the year prior while at Harvard University. At a noodle bar on University Avenue in Palo Alto, Zuckerberg tried to recruit Systrom, who had a passion for photography and had developed on the side a website called Photobox. Zuckerberg offered him a once-in-a-lifetime offer to step in at the ground floor of something that could be huge. Afterward he talked to one of his mentors, who said, "Why waste your potential for somebody else's vision? Don't do this Facebook thing."[67] He declined the offer. Their paths would cross again five years later.

Kevin Systrom and Mike Krieger would go on to found Instagram in 2010. The service originated with the idea to enable people to easily share high-quality photo moments via an app made for a select group that would connect people around their interests. Systrom had a passion for photos, and he and Krieger saw the confluence between the rise of apps and the emergence of people taking photos with their phones rather than their cameras. The company quickly took off—faster than they had prepared for—and attracted a leading angel investor in Marc Andreessen.

Within a couple of months, Instagram got on the radar of Mark Zuckerberg, who quickly saw both the potential and the threat to Facebook that Instagram represented. As Instagram had also been approached by Twitter, Zuckerberg reached out to Systrom and Krieger with the offer to buy Instagram and have them continue to pursue their dream but within the auspices of the Facebook organization. Zuckerberg wanted to close the deal in just a weekend, so he made a $1 billion offer, which at the time was seen as outrageous for a start-up with just eleven employees. Systrom, Krieger, and the other shareholders accepted the offer.

After the deal was announced, the Instagram team was driven via one of the many Facebook shuttles to Facebook's gigantic campus in Menlo Park (in the Silicon Valley). There

---

67 S. Frier, *No Filter: The Inside Story of Instagram* (Simon & Schuster, 2020).

they were shown to an office tucked somewhere deep in the middle of the sprawling campus, which would be their new office home. The Instagrammers were overwhelmed and felt a bit like they were drowning in this new Facebook world. It was a completely different culture and environment. There were Facebook posters everywhere. There were many restaurants, dry-cleaning services, etc., which was very different from what the eleven Instagrammers had started as their own culture. Also, many Facebookers looked with disdain on the new Instagram addition. The $1 billion price tag was seen as over the top, and everybody was focused on making Facebook a success—and definitely not this new start-up, Instagram. When an Instagram engineer was invited for lunch by the Facebook Camera team (the group who had launched an Instagram copycat app), they said, "Our job is to kill you, guys." When Instagram met with Facebook's all-star growth team, they were told that they wouldn't get any help adding users unless they could demonstrate—through data—that the product wasn't competing with Facebook.

Krieger and Systrom really wanted to make Instagram a success within the Facebook environment, but they didn't want to get swallowed up in the process. How could they keep their identity while navigating the political currents of such a large organization? They had to do something to protect their own unique culture and approaches. Their ambition was to protect the pristine creative paradise they had created on Instagram. They hired a designer to differentiate their offices from the Facebook look and feel and protect their own unique, more creative, and quality-focused culture. They even brought in photography books and old cameras. They also decided to codify their own culture with values such as "community first," "simplicity matters," and "inspire creativity." They also changed how they would measure success and began to move away from Facebook's metric of time spent in app and toward post quality and the number of posts shared. Instagram wanted to maintain its thoughtful design and simplicity by focusing on brand preservation and training its biggest users to use the app to build a culture of quality.

It was one thing to protect their own culture and approach, but Instagram also needed to secure the right level of support in what seemed like a more hostile corporate environment. For them to succeed, they needed to tap into Facebook's network of talent, the scalability of new features, and their ability to do international rollouts. One of the first things they realized was that only 10 percent of Facebookers actually had an Instagram account. They launched an outreach campaign where they opened their doors to their Facebook colleagues and tempted them with free coffee and muffins so that they would engage with them. They also hired selectively from the Facebook side, bringing in new analytical skills that would help them grow—data analysis was the language in Facebook to secure resources. They also wisely secured a very senior Facebooker who became their mentor and sponsor to guide them through the world of Facebook.

While they struggled to find their footing and protect their way of doing things, Krieger and Systrom realized that they needed to go on the offensive so as not to get marginalized and become irrelevant in the rapidly growing Facebook environment. They asked themselves what earned respect from the Facebook leaders and from Mark Zuckerberg. They realized that this was countering competitive threats and demonstrating profit growth. So they started to do both.

Systrom and Krieger found an opportunity to make an impression with the rise of the new six-second-long video platform called Vine. Twitter had purchased Vine, and the app was seeing great success. To deflate Facebook's nemesis, Twitter, Instagram set off on a brutal sprint to launch their own fifteen-second video feature. After the new Instagram Story product launched with great aplomb, Zuckerberg gave the floor to Systrom—a sign of respect. The Instagram team managed to continually deflate the competition, demonstrating their ability to innovate and find a strong future position, but they still weren't able to turn a profit.

To try to begin making any money for Facebook, they decided to develop advertising for Instagram. These ads needed to look like Instagram posts and needed to be visually pleasing to fit the app. They ran their first ad on November 1, 2013. They began by focusing on only one brand a day. Zuckerberg felt that Instagram now had enough followers to earn some money back and thus urged Systrom to increase Instagram's ad frequency. This change was about personalization and the ability to offer advertisers the opportunity to put ads across the different Facebook platforms (which now included Instagram).

Systrom was called into a meeting with Facebook's leadership team and shown a chart that depicted the target goals for Instagram's ad revenue—a steep curve of $1 billion in targeted advertising growth. The $1 billion target of ad revenues would ultimately become a delicate political exchange between Instagram and Facebook. Instagram's square photos were iconic, but advertisers on Facebook tended to utilize horizontal rectangular formats. Instagram ads were also a higher resolution, which made using images across the two platforms difficult. Systrom was able to convince Facebook to ask advertisers to upgrade the photo quality of their ads so that they could be used on both Facebook and Instagram without diluting the quality of Instagram ads.

Systrom and Krieger were able to create unprecedented growth for Instagram in the years that followed their acquisition of Facebook in 2010. By 2018 they had broken one billion users and were closing in on having $10 billion in revenue. It has become a large part of the Facebook ecosystem. They had secured their own offices on the Facebook campus.

The previously scoffed-at $1 billion acquisition price was now seen, in hindsight, as an absolute bargain. Systrom and Krieger had succeeded where the leaders of companies who had been acquired by Facebook failed.

Most left quickly, unable to adapt and navigate the political field effectively. Systrom and Krieger persisted.

Instagram had become so large that counterforces had started to take shape around the organization—it was now seen as a threat to the Facebook platform itself. Social media platforms are well aware that people have only so many minutes a day to spend online. After Instagram reached one billion users, Facebook's head of growth assessed all the ways Instagram's growth was helped by the Facebook app and ultimately decided to switch some of these features off. Additionally Instagram was also no longer allowed to run free promotions within the Facebook news feed. The budget for adding new FTEs to the now eight-hundred-person Instagram organization was also curtailed. Krieger was now spending a significant amount of time dealing with bureaucracy while shuttling back and forth to Facebook's HQ.[68] One morning in late September of 2019, Systrom and Krieger abruptly resigned.

10.2 What Is the Politics and Power Wing on the Transformational Flywheel?

Politics and power dynamics are always present when people work together to get something done. What are politics? *Politics* is defined by the *Oxford Dictionary* as activities aimed at improving someone's status or increasing someone's power within an organization. What is

---

[68] N. Thompson et al., "Fifteen Months of Fresh Hell Inside Facebook," *Wired*, 2019.

power? *Power* is defined as the capacity of an individual to influence the actions, beliefs, or conduct of others. So why are these forces so important in a transformational situation?

In a transformational situation, it's key to have enough political support for the transformational change agenda and, as a leader, enough personal power to enact that agenda if the political will exists. Power needs to be distributed with the right delegation/allocation in an organization. If power is appropriately balanced, it allows the leader to use the power to influence beliefs and behaviors. The power of a leader, their political support, and the distribution of power are all interconnected. When, for example, the power a leader has is used to successfully create progress for the change agenda, their level of political support will likely increase, and this allows him to make internal power allocational changes in an organization and distribute power more effectively. As you can see in the Instagram case, for many years the leadership team was very successful in expanding their influence within Facebook and using that to build their business—which led in itself to more political clout. All in all it's important to be aware of and manage these forces as a leader in a transformation.

> It's key to have enough political support for the transformational change agenda and, as a leader, enough personal power to enact that agenda if the political will exists.

So where does political support come from? In our experience it typically comes from three levels: the leader's superior, his or her team and peers, and the broader organization he or she is responsible for. The question is, what level of support is there for the leader and for the transformational agenda? A leader can be liked, but if the change agenda is perceived as wrong or unsuccessful, political support erodes. Even if the change agenda is right, political support might spiral in the wrong direction if the leader is not respected or liked. This can be a tricky dynamic, as was demonstrated in the case of Steve Jobs, who was so unpopular that he was fired from his CEO position at Apple in 1985. When he gloriously returned in 1997 and transformed the company, he did so by cultivating a much stronger political support base.

Another important dimension is, of course, how a leader harnesses his or her formal and informal powers and how they use this to make the transformational agenda happen. Prof. Craig Barkacs of the University of San Diego[69] recently published an article laying out ten arenas of power that every leader must negotiate:

- **Legitimate power:** This is the power a leader gets by having a rank, status, and title.

- **Reward power:** This is the power to grant benefits to others such as hiring, promotions, increased pay, etc.

- **Coercive power:** This is the power to be able to punish someone in an organization—such as demotion, write-ups, and firing.

- **Expert power:** This is the power of having specialized knowledge in a valued area.

- **Referent power:** This is the power of admiration and likability that is not related to rank and status.

- **Informational power:** This is the power that comes with specialized knowledge in a specific area. A person with informational power knows "how things really work" in an organization.

---

69 C. Barkacs, "The Ten Sources of Power and How Anyone Can Use Them," University of San Diego, 2021.

- **Network power:** The power comes with the strength of a person's network professionally and personally.

- **Centrality power:** The power comes from "being in the loop."

- **Framing power:** This is the power to use language to frame things in a way so as to influence how people view them.

- **Agenda power:** This is the power of having the ability to influence what is or isn't acted upon and, therefore, what gets attention, priority, and resources.

Strengthening these powers can be helpful if they are used as a means to achieve a successful transformation. Finding the right balance is key. If too many decisions are going over the leadership desk, the organization gets disempowered, and the leader becomes a bottleneck. On the other hand, if a leader allocates too much the decision-making process, political tensions might arise on the levels beneath him.

Next to political support and a personal power base, it is important to decide how power and influence are allocated in an organization.[70] The status quo exists because certain power structures are currently present. To make change happen, this often has to change. Who and what functions should be assigned in the leadership team, and who in the organization can decide which endeavors are most important? In the case of the Microsoft transformation that Satya Nadella started, he felt that Microsoft should work with other technology partners in the technology ecosystem. To facilitate this he created a new position in his management team and hired a heavy-hitting, experienced leader for shifting power dynamics.

---

[70] B. Kuhel, "Power vs. Influence: Knowing the Difference Could Make or Break Your Company," *Forbes*, 2017.

So in a strong politics and power wing in the Transformational Flywheel, leaders have secured political support, harnessed the resulting power, and used that power to break the status quo. As a result they are able to delegate powers in such a way that it supports not the past but the direction that leads to the future.

> ### MARCO: ALIGNING POWER TO THE TRANSFORMATION WHILE REDUCING POLITICKING
>
> As we have explored in this chapter, there are three levels of power and politics to be aware of. Managing all three in parallel is the key to a successful transformation—but not easy. Let me share some examples of times when all three levels needed to improve.
>
> In one of my latest transformational leadership roles, I had to address all three aspects to enhance the power wing. In terms of stakeholder support, when I stepped in, there had been a change in the organization's ownership and, as a result, in supervisory board compensation. Earlier in my career, I had made the mistake of focusing too heavily on driving a transformation and too little on keeping all key stakeholders on board. Therefore, in this case, I immediately set up an intensive meeting rhythm with the key supervisory board members. In these meetings the transformation was always on the agenda. We consistently zoomed out to see the big picture of the transformation and looked at the road map, an overview of all initiatives, status, progress, and issues. We complemented this with

> targeted deep dives on initiatives. Several of my management team members felt as if it was almost too much, but I learned that when the going gets tough—which always does at some point in a transformation—this alignment is key and will allow for speed in a transformation.
>
> In terms of power allocation within the organization, it was not clear who actually had what decision rights, which created a lot of tension. It was also unclear how tensions between the different parts of the business would be resolved. To unlock this part of the flywheel, we delegated the proper decision rights to the appropriate parts of the business and functions and defined clear forums to discuss possible conflicts to find alignment and a way to escalate if needed so that decisions could always be made. In my experience, organizing this properly gives a lot of oxygen to an organization and takes out a lot of politics.

10.3 Why Are Politics and Power Important?

Why are power and politics so important during a transformation? The simplest answer is that when these factors are not aligned with the transformation, a leader is likely to fail; and when they are, the Transformational Flywheel gets a strong boost of momentum.

If a leader can't get enough political support from his superiors, his peers, his team, or the wider organization, it is almost impossible to make change happen, even if you have the best perspectives, a clear future position, priorities, and people.[71] As change is always a bit messy and since you need to invest before you experience positive outcomes, support is needed as those outcomes manifest. However, we have also seen leaders who spend too much time on "playing" politics and thus compromise the transformational agenda by being unwilling to make tough decisions and engaging in fussy communication. By trying to please all, you please none. Great change leaders have a sense of how to navigate this properly, creating and spending political goodwill wisely.

For example, when Iger took over as the CEO of the Walt Disney Company, he managed his political power more wisely than Eisner, whom he was replacing. Eisner had always had a fraught relationship with Roy Disney, and Disney had consequently criticized many of Eisner's decisions in a public forum.[72] Disney truly did disagree with Eisner's strategies, but his dislike of Eisner, whom he felt treated him disrespectfully, likely made him especially vocal. Iger kept the heir to the Disney name on his side by giving him a position of respect within the organization—although Roy didn't have a formal role in the company, when Iger took over as CEO, he immediately visited Disney and asked him to be an informal consultant and even offered him a physical office at the Disney headquarters. Extending this respect was an effective management of politicking that also allowed Iger to maintain his power base in other areas.

The same sorts of calculations are needed for your personal power base. If a leader doesn't harness their own power and actively use it to advance the change, he or she will lose momentum with the change program. A leader with too little power inevitably creates a vacuum that will be filled by people below him or absorbed by those above him in the organization. These impositions will often cause tension, as

---

71 A. Zaleznik, "Power and Politics in Organizational Life," *Harvard Business Review*, 1970.

72 Iger, *Ride of a Lifetime*.

people will begin to consolidate power within their own small fiefdoms and no longer act to the benefit of the whole organization. On the other extreme, however, if a leader is only focused on harnessing power for themselves and is not delegating power to those who will drive the change priorities, they will create a Sun King syndrome, where an organization becomes stifled because all the decision-making power rests with one person. Finding the right balance is key.

It is critical that powers are distributed to the right places in an organization. To empower the right people and parts of the organization is key—when status quo power allocations stay static, a transformation will fail. Some change is often needed. Iger's transformation of the Walt Disney Company, for example, is an excellent example of redistributing power effectively. Iger realized that the strategy and planning department had an outsize amount of influence that was stifling change. Iger reorganized so that other divisions within the organization, especially the movies division, received additional support and resources. The subsequent transformation of the company and the second renaissance in Disney films speak volumes as to the effectiveness of placing power.

How do you currently score? How reliable is your political support? How much power do you hold, and how have you allocated powers in the organization? Is there room to improve?

10.4 How Do You Score on the Politics and Power Wing?

How strong is the progress wing of your politics and power flywheel? Is it in full force, or is there room to find the next gear or to shift all the way into sixth gear? How would management and your employees rate the strength of getting things done in the business? How would they evaluate the political situation in your organization?

- **Level 1. No or limited power.** At this level there is no overall political support for the leader and no will to drive the transformative agenda. Powers are not delegated to the right people or divisions. Different departments and senior leaders are focused on optimizing their own powers. Political games are absorbing a lot of time. There is a lot of mistrust, and people within the organization are constantly looking over their shoulder. Key superiors have not allocated enough powers to the leader, and they themselves are divided. The status quo areas of the organization still have a lot of power, and new initiative areas are therefore starved of resources and attention. The wider organization has a fear of change. The leadership has only a limited awareness of these problems and is thus unable to manage these forces. The political situation is such that there might be a culture of vindictiveness and a perceived sense of victimization.

- **Level 2. Some power.** At this level the leader has been allocated some powers from his superiors to make the change happen, but the organization has not fully committed. The majority of the superiors/owners support the change, but there are still several skeptical forces waiting to see what happens and are thus hesitant to commit—especially when setbacks occur. The wider organization has a "wait and see" attitude. The governance processes are not fully effective. The leader has good support from several key peers, but some only pay lip service or are even openly hostile. The leader generally has strong support among his team, although there are several rivals who have an eye on the leader's position and intend to take it sometime in the future. Although new initiatives have been started and are making some headway, the traditionally powerful departments and managers are striving to hold on to their status quo powers, consequently creating continuous tensions that clash with the new initiatives. The organization is factional and politically divided, which creates a situation where it is difficult to get things done. It takes a lot of energy to get the right resources to the right parts of the organization. Many hide still behind inherited formalities. The leader neglects politics and power delegation until there is an urgent problem that must be resolved.

- **Level 3. Good power.** The leader has the full backing and support of his superiors/investors. There is a level of professional trust and the organization engages in proper governance processes. The leader has support from his key peers, and their leadership team is low on divisive politics. There is a sense of trust and a feeling that power is properly delegated. There are larger pockets of support for the change in the wider organization, and only a smaller group is critical and holding on to the past power/political structures. New initiatives get the proper empowerment and attention, but some tough decisions are still avoided, especially when they require reallocating the formal and informal powers of different departments. This still creates unproductive tensions, and there is still an undercurrent of politicking and power games. Key trade-off issues often create personal emotional tensions among leaders, but these issues are at least discussed. While there are still some remnants of the past, the point of no return to the old power structures has been passed. At this level the leadership still harbors several blind spots in relation to the counterforces working against their agenda. The leader and their trusted team have ad hoc discussions about the politics and power landscape of the company. They are able to identify the hot spot areas, but they have not yet learned to manage with a disciplined process.

- **Level 4. Transformative power.** There is a continuous effort by the leader to build a strong coalition of owners/superiors who support the transformative agenda. Their interests are aligned with the outcome of the change, and there is a respected and trusted relationship between these key stakeholders and the change leader. The change leader has a good standing among their peers and their team and with the wider organization. These parties, consequently, fully support the change agenda. Powers are properly delegated to the right people and departments to make change happen. The counterforces have been broken. The organization does not have significant political infighting and is thus collectively focused on making the overall vision work. It's an environment where things get done, and there is focus on progress as well as a sense of meritocracy. The leader and his trusted core team are proactively monitoring and managing the politics and power dimensions.

POLITICAL WING

	WING-POWER LEVEL	YOUR SCORE?
LEVEL 4	TRANSFORMATIVE POWER	
LEVEL 3	GOOD POWER	
LEVEL 2	SOME POWER	
LEVEL 1	NO POWER	

PETER: HOW COUNTRY AND CULTURE IMPACT THE ACCEPTANCE OF POWER

Delegating power happens at least partially in a cultural context. This needs to be taken into account since national cultures often have different social expectations of how power will be reflected in organization and personal interactions.

I was once part of a transformation catalyzed by a merger between two international banks—one Dutch and one Italian. Each country had different concepts on how hierarchical power should influence professional and social interactions. In Italy the power distance index is relatively higher—meaning expressions of power and hierarchy are more accepted and more visibly part of the culture. In the Netherlands the power distance is significantly lower—meaning that power-based inequality is less accepted. These conflicting national tolerances to power were fully reflected in the corporate cultures of both these merging banks.

As I oversaw a cultural change program, I witnessed cultural clashes because of these different attitudes. In the Italian bank, there was more acceptance of a distance between those of lower and higher levels, and decision-making was governed by those on the highest level. This led to all kinds of challenges in governance and in formal and informal power.

I experienced this firsthand when the bank was celebrating the end of the Volvo Ocean Race—sailing's greatest round-the-world challenge. This was to be celebrated by all branches worldwide and therefore also in Italy. Everything was prepared, but the highest Italian boss decided to cancel the party at the last moment. After that happened someone from my department came to me and claimed that this was a power play. This executive wanted to show the company who was boss and who held the most power.

There was an exchange of Dutch managers to the Italian branches of the company. This led to all kinds of challenges in governance and in formal and informal power. Eventually there was a local manager from the Italian division who was in charge and managing and determining everything. The transformation became bogged down because of this difference in governance style that trended toward being top-down.

Eventually the shareholders stopped the transformation because of this infighting and consequently sold parts of the bank—which made this transformation one of the most interesting power and political examples of how not to do a transformation.

10.5 How to Strengthen the Politics and Power Wing

Managing the delicate balance of power and politics is as much of an art as it is a science. The first step to strengthening this wing on the flywheel is, of course, to increase your awareness of how power is currently distributed. Then comes action. It is, however, good to keep in mind that there's not a simple fix in terms of power—this wing requires consistent adjustments and corrections. When looking to address this wing of the flywheel, there are three different power layers (stakeholders, your own power base, and the delegation of powers) that will require your attention:

1. **Secure Key Stakeholders' Support.** Who are your key stakeholders? The first step in becoming aware of the political dynamic of your organization is to make a transparent overview of who your key stakeholders are. Only then can you begin to actively manage it. Defining their interest and taking steps to determine the importance they have toward your transformation is a good next step. Outline an effective rhythm of meetings and updates for each of the different stakeholders. Some might need to be very closely involved and engaged, while others might just want to be informed. Asking them explicitly what they expect and not assuming can make a big difference. Once you have a rhythm going, it's helpful to check back in with everyone twice a year to gauge their level of engagement and that they are being provided with the necessary information to secure their support.

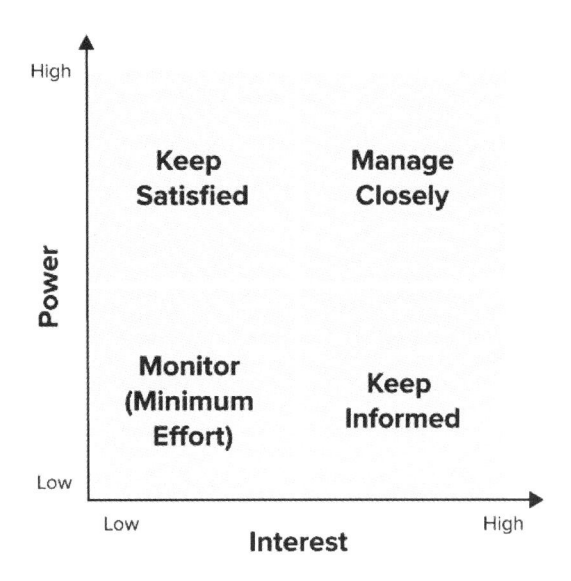

```
                    High
                     ^
                     |
                     |  Keep          Manage
                     |  Satisfied     Closely
              Power  |
                     |
                     |  Monitor       Keep
                     |  (Minimum      Informed
                     |  Effort)
                     |
                    Low
                     +----------------------->
                       Low              High
                            Interest
```

2. **Your Own Power Base.** It is also fundamental to assess and manage your own power base. As mentioned earlier in the chapter via Professor Barkacs's list, there are a lot of different sources of power. Again when you're looking to increase your influence within the organization, the first step is to increase your awareness of your current level of power and influence. How aware are you of your power sources? Which score high, and which score low? Once you have increased your awareness and begin to take concrete action, reviewing your power base every six months should become a habit.

3. **Delegation of Powers in the Organization.** Becoming aware of the different power structures in your organization and then shifting to accommodate the organizational change is key in any transformation. In the first step, it's good to map the key meetings and key boards who have decision rights. Map participants, how decisions are made, and who sets the agenda. It's also important

to map which leaders can make key decisions (and in what areas) inside the current power structure. Once you have the overview, it is helpful to define the biggest pain points or misalignments with the transformative agenda. Based on that, it can be helpful to take a white sheet of paper and design, from scratch, what the ideal power structure would look like. You can think about changing reporting lines; delayering an organization; changing decision management, committee memberships, or remits; and rotating certain individuals to other roles. This is then followed by creating buy-in and a migration path to court key individuals. Some decisions on, for example, who sits in the top team, their responsibilities, and the key decision-driving meetings might need to be shifted to optimize the delegation of power in a transforming organization.

References

Frier, S. *No Filter: The Inside Story of Instagram*. Simon & Schuster, 2020.

Thompson, N., and F. Vogelstein. "Fifteen Months of Fresh Hell Inside Facebook." *Wired*, 2019. https://www.wired.com/story/facebook-mark-zuckerberg-15-months-of-fresh-hell/.

Barkacs, C. "The Ten Sources of Power and How Anyone Can Use Them." University of San Diego, 2021. https://www.sandiego.edu/news/detail.php?_focus=80785.

Kuhel, B. "Power vs. Influence: Knowing the Difference Could Make or Break Your Company." *Forbes*, 2017. https://www.forbes.com/sites/forbescoachescouncil/2017/11/02/power-vs-influence-knowing-the-difference-could-make-or-break-your-company/?sh=6778812357c7.

Zaleznik, A. "Power and Politics in Organizational Life." *Harvard Business Review*, 1970. https://hbr.org/1970/05/power-and-politics-in-organizational-life.

Iger, R. *The Ride of a Lifetime: Lessons Learned from Fifteen Years as CEO of the Walt Disney Company*. Penguin Random House LLC, 2019.

INNER GAME POWER

- 1. PURPOSE
- 2. PERSPECTIVE
- 3. POSITION
- 4. PRIORITIES
- 5. PEOPLE
- 6. PRINCIPLES
- 7. PROMOTION
- 8. PROGRESS
- 9. PASSION
- 10. POLITICAL
- **11. PARTY**
- 12. PAY-OFF

CHAPTER 11

PARTY

Fun is one of the most important—and underrated—ingredients in any successful venture. If you're not having fun, then it's probably time to call it quits and try something else.

—RICHARD BRANSON

11.1 INTRODUCTION: VIRGIN

A gaggle of journalists and photographers, a troupe of entertainers, and the Virgin Group management streamed down the aisle of a massive Boeing 747-200 and began to take their seats. As the aisles filled, the aircraft switched on its cutting-edge engines. This was a moment of truth—only two days beforehand, the plane had billowed smoke and flames during a test flight, resulting in the destruction of an engine, causing a £600,000 budget blowout. As a result the permits to take off and land between Gatwick and Newark, New Jersey, had been painful to arrange. Worse still, one of Virgin Atlantic's cofounders was doing everything in his power to stop the flight from taking off at all. Safe to say that preparation for the whole endeavor could be described as a logistical nightmare. The year was 1984, and in the middle of British summer, Virgin Atlantic's maiden voyage was about to begin.

As the plane was hurtling down the rapidly tapering runway of Gatwick International Airport, an announcement came over the intercom. "Since this is our first flight, we thought you might like to share our view from the flight deck and see what really happens when we take off." The inflight entertainment turned on. On each screen were the pilot, the copilot, and a view below them where the runway was rapidly turning into a blur. This seemed like a normal information video for a corporate event—except that it soon became clear that neither pilot was paying much attention to what was happening at all. In fact, they didn't really look like pilots either. As the plane left the tarmac, the copilot removed a joint from behind his ear and passed it to the copilot. Rather than surveying the instruments or working the controls, the duo proceeded to sit back in their chairs and admire the blue abyss.

There was an understandable air of apprehension among the passengers. A deathly hush filled the cabin. Everybody knew that Richard Branson was a joker, but hiring a couple of stoners to captain the maiden voyage of his airline was a bit much. As panic began to hit a climax, Ian Botham and Viv Richards, two famous cricketers, revealed themselves. The bearded engineer, who was Branson himself, turned around and smirked at the camera. People began to realize that the video had been prefilmed as a spoof, and as the 747 began its journey across the Atlantic, the cabin roared with laughter. What followed was an eight-hour party. Fueled by some seventy bottles of champagne, people danced in the aisles as Madonna's new hit "Like a Virgin" pumped through the cabin.[73]

As the plane touched down in New Jersey, Richard shook some hands, and then he was on an immediate flight back to the UK. Exhausted from the all-nighter, Branson fell into a deep sleep for the first time in weeks. He felt that nothing could go wrong. "A bad mistake," he later recounted. As he arrived home, his account manager at Coutts & Co. was waiting for him and told him that Virgin's line of credit would not be extended. The group was essentially being forced into instant insolvency. Reeling from the party, he still snapped into action once more.

As they launched a new airline with one plane and fought against the powerful British Airways, Virgin needed continuous positive energy to overcome all the seemingly impossible obstacles. This positive energy, at least in part, would come from Virgin's use of celebration. Richard Branson is not unique in his desire to party, but his strategic use of celebration stands out. He was able to create value even in the toughest of times, which is exceedingly rare. From the humble start of his entrepreneurial activities as an editor for student newspapers and magazines to his

---

[73] R. Branson, *Losing My Virginity* (Virgin Books, 2010), p. 207.

founding of Virgin Records, Branson always celebrated milestones, large and small.

A lot of things that Virgin does are fueled by a philosophy of enjoyment and celebration. This is celebrating not merely for the sake of it but also because it's an essential element of their market position, value proposition, and employee engagement strategy. Milestones, big and small, are followed by a party—and many of those parties take place on a grand scale when Branson launches his businesses. For example, in those early years, Virgin would throw legendary, outlandish parties for their employees at their Oxfordshire countryside recording studio. It was said that if you remembered the party, you probably were not actually there. They had also purchased a rooftop garden venue in Kensington in 1981, which would go on to play host to many of the company's big bashes. The garden was even home to four resident flamingos and was frequented by many celebrity guests including the duchess of Cambridge, Madonna, and even the group Queen. Even for formal events—like when Virgin took over a high street bank—Branson ensured that the management team was able to cut loose. To celebrate the takeover, Branson and Virgin Money CEO Jayne-Anne Gadhia threw a bank-

> Strategically celebrating, even just the small victories, is an integral factor of successful transformation.

sponsored megabash street party and gave everyone an opportunity to behave in very unbankerlike ways.

"Fun is one of the most important—and underrated—ingredients in any successful venture. If you're not having fun, then it's probably time to call it quits and try something else," he said.[74] And because of it, Virgin managed to shine a new light into stagnant industries the world over and created a unique culture. While Virgin may be one of the most extravagant cases in point, the principles that underpin this case are widely transferable. Strategically celebrating, even just the small victories, is an integral factor of successful transformation.

11.2 What Is the Party Wing on the Transformational Flywheel?

In the Flywheel of Transformation, the party wing is about celebrating progress in every form. Changing an organization is hard, and celebrating milestones is a powerful way to create a sense of achievement, to encourage social bonding, and to provide a moment for recharging. For many organizations, however, regular celebrations are not common practice, perhaps due to the belief that celebration should not be done too frequently. At times celebration can even be seen as unprofessional. But is this the right way to go about it, or is this attitude a missed opportunity to fuel a transformation?

---

74   R. Branson, *The Virgin Way: Everything I Know about Leadership* (Portfolio, 2014).

Take, for example, how celebration is frequently used in the game of soccer. In this sport, teams celebrate expressively and at regular intervals. Teams don't wait until the end of the season to celebrate. They don't even wait until the end of the many games they play each year. They celebrate goals in each game, even when they are 0–3 behind or when they have scored a goal just five minutes before. Players celebrate these moments—often and without limits. Teammates run to each other and create a microexpressive party moment. Quite often these moments happen multiple times on a weekly basis. How often do you celebrate progress with your business team?

You can use celebrations not only when the transformation is complete, or once a year at some annual corporate event, but also when smaller milestones are achieved. It will create more energy and encourage social bonding for the team. People have an inherent need to feel like they are making meaningful progress in their work.[75] Celebrations are one way to do this because they recognize the efforts members of the team have put into the change effort.

In the context of an organizational change effort, we define *party* as any moment to celebrate progress made as an individual or team or by the organization. These celebration moments can range from small, sporadic moments to large events that can be either formal or informal. Regardless of their size, when a team accomplishes a goal, it should be celebrated.[76] There are endless examples of ways to celebrate progress during a transformation, but here are a few:

- Formal annual Christmas party
- Quarterly office drinks
- Weekly MVP awards

---

[75] T. Amabile et al., "The Power of Small Wins," *Harvard Business Review*, 2011.

[76] T. Gimbel, "Why Corporate Celebrations Are Important," *Inc.*, 2017.

- Pizza party
- Summer drinks
- Cake and coffee
- Standing ovations for great performing individuals or teams
- Team performance awards
- Starting meetings with music
- Product launch party

In order to have transformative power in the party wing of your flywheel, celebrations should be strategically, tactically, and spontaneously used to propel the change effort forward.

MARCO: THE POWER OF CELEBRATING SMALL WINS

Celebrations are essential for giving energy to a transformation, and I am continually experimenting with new ways to create meaningful and authentic experiences that celebrate progress.

I saw the power of celebration very early in my career, when I had just transferred from McKinsey's Chicago office to their office in San Francisco and stepped in as the de facto COO for almost a year for a new start-up in our McKinsey incubator for start-ups. It was a unique opportunity to work alongside two successful serial entrepreneurs. Together we made the business plan, raised funds from investors in New York, and recruited a development, sales, and marketing team. Every week we brought the rapidly growing team together to share progress, celebrate weekly deliverables, and give an award to the Most Valuable Player (MVP) of the week, which was a silly puppet. This ritual created a sense of momentum and made our teams across the organization aware of all the progress we'd achieved.

Now two decades later, I have continuously evolved the approach to celebrating and encouraging progress in a transformation. Often I initially get skeptical responses when I suggest starting some celebration practices. Somehow celebration is not perceived as professional or is seen as something that is just not done. I often use the metaphor of how soccer teams celebrate weekly every goal to keep team momentum. But once people do it a few times, they normally start to appreciate it and actually love it. Let me share some practices that I have been using in my recent leadership:

- Every week in the executive board meeting, we get a pulse on how everyone is feeling by asking them to rate their emotional state on a scale of 1 to 10. This process is usually followed by everybody sharing a piece of progress over the last week. After that we do a quick vote by finger-pointing on who deserves the MVP award for the week.
- At the end of each month, we spontaneously call via Zoom (as an executive board) several people anywhere in the organization at any level who have reached an important progress milestone. It can be recognition for completing a project, landing a new client, improving

supplier contracts, or anything else similar. Afterward people are normally flabbergasted by seeing the leadership team and hearing us thank them. We also stand up and give them a standing ovation.

- In a transformation the continuous delivery of change initiatives is key. In one situation we created a yearly project, Olympics. A team would get a gold medal when they delivered a project within the spec, time frame, and budget and with a high team engagement score.
- In another situation we created a fun competition based on KPI scores related to our priorities ordered by country. We did it in such a way that everybody could win if they improved their KPIs at a certain rate. They could win Champion League cup-size trophies if their numbers reached certain targets.
- We sent cakes around the world to teams who had achieved an important milestone.
- We spontaneously threw a food truck Christmas festival for all headquarter employees to thank everyone for the great progress we'd made.

These are just a few examples, and there are endless ways to celebrate progress. Without celebrating milestones and microwins, it becomes challenging to win the marathon that a transformation usually is.

11.3 Why Is Partying So Important in a Transformation?

Why can partying be so powerful in a transformational situation? Changing an organization is often hard and cannot be achieved by a quick fix. Identifying milestones and moments to celebrate can create positive energy for several reasons:

- Celebration creates connection among people. It is part of every culture. In moments of celebration, positive emotions are shared, and hierarchies disappear. It creates a general sense of goodwill among colleagues.

- Celebration builds momentum. Having moments of celebrating achievements in line with progress creates a sense of accomplishment and increased confidence. It's like climbing a mountain and focusing only on the peak; you never realize the ground you've gained until you look back down.

- Celebration of milestones generates focus and anticipation. It creates motivation to reach the milestone because something positive is waiting there for you.

- Celebration of milestones is also a signpost. Celebrating is a way of setting markers to the broader organization on what matters and where the organization is heading. What's not celebrated is a marker to the organization as much as what is.

- Celebration is a way of recharging. Spirits are often lifted after a party moment. People find the energy to be more resourceful and see things in a different, more positive light.

Teresa M. Amabile and Steven J. Kramer published an article in the *Harvard Business Review* entitled "The Power of Small Wins" that supports the belief that recognizing progress and celebrating microprogress moments is an important ingredient in transformative business teams. They write, "Because inner work life has such a potent effect on creativity and productivity, and because small but consistent steps forward, shared by many people, can accumulate into excellent execution, progress events that often go unnoticed are critical to the overall performance of organizations."[77]

It is, however, important that celebrations are done with the right intentions. It has to come from the heart in order to not be seen as a gimmick. A self-organized and leadership-led action is often better than spending money on a flashy event organized by a third party.

Furthermore, it's critical that the right moments, people, and teams are celebrated. If superficial progress or people who haven't contributed to the transformation are celebrated, it confuses an organization and can even create cynicism. The party moments have to support and be aligned with the Transformational Flywheel.

11.4 How Strong Is Your Party Wing?

How strong is your party wing in the Flywheel of Transformation? How is your personal attitude toward celebrating? How would your team and other employees rate this aspect of your corporate culture? To help you assess where you currently stand, we have defined four different levels of power in this wing:

- **Level 1. No or limited power.** There is an attitude among the leaders that celebrations are not compatible with work. There have been no celebrations during the transformation, no moments during the intermediate milestones, and no spontaneous celebrations after moments of success. The transfor-

---

[77] Amabile et al., "Power of Small Wins."

mational journey feels like an endless road because milestones pass by unmarked.

- **Level 2. Some power.** There is an attitude that it is good to have some standard moments to celebrate—such as an annual Christmas party. Although the party is not related to the achievements and progress of the transformation, it highlights some moments of progress to create a sense of momentum and achievement. However, these events are often outsourced to a third party and feel slightly artificial.

- **Level 3. Good power.** There is an attitude that celebrations and the recognition of progress are a source of positive energy toward achieving change. There are regular, separate celebration moments scattered over the year. Some of these events are formal, and some are more spontaneous. They can range from celebratory evening events and galas to pizza parties. Key achievement milestones, like when a new product launches or when new customers come on board, are celebrated.

- **Level 4. Transformative power.** There is an understanding and attitude that celebrations are fundamental and important to create, keep, and reenergize the change momentum in a transformation. There is a belief that fun and positivity differentiate the company and its culture. Celebration moments are genuine and not cookie-cutter events. They are unique to the company. The senior leadership is actively engaged in creating and participating in party moments.

What is your current score on this wing of the Flywheel of Transformation?

WING-POWER LEVEL		YOUR SCORE?
LEVEL 4	TRANSFORMATIVE POWER	
LEVEL 3	GOOD POWER	
LEVEL 2	SOME POWER	
LEVEL 1	NO POWER	

PARTY WING

PETER: OPENING UP YOUR CELEBRATION MINDSET

Since transformations are full of ups and downs, it is important to celebrate even more regularly than in ongoing business.

Let me share an example. I once worked with a trading company that had rapidly grown from a start-up to a reasonably sized company. They were going through a transformation that involved expansion and a transition to digital platforms. Something, however, was missing: they had no party culture at all. Nothing was celebrated, there was no recognition of people, and no successes, large or small, were celebrated.

Neither the CEO nor the HR director were used to celebrating successes. For the CEO this pattern stemmed from his own childhood. He was educated in a culture that is deferent to authority. This meant, for him, that there was never a "good reason" to celebrate. The HR director had also never celebrated through his whole career. In the past his managers had taken all the credit for his success for themselves. As a result the HR director was directly copying his management style from his previous working experiences, and he was taking the success of his subordinates as his own. Both played a key role in suppressing the celebration of success at this organization.

This had been a blind spot since they were very focused on digital transformation, on hiring people, on new processes, on new systems, and on new business. To address this situation, we worked with the CEO and the HR director on how to recognize the need for celebration. We worked on different aspects of his work culture to unlock the attitude to celebrate more. In our experience there are different ways to shift your attitude toward an emphasis on celebration:

- First, you need to be able to receive compliments and have the motivation to celebrate. If you can't receive compliments, you will struggle to give them. How do you react when you receive a compliment?
- Second, it's important to find a role model. You need to have examples for celebrating successes and personal stories of celebration that show you know how to do it. If you haven't had them, it makes it seem as if there are no role models to set the tone at the company.
- Third, try multiple things in a low-risk, experimental environment. Perhaps some won't work, but it's important to test and learn what works. What have you got to lose by trying?

- Last, you need to go in with the spirit of a cheerleader, knowing how to be happy and enthusiastic.

When these leaders became aware of the importance of celebration, they both made a big difference when they started putting more focus on building a culture that celebrates. This increased the level of motivation in the team and had a positive effect on the transformation process and accelerated the drive toward change.

11.5 How to Strengthen Your Party Wing

If you assess that there is an opportunity to bring more force into your party wing, how can you go about doing so? In our experience there are several steps you might want to consider:

- Check your belief set and biases first. Is there something you believe that could be holding you back?

- Ask yourself if you have the right intentions. Do you have a mindset where you really want to celebrate and thank those who make things happen for the good of the whole organization?

- It's, of course, key to focus on transformative progress milestones. Define visible milestones for the transformational journey. This allows you to celebrate progress with regularity.

- Make sure that celebrations are timely. For example, if a project is completed in February, don't wait until the end of the year or for a Christmas party to celebrate this achievement.

- Brainstorm creative ways to celebrate, from small things like standing ovations and highlighting teams in a newsletter or video cast to larger, more formal events.

- Create a solid road map of celebration moments for the year and allocate responsibilities and bake it into the planning and review loops. This builds up rhythm and generates momentum.

- Participate in several celebrations as a senior leader to model behavior and inject real happiness and appreciation for the progress.

- Communicate about the celebration moments in the organization, following the celebration moments with pictures, videos, or other documentation.

- Have fun with it! It has to come from the heart.

The importance of celebrating achievements step-by-step is recognized by many successful transformations. The best thing is that celebrations don't have to be huge, but small tokens of appreciation are also appreciated. To solve big problems, you want to look for small wins. Research has shown that positive emotions create strong motivation.[78]

> To solve big problems, you want to look for small wins.

---

78 T. Amabile et al., *The Progress Principle: Using Small Wins to Ignite Joy, Engagement and Creativity at Work*, (Harvard Business Review Press, 2011).

References

Branson, R. *Losing My Virginity*. Virgin Books, 2010.

———. *The Virgin Way: Everything I Know about Leadership*. Portfolio, 2014.

Amabile, T., and S. Kramer. "The Power of Small Wins." *Harvard Business Review*, 2011. https://hbr.org/2011/05/the-power-of-small-wins.

Gimbel, T. "Why Corporate Celebrations Are Important." *Inc.*, 2017. https://www.inc.com/tom-gimbel/why-corporate-celebrations-are-important.html.

Taylor, B. "To Solve Big Problems, Look for Small Wins." *Harvard Business Review*, 2020. https://hbr.org/2020/06/to-solve-big-problems-look-for-small-wins.

Amabile, T., and S. Kramer. *The Progress Principle: Using Small Wins to Ignite Joy, Engagement and Creativity at Work*. Harvard Business Review Press, 2011.

12. PAY-OFF

INNER GAME POWER

1. PURPOSE
2. PERSPECTIVE
3. POSITION
4. PRIORITIES
5. PEOPLE
6. PRINCIPLES
7. PROMOTION
8. PROGRESS
9. PASSION
10. POLITICAL
11. PARTY
12. PAY-OFF

CHAPTER 12

PAY-OFF

Of course, it is not the employer who pays wages. He only handles the money. It is the product that pays wages, and it is the management that arranges the production so that the product may pay the wages.

—HENRY FORD

12.1 UNION SQUARE HOSPITALITY GROUP

New York City has become the epicenter for gastronomy due to its diversity of cuisine types, the local talent, the international chefs, and the drive of local restaurant entrepreneurs. This, however, was not always the case. When Danny Meyer, who is today the head of the Union Square Hospitality Group (USHG) and is now known as one of America's most prolific restaurateurs, was opening his first restaurant, the scene was entirely different.

In the 1980s New York's culinary scene was characterized by its bottomless coffee and the classic corned beef hash. Meyer, who was a passionate foodie avant la lettre, gave up a secure job to start a restaurant in a backwater area of Union Square in New York. Using his focused and clear philosophy, the USHG grew to become one of the most admired restaurant groups in New York.

In the decades since, he has launched several new innovative restaurant concepts that challenged outdated beliefs driven with his unique philosophy and his multistakeholder focus. He shepherded the now iconic restaurants including Union Square Café, Gramercy Tavern, Blue Smoke, Jazz Standard, Tabla, the Modern, Café 2, and Terrace 5 at New York's MoMA, which are all part of USHG. From the best hamburger stand in New York to Michelin star restaurants, each was built by Meyer from the ground up. People drive hours to have dinner in his restaurants and line up in rows behind the original Shake Shack in Madison Square Park. These restaurants have created not only a high level of repeat guests but also a workforce of highly engaged employees with extensive community involvement. His group now has more than twenty restaurants, and the Shake Shack has expanded into a fast, casual restaurant chain with a market cap of several billion. Many say that Meyer didn't take advantage of a rising tide of better food and dining in New York, but he was, in actuality, one of the instigating forces behind the cultural change.

One of the elements behind the success of each of these unique restaurants is Meyer's belief that a restaurant should fulfill basic needs we had as a newborn child. The "first four gifts of life," as he calls them, that a baby will experience are eye contact, a smile, a hug, and good food.

Nothing will ever replace shaking people's hands, smiling at them, and looking them in the eye. Virtually nothing else is as important as how one is made to feel in a business transaction, he says, and these four components comprise the basics of hospitality.

Meyer, going against the grain at the time, wanted to provide a place where people could come not only to be served quality food but just as importantly to feel at home. He believes that his success in business has been due to his understanding of the difference between service and hospitality. "Service without a soul is quickly forgotten by the guest."[79] While today that may sound logical, at the time, it was not a matter that was considered in the service industry. Next to this belief in "service with soul," he focused on developing new, innovative concepts where he could combine unexpected elements from other concepts. For example, his first restaurant on Union Square combined outstanding hospitality with high-quality food you normally would find in a white-tablecloth restaurant.

The virtuous cycle of enlightened hospitality has been the "single greatest contribution to the ongoing success of our company," says Meyer.[80] By prioritizing their five primary stakeholders in the following order, USHG created a framework for ensuring that their excellence, success, and soul are sustained and nourished:

1. Employees

---

[79] D. Meyer, *Setting the Table: The Transforming Power of Hospitality in Business*, Ecco, 2008, p. 65.

[80] Ibid., p. 237.

2. Guests
3. Community
4. Suppliers
5. Investors

Everything USHG does, Meyer says, is built on this logic. They're the guiding principles for "practically every decision" the company makes, and those decisions are scrutinized by whether they put employees first and investors last. This logic not only created value for all stakeholders involved but it also was significantly different from most other contemporary hospitality businesses.

Employees in the USHG knew that to consistently provide hospitality in its highest form, they had to put their teammates' happiness above that of their guests.' Before investors had the chance to invest, they had to understand that their interests would always come after those of the community. Many of these decisions would mean forgoing short-term profits in favor of long-term sustainable returns. This might be a tough sell to some, but Meyer says that by prioritizing their five stakeholder groups in this way, the USHG has been able to build loyalty where it most counts.

Employees. While the saying may be "The customer is always right," in Meyer's world this is factually incorrect. At all of USHG's restaurants, the customer comes second—perhaps a close second—but it's employees who are number one priority. After all, how can you look after someone else before looking after yourself first? While this belief still seems crazy to many industry veterans, it enabled USHG to set in place many bold—and at times controversial—policies, including a smoking ban across all their restaurants, a ban on tipping, and an increased minimum wage of $15 per hour. Meyer wanted employees to see his businesses as an opportunity to build a career, rather than as a temporary job for passers-through. He ensures that there are opportunities not only to work but also to grow within the company. And although he admits that there's only so much space for entrepreneurs to grow within the company itself, Meyer often backs his staff to open their own concepts under the USHG brand.

Guests. Much of USHG's success can be attributed to the warmth that each guest receives upon walking through the door. But it doesn't end there. His entire focus was to create a place where people would feel welcome and at home. To deliver on this promise, his staff took notes on every guest—including where they came from, why they needed the reservation, and other related information—so that when they entered a restaurant, the waiters knew as much as possible about the guests. They spent a ton of time on seating plans to make sure that they could facilitate connections while dining. The USHG also took great pains to correct anything that went wrong during a meal. One interesting policy paints an accurate representation of the policy: if something was wrong with someone's meal, the customer would receive a small complimentary meal so that they could still dine at the same time as their companions while their meal was being fixed. Another way he put guests first was by empowering the solo diner. In many restaurants at the time, guests who dined alone weren't welcome. They didn't spend enough, and they used up valuable space. However, Union Square Café found this unacceptable. To serve this niche clientele, Meyer created a special bar that allowed diners to enjoy their meals alone and offered solo diners the chance to mingle if they were so inclined.

Community. A rising tide lifts all boats.[81] To offer exceptional value, Meyer had to make compromises. But compromises don't always have to be a win-lose situation. In Meyer's case he knew he couldn't have the highest quality of food and service while having the prime New York locations as well. Rather than see this as a hindrance, Meyer saw it as an opportunity—an opportunity to help flourish areas that have often been overlooked or undernourished by New York's top restaurants. He had a vision that each of his restaurants should uplift the entire community in which they were located. In the late '80s and early '90s, Union Square was considered a shabby area. Most restaurateurs would have turned their noses up at the mere suggestion of a fine-dining establishment located in Union Square. But to Meyer it was an obvious choice. "I am convinced that doing things that make sense for the community leads to doing well as a business," Meyer says. This philosophy has become embedded in every restaurant he has opened. Shake Shack started as part of an initiative to revitalize the degenerating Madison Square Park. They also prepared meals for local hospices and nursing homes, participated

---

81 Ibid., p. 251.

in hunger-relief events, and threw charity events that donated the profits to New York–based NGOs. But perhaps Union Square is the greatest example of all: what was once a dangerous place for many is now one of the busiest retail destinations in Manhattan.

Suppliers. At USHG taking care of suppliers has become part of who they are. In many cases investors will always come before their suppliers. But in order to hold up the reputation and the relationship, Meyer always insisted on putting suppliers before investors. To ensure that this carried through the value chain, all of USHG's restaurants focused on building loyal and respectful relationships with suppliers as opposed to squeezing their suppliers and getting the best deals. Believing in a win-win scenario, they also tried to adhere to the payment terms; and if there was an issue, they would address it up front. They also tried to bring suppliers into their community efforts, creating value across the community as a whole. [insert example of FIJI water here] It was part of Meyer's philosophy to "share our strengths."

Investors. Investors come last according to Meyer's "enlightened hospitality" logic—not because he doesn't want to earn money but because he knows that excelling at earning is only possible if all the other pieces of the puzzle are in place. In the long term, your investors are only looked after if you've looked after everyone else first. If you care for your investors' interests first, then you can make money quicker. But eventually you're likely to have a revolving door of staff who will leave, they won't make

> their customers happy, and people won't feel proud or enthusiastic. Investors had to buy into the business, the employees, the guests, the community, and the suppliers; they needed to feel their part in the ecosystem in order to have a part in the cycle.
>
> By prioritizing and taking care of these five stakeholders' respective interests, USHG has built a business model designed with long-term sustainable profitability in mind.

12.2 What Is Pay-Off in the Flywheel of Transformation?

Pay-off is the rewards and benefits for all stakeholders that result from being involved in the transformational journey ahead. The goal of any transformation is to shift a business toward a profitable future course and create more value for all stakeholders.

In the context of our flywheel, we have defined the strength of the pay-off wing as the extent to which all key stakeholders expect to gain more value by the end of the transformation phase while knowing that they have to invest before they see a return. Any change requires a leader to not just deal with the natural resistance to change but also actively increase the willingness to change. These two forces always exist at the same time; the question, however, is, which one outweighs the other?

So what and who are the critical stakeholders in every transformation? We have found the enlightened hospitality framework of USHG to be helpful as a reference. It shows the five categories involved in any business venture or change endeavor—namely, each other (employees, the team), guests (customers), community, suppliers, and investors while also illustrating the dynamic between the different stakeholder groups.

What, then, is the pay-off for each of the stakeholders for being part of the business and the change journey ahead? Particularly, what is the pay-off when you face an uncertain change journey ahead where stakeholders are asked to do more or to give up something as part of that journey?

The pay-off should have a perceived value that is greater than the perceived time, effort, and resources each stakeholder group gives to the organization. A strong pay-off wing in the flywheel means that the pay-off is well managed, clearly communicated, and properly balanced across all the key stakeholders.

When one or more stakeholder groups don't see the value in the transformation, this will create a situation where the resistance to change is higher than the appetite for change. Or worse still, that stakeholder group will vote with their feet and shift their commitment and resources away toward other opportunities. For example, if the quality of the product or service is reduced to get higher investor returns, customers will start leaving.

How does the value manifest itself for the different stakeholder groups?

- **Employees.** Employees commit their time, energy, intellect, and social focus. In return they receive a salary, work experience, learning opportunities, and future career options. In the case of USHG, the process value next to salary is high, as employees experience an engaging team experience, learning and development, a feeling of achievement, the possibility of career advancement, and the satisfaction of warm, appreciative customer interactions.

- **Customers.** Next to their money, customers spend their time and often other things to experience the benefits of an interaction. The benefits often go beyond the service or product. At USHG, for instance, they get much more in return than just a delicious meal. They get an experience of ambiance, world-class customer service, and some bragging rights of having been to a top-tier restaurant.

- **Community.** Our definition of *community* is not constrained to just the literal area in which a business operates but we also use the term to refer to society at large. Businesses use many resources from a community, including the infrastructure, laws, markets, security, and other parts of the social and commercial fabric. What does it give back beyond providing great products and services, taxes, jobs, and paying suppliers? How is more value created for a community? How active is the business driving, for example, the ESG (environmental, social, and corporate governance) agenda? In the case of USHG, they were very active in adding value not only in the local community but also in national charity activities.

SALESFORCE.COM: A CASE STUDY

When Marc Benioff started Salesforce.com, he wanted to have an impact beyond just creating a leading CRM cloud software company. Right when Salesforce.com was founded, when the company had just a few people and it was not even a certainty that it would even survive, he created the 1-1-1 model. This was an initiative intended to ensure that Salesforce would give back to society as an organization. The 1-1-1 model is shorthand for the following:

- One percent of founding stock is allocated to a fund that is spent on charity and community projects.
- One percent of the products and services are given to nonprofit organizations.
- One percent of employee time (several days a year per employee) can be spent on community initiatives.

This program enhances Salesforce.com's social standing and provides resources to help others with time, products, and financial assistance. It also has had a positive impact and employee engagement and the overall culture of the organization. Two decades after Salesforce first introduced their simple yet innovative commitment to the community, over 8,500 companies had engaged in pledging 1 percent.[82]

- **Suppliers**. Every organization leans on the support of many different suppliers—some very industry specific and others more general. They range from raw material providers to real estate providers, from content creators to legal advisors. They provide value in the form of products and services. And in return they are financially compensated. But are they treated as part of the larger team, or are they kept at arm's length in a relationship that is merely transactional? Can more value be created by treating this relationship differently? For example, in the case of Zappos, Tony Hsieh and his team decided to treat their suppliers with the utmost respect, ensuring that

---

82 A. Aziz, "The Power of Purpose: How Salesforce and the Pledge 1% Model Is Inspiring Silicon Valley to Do Good," *Forbes*, 2019.

they were always paid on time and bringing them into the organization's success by giving them unique access to their data.[83] This dynamic ultimately created much more value for both parties.

- **Investors.** Every business requires capital to fund its operations and growth. Can you create more attractive returns by growing the business or acting more efficiently with your resources? Next to providing an attractive investment return, are there other ways to create value for investors?

For an organization's transformation to be successful, it must be clear what the change program's benefits are for all stakeholders involved and why this is more attractive than the trajectory of the status quo. Is this value well communicated? Do the expected benefits outweigh the extra effort required? Does each group of stakeholders already see and experience part of the benefits during the journey, or will they only experience this value at the end?

MARCO: CREATING VALUE FOR ALL STAKEHOLDERS IN A TRANSFORMATION

As mentioned in this chapter, an organization is there to create value for all its stakeholders. Normally at the end of a transformation, all key stakeholders should see a higher value toward the future for being part of the business.

Let me share an example. When I was a partner at McKinsey, we regularly did pro bono work for nonprofit institutions like NGOs. At some point I was asked to

---

83 Hsieh, *Delivering Happiness*.

help one of the world's larger family charity funds. Over several generations a large charity fund was created by the expanding family by allocating a certain percentage of the yearly profits of their large business portfolio to this fund. The large fund was annually allocating grants around the world to other NGOs and specific projects. It maintained multiple offices around the world and retained a professional and dedicated staff.

Although substantial amounts were allocated each year, there was a sense that not enough value was being created for its stakeholders. When we spoke to the family members, the NGO professional, and the receivers of grants, they all seemed frustrated that the NGO was not living up to its full potential and not delivering on their individual visions.

Upon investigation it turned out that one of the main reasons for the lack of success was the charity's scattered approach. Because many family members had their own ideas about which causes to support and where to allocate grants, the charity had become active in more than thirty countries. As a result they felt they had failed to capture the opportunity to make a real difference in any one place. This approach also led the professional staff to become overextended in their duties and to subsequently feel unfulfilled. They were unable to follow up opportunities, build expertise, or support local initiatives in developing countries. They found that they were essentially offering financial support but no follow-up, best practices, or cross learning. Many of the family's multigenerational donors felt distanced. They were not well informed enough about the initiatives they were funding, which led to them questioning why so much funding was being allocated each year even as they saw a lack of impact.

By leveraging several wings of the flywheel, we were able to help transform this NGO and give it the force to once again make a positive impact. We started by clarifying the purpose of the charity with the family and then codifying this. We also helped set the future position so that the organization could become a real cutting-edge social investment fund. We united the family by increasing the communication between the older and younger generations. To achieve this we undertook a broad survey polling all of the family members. They could select their major priorities in terms of which endeavors were most important and which regions were most in need of assistance. As a consequence we were able to select a few major topics—like healthcare and education—and then focused on fewer than ten countries in which the charity was active. Furthermore, we formalized more professional return-on-investment reporting and launched an initiative to implement it. Also, the family's governance of the charity was professionalized with a rotating leadership and a good mix of the different generations involved. The NGO setup and leadership team was also reorganized. The internal promotion of the charity to the family members was stepped up as well, and during the yearly family retreat, a whole session was used on the charity and how it was making a difference, as well as regular newsletters and videos.

Although most of the NGO staff and family members, as well as grant recipients, started to see this as a real added value improvement, there was still a subgroup who felt that they were losing out. This was a group of family members who, in the past, had been able to secure grants for their personal interest projects by going directly to the NGO leadership. This protocol breaking, however, had led to the aforementioned scattershot approach, the inability to focus, and unprofessionalism in a number of areas. To ensure that all key stakeholders saw more value in the transformation, we agreed to use 20 percent of the yearly grant capacity for individual projects of interest selected by family members—to moderate this better, we created a professional request process. With this move we managed to bring everybody on board with the changes we'd enacted.

This transformation has led to not only a substantial increase in the positive impact that this NGO has had on society but also more unity, pride, and a deeper connection among the different generations of family members and staff who make up this organization. Ultimately there was a pay-off for all stakeholders who put so much effort into doing good for the world.

12.3 Why Is Pay-Off Important?

If all stakeholders see attractive returns as part of the transformational journey, the flywheel receives a lot of power. On the other hand, if one or more of the categories of stakeholders don't see the benefits of actively participating in the change journey, a change effort is threatened with doom by a lack of effort and investment.

- If the senior leaders involved in a change program are offered attractive returns as an incentive to achieve a transformation, it will motivate them to go the extra mile. If incentives are not apparent, difficult decisions might be avoided, and the path of least resistance—merely optimizing instead of transforming—is likely to be the path they choose.

- If you reward clients with better products and services or with lower costs, they will pay the organization back with loyalty and word-of-mouth praise. If not, the experience of receiving a reduced pay-off will cause them to look for alternatives to your product or service.

- If a transformation creates value for employees by creating interesting work, growth opportunities, good salaries, and a great work culture, you can ask them to go through the change journey. If not, the status quo, where their present jobs are meeting their needs, keeps its appeal. This may cause even the best-laid change plans to stay as just that—plans.

- If you reward the community and give back to the world, you will engender support from your employees, customers, and society. If you are not offering a community pay-off, the good you have generated among your community will remain static. This consequently means that you will not necessarily receive community-based support for your change endeavors. If the community sees the possibility of a public good in the form of a product, service, or relationship, they are much more likely to aid an organization in their transformation.

- If you reward your suppliers with growth, a cooperative and respectful partner, smooth logistics, and fair payments, you will get more value-add than just the product/service a supplier provides. Providing your suppliers with a clear pay-off will create more partnership-driven business improvements. If not, your suppliers might not go the extra mile for your organization when the time comes, and you might miss a competitive edge one of your suppliers might have provided.

- If there's an attractive return for the shareholders, they will invest. If not, they simply won't. It's imperative to make it clear that the long-term pay-off of a transformation trumps short-term profit. Communication and clarity are as much a part of this dynamic as the promise of a material return. Otherwise, investors might be unwilling to engage in short-term losses in favor of the future return.

Of course, in a transformation, return on investment may not always be (at least in the short term) the best way to improve the value equation for all stakeholders. Hypothetically it might be that certain stakeholders have profited disproportionately even while others have been squeezed—which might have created the need for a transformation in the first place. Profit for investors might not always be an indicator of health—for instance, when all profits have been divided out to investors for years at the expense of investments in improving the customer experience, it might be right to make a shift. Or if the salaries in an organization have risen to an uncompetitive level and caused the prices offered to customers to become uncompetitive, some reset in compensation might be needed. Conversely there might be customer groups who are receiving a deal that is quite literally "too good to be true," and a price increase might be the right course of action.

Thinking deliberately about what the pay-off levels are for all the stakeholders and what the level should be once the transformation succeeds is integral. Are there gaps that need to be addressed? Can this wing be strengthened in your flywheel?

12.4 How Strong Is Your Pay-Off Wing?

How strong is the pay-off wing in your Transformational Flywheel? How deliberately are you managing this wing? How would each of your stakeholders rate you? To help you assess where you stand, we have defined four different levels of power for this wing.

- **Level 1. No or limited power.** It's unclear how there will be enough pay-off for key stakeholders. There might be a transformation plan, but stakeholders don't see what's in it for them, and several may even see a serious reduction in the apparent long-term pay-off. There is no clear strategy, management, or communication with stakeholders. Therefore, stakeholder forces are not aligned, and the short-term status quo is holding firm, making change challenging.

- **Level 2. Some power.** Investors and management are able to envision the possible pay-off from the change program, but they are mostly focused on financial performance, and some stakeholders feel as if they are losing out in order for others to win. The playing field seems uneven to these stakeholders.

There is no deliberate stakeholder management process in place by senior management, and consequently communication about the possible benefits of the change program is more ad hoc.

- **Level 3. Good power.** At this level there is a clear understanding of the attractive pay-off for all stakeholders, and there is a regular review of how this program is progressing toward a pay-off. There is a right balance between short-term pain and long-term gain. There is active communication with each of the stakeholder groups. It's very professionally managed, but the real, deeper intent and passion for this might be trailing behind the message. Rather, this change program is seen as something that you *should* do and not something you want to do and be.

- **Level 4. Transformative power.** At this level of the pay-off wing, there is a clear understanding of how to create attractive trade-offs for all stakeholders along with a stable balance between short-term pain and long-term gain. All of this is scaffolded by clear, engaging communications. The broader pay-off is also focused as part of the core competitive edge of the organization, like it does with USHG. It's part of all day-to-day decisions, of operational processes, and of the key values and beliefs of the company. It's done with a powerful intent and a deep set of core beliefs.

WING-POWER LEVEL		YOUR SCORE?
LEVEL 4	TRANSFORMATIVE POWER	
LEVEL 3	GOOD POWER	
LEVEL 2	SOME POWER	
LEVEL 1	NO POWER	

PAY-OFF WING

PETER: UNDERSTANDING THE NEED TO OFFER A MEANINGFUL PAY-OFF FOR YOUR TEAM

A transformation needs to create a proper level of pay-off for all stakeholders, including you, the leader. The pay-off needs can be material, but they, of course, can also be immaterial benefits like reputation, experience, and credibility. It starts with your own drive toward the pay-off you might ultimately receive. Are you fully motivated for the journey ahead? If you are not fully motivated, others will sense this. But just as importantly, you need to motivate your key stakeholders and make sure they see the value of this pay-off as well. If you forget that people have different desires and ways of feeling rewarded, you cannot

> Motivate your key stakeholders and make sure they see the value of this pay-off.

recognize other people's needs and thus cannot offer them an incentive that will keep them motivated. It's important, therefore, to take different views of the world into account in case your individual worldview would not lend itself to seeing what an incentive to another person might be.

Let me demonstrate with an example. I once coached a CEO who was a natural leader. He was in the right position and had the right personality to lead the transformation that he was intent on creating. The company had a very conservative profile, and he was brought in to make the company more digital, more proactive, and more international. His profile was such that he had traits from the creative, enthusiastic, action-driven personality. It looked like a great match.

The CEO thought he was doing a great job because he felt that his enthusiasm always had a positive effect on people. After a while, however, it became more and more difficult to motivate his team and even their customers. At first he blamed it on the sales manager, but it was only when some key staff members were completely unmotivated and customers started to make negative comments that he realized the need to change. To address this situation, this CEO and I began to look at the reward needs from different perceptual positions. We worked with the notion that there are three positions from which you can think, feel, see, and experience the world:

1. The world according to yourself (in this case the CEO's own perspective)

> 2. The world according to someone else (looking through the eyes of the stakeholders)
> 3. The objective, reflective, and neutral camera perspective (taking a third-party view and looking at yourself interacting with the different stakeholders)
>
> After doing this exercise for important team members, customers, and shareholders, his awareness increased. Now he could better understand what the different stakeholders needed in order to stoke enthusiasm for the change journey. An action plan was made in which he diversified the ways of rewarding the team, the customers, the shareholders, and all other stakeholders with both material and intangible rewards.
>
> After seeing that he was taking care of his stakeholders, the shareholders took care of him, which propelled the transformation.

12.5 How to Strengthen the Pay-Off Wing

How can you ensure that the level of pay-off is correct for the stakeholders of your business? Here are some steps to make this wing of the flywheel stronger.

1. Start with awareness. Assess what the current value equation is for each of your key stakeholders. Compare this to the value equation they have on the current trajectory following the status quo. Where do you score in the table provided in 12.4? Is there a

burning desire for transformation? Have you put yourself in each of the stakeholders' shoes? How do you know how everybody feels? Where are the biggest gaps/issues?

2. Set an ambition level in terms of what changes you intend to make in the organization's pay-off wing. Do you need to fix some major gaps, or do you need to set a pay-off that is desirable for all the key stakeholders (like in the USHG case study)?

3. Set a deliberate logic of prioritization. USHG made a hard call on their priorities. Ask yourself, "Which stakeholder group needs to be addressed first, which second, etc.?" Define your logic and codify it into action.

4. Define clear targets, strategies, and action plans by stakeholder groups as part of the overall transformation strategy.

5. Set up clear communication strategies for all key stakeholder groups. Explain why the status quo is not the future, what an attractive future looks like, what action is needed for that future, and what is required from the stakeholders. Don't forget to communicate the incentives for the stakeholders as well.

6. Manage the pay-off wing. Allocate responsibilities; decide on temperature-checking approaches to check in with shareholders to see how they're feeling about progress. Go and visit customers; do roundtables and surveys. If you rely solely on reports, you don't really know the condition of the endeavor because the moment that you see it in numbers, you're too late. It's important to make the pay-off wing part of the management agenda meeting rhythm.

References

Meyer, D. *Setting the Table: The Transforming Power of Hospitality in Business*. Ecco, 2008.

Heskett, J., E. Sasser Jr., and L. Schlesinger. *The Service Profit Chain: How Leading Companies Link Profit and Growth to Loyalty, Satisfaction, and Value*. New York: Free Press, 1997.

Aziz, A. "The Power of Purpose: How Salesforce and the Pledge 1% Model Is Inspiring Silicon Valley to Do Good." *Forbes*, 2019. https://www.forbes.com/sites/afdhelaziz/2019/04/18/the-power-of-purpose-how-salesforce-and-the-pledge-1-model-is-inspiring-silicon-valley-to-do-good/?sh=53fc300d543d.

Hsieh, T. *Delivering Happiness: A Path to Profits, Passion, and Purpose*. Hachette Book Group, 2010.

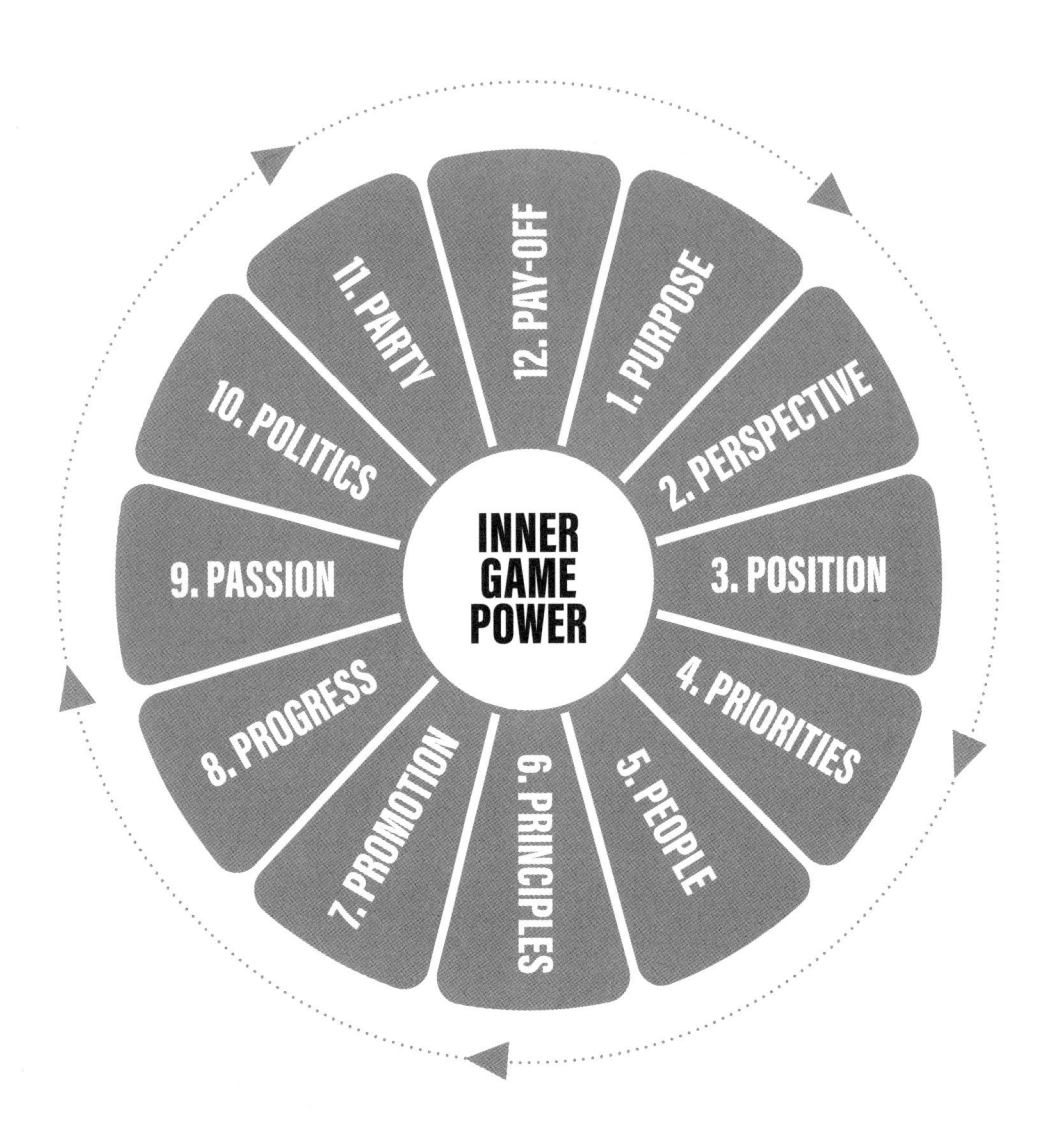

INNER GAME POWER

1. PURPOSE
2. PERSPECTIVE
3. POSITION
4. PRIORITIES
5. PEOPLE
6. PRINCIPLES
7. PROMOTION
8. PROGRESS
9. PASSION
10. POLITICS
11. PARTY
12. PAY-OFF

CHAPTER 13

THE INNER GAME

The outer game is won by winning the inner game as well.

—MARCO VAN KALLEVEEN AND PETER KOIJEN

13.1 Introduction

Transforming an organization is a demanding and energy-intensive endeavor. It requires leaders to bring their A game for an extended period of time. To succeed at the external transformational business challenge—the outer game—a leader must harness their inner game. To give you some examples, let's review some of the practices the leaders from our earlier case studies utilized as they transformed their organizations.

- **Steve Jobs - Apple.** Steve Jobs transformed Apple into the most valuable company in the world despite taking it over as it sat on the brink of bankruptcy. During his time as CEO, he pioneered the use of Zen mindfulness meditation to reduce stress, gain clarity, and empower his creativity. His biographer, Walter Isaacson, shared the following quote from Jobs, one that we believe sums up his ideas nicely: "If you sit and observe, you will see how restless your mind is. If you try to calm it, it only makes it worse, but over time it does calm, and when it does, there's room to hear more subtle things—that's when your intuition starts to blossom, and you start to see things more clearly and be in the present more."[84]

- **Bob Iger - Disney.** Bob Iger, who led the transformation as CEO of Disney, has indicated in interviews that he wakes up at four fifteen in the morning and then avoids looking at his phone until after his workout. "I create a firewall with technology, by the way, in that I try to exercise and think before I read," Iger told *Vanity Fair* in 2018. "Because if I read, it throws me off, it's distracting. I'm immediately thinking about someone else's thoughts instead of my own. I like being alone with my own thoughts, and it gives me an opportunity to not just replenish but to organize, and it's important."[85]

- **Satya Nadella - Microsoft.** Satya Nadella, who fundamentally transformed Microsoft to become one of the most valuable companies in the world again, has two fixed things in his daily morning routine, namely, exercise and self-reflection. He shared that he normally wakes up at seven in the morning after eight hours of sleep and starts the day by asking himself, "What are you thankful for?" "It's just grounding. It gives you the ability to get up in the morning and orient yourself for the day," he told LinkedIn's *Hello Monday* podcast. Then he

---

84 G. James, "How Steve Jobs Trained His Own Brain," *Inc.*, 2015.
85 "Bob Iger: Daily Routine," Balance the Grind, 2020.

gets his exercise: "It doesn't matter where I am, what time zone, how late I get in, I get up and go to the gym."[86]

- **Marc Benioff - Salesforce.com.** Marc Benioff, who transformed the CRM software industry and built Salesforce.com into a global leader, continuously invests in his inner game. In an interview in 2019, he mentioned how important reading has been in shaping his approach to business and life. He mentioned books like Harold Geneen's *Managing* and *The Good Heart* by the Dalai Lama. He described how he had adopted a low-sugar diet and was using his Peloton cycle for forty-five-minute rides.

> Leaders explored various experiences and found practices that worked for them and helped bring their best inner game to a transformational endeavor.

He also claimed that one of the best investments he ever made was in Hei meditation practice. He typically meditates every morning for thirty to sixty minutes.

These leaders created routines that sustained them and enabled them to bring the peak of their abilities for an extended period of time—thus winning their inner game. While some have pushed these habits to some unusual extremes, like waking up at four fifteen to take an ice bath, that is not the secret to having a strong inner game. What's important is that these leaders explored various experiences and found practices that worked for them and helped bring their best inner game to a transformational endeavor.

---

86 C. Stieg, "Microsoft CEO's Two Morning Rituals to Help 'Orient Yourself for the Day.'" CNBC, 2019.

How strong is your current inner game? What routines are you investing in to aid you in harnessing your inner game even more?

13.2 The Six Inner Game Forces

Although the main focus of this book is how to make the Transformational Flywheel gain momentum—to tend to the external game—it is also important to increase your awareness of what we call the inner game so that it can be enhanced. At the end of each of the specific flywheel chapters, we have shared some specific inner game suggestions. In this chapter we wanted to share some strategies for enhancing the foundational forces of your inner game. There are, of course, many different aspects in which leaders can invest to increase their inner game, but in our experience, there are six forces that stand out as being essential.

THE SIX INNER GAME FORCES

1. Health and Fitness
2. Emotional Fuel
3. Mental Strength
4. Knowing Yourself
5. Empowering Beliefs
6. Motivation Force

6 Inner Game Forces:
1. Health and Fitness
2. Emotional Fuel
3. Mental Strength
4. Knowing Yourself
5. Empowering Beliefs
6. Motivation Force

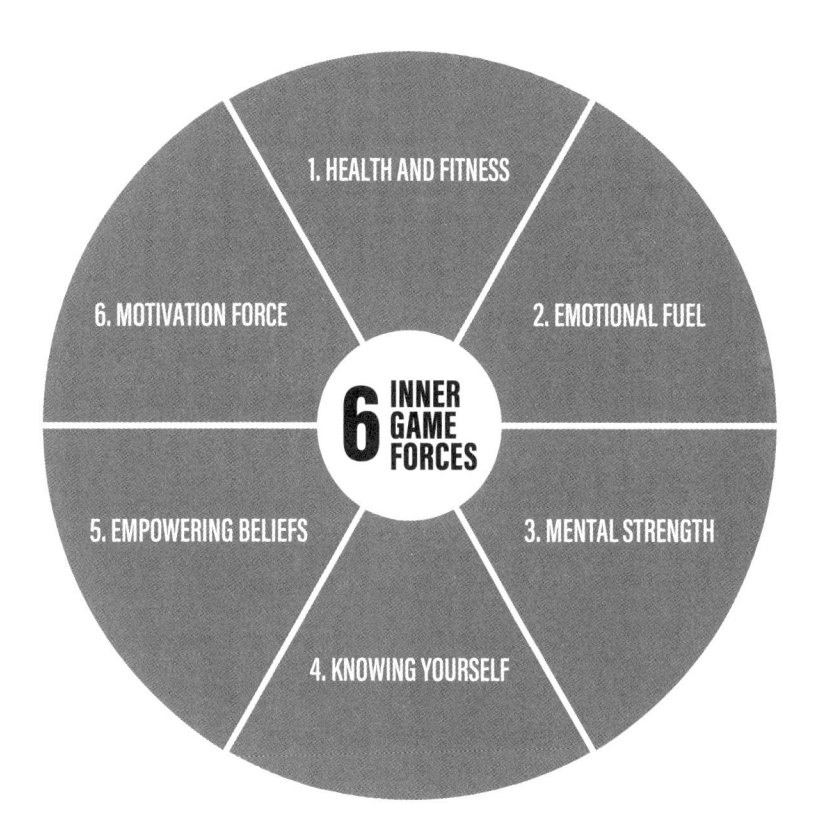

Let us dive into the high level on the what, why, and how involved in each of these six aspects of inner game power.

1. Health and Fitness

Many successful leaders consciously invest in their health and fitness to sustain their high levels of energy and vitality. This practice gives you the energy and stamina needed to set direction, motivate others, and resolve issues. It also has a positive impact on our cognitive processing.[87] This has been demonstrated by research published in the *Journal of Managerial Psychology*, which followed over six hundred

---

[87] Candice L. Hogan et al., "Exercise Holds Immediate Benefits for Affect and Cognition in Younger and Older Adults," *Psychology and Aging* (2013).

senior executives over the course of a few years.[88] Prior to attending, the participants completed a health and physical activity questionnaire that included questions about their exercise routine, diet, physical health, and vices such as smoking. Each participant's performance was then rated by their peers. The results were striking: senior executives who exercised regularly were rated significantly higher than nonexercisers on various leadership indices.

Given the importance, how do you rate your health and fitness?

- **Weak Inner Game:** Unhealthy lifestyle and habits, low energy and vitality

- **Some Inner Game:** Having some good and bad practices—health is not a top priority

- **Good Inner Game:** Living relatively healthily and working on fitness as a priority

- **Outstanding Inner Game:** Living like an athlete with an abundance of energy and vitality

If you want to increase your inner game in the arena of your health and fitness, you likely know what to do. The issue is often not a lack of knowing what to do. Most know what drives improved health and fitness, such as quality of sleep, healthy nutrition, drinking sufficient amount of water, regular exercise, breathing exercise, limiting vices such as alcohol and smoking, and so on. There are over ten thousand books on Amazon on these topics, and the availability of exercise programs and fitness studies is endless and often close to work and home.

---

88   S. McDowell-Larsen et al., "Fitness and Leadership: Is There a Relationship? Regular Exercise Correlates with Higher Leadership Ratings in Senior-Level Executives," *Journal of Managerial Psychology* (2002).

There are, however, typically two things standing in the way: not making and keeping health a priority because there are so many other demands and the challenge and time investment involved in changing habits. According to a 2009 study in the *European Journal of Social Psychology*, it takes, on average, sixty-six days for a new behavior to become automatic.[89]

If you want to shift gears, there are several methods you might consider as a means of doing so. You'll need to create a very clear and compelling *why* if you want to improve your health and fitness. If the why is strong enough, the what and how will follow. Allocate fixed, nonnegotiable times for activities like healthy eating and exercise. Focus on changing one habit at a time. Set measurable targets and break your journey down in bite-size steps. Track progress, make the process fun, and celebrate small wins. Surround yourself with like-minded people. The list of what you can do is endless, but you need to formulate a specific plan and stick to it to reach the next level of this inner game lever.

2. Emotional Fuel

A leader needs a significant amount of emotional fuel to make a transformation succeed. A strong inner game, therefore, will be characterized by empowering emotions like confidence, curiosity, creativity, passion, kindness, gratitude, and determination. A strong transformation leader will be able to deal with disempowering emotions like fear, worry, and stress. Research published in the *Journal of Leadership and Organizational Studies* shows that "leaders who use emotion regulation

---

[89]   P. Lally et al., "How Are Habits Formed: Modelling Habit Formation in the Real World," *European Journal of Social Psychology* (2010).

effectively may be able to improve their effect, the quality of their relationships, and organizational outcomes."[90]

Why is emotional health so important? If you are in a positive and resilient emotional state, challenges and problems are much easier to address. Also, emotions are contagious; worry and fear spread, as do optimism, confidence, and a sense of curiosity. A study in *Scientific American Mind* suggests that negative emotions can be more contagious than the common cold.[91] Research also shows that teams are influenced by the emotions of their peers and that a leader's mood can have a spark effect that activates a positive feedback loop.[92]

How would you rate your emotional state?

- **Weak Inner Game:** Feeling emotions that are predominantly disempowering like stress and worry

- **Some Inner Game:** Having some awareness of your emotions but not taking control

- **Good Inner Game:** Living most of the time in a positive state but with periods of negativity

- **Outstanding Inner Game:** Living almost always in a positive emotional state

If you want to raise your inner emotional game, you might consider two steps: increasing your awareness and managing your emotions better.

---

[90] A. Haver et al., "Emotion Regulation and Its Implications for Leadership: An Integrative Review and Future Research Agenda," *Journal of Leadership and Organizational Studies* (2013).

[91] G. Lewandowski Jr. et al., "Is a Bad Mood Contagious?," *Scientific American Mind*, 2012.

[92] T. Sy, "Contagious Leaders and Followers: Exploring Multistage Mood Contagion in a Leader Activation and Member Propagation (LAMP) Model," *Organizational Behavior and Human Decision Processes* (November 2013).

Awareness. Having a strong inner game requires a high level of awareness. One way to do this is by measuring your emotional state regularly. This process of emotional measurement is greatly aided by good labels for the emotions you regularly feel as well as some scale for intensity with which you feel these emotions. For example, consider the emotion *happiness* on a scale of one to five: (1) content, (2) positive, (3) smiling, (4) elevated, (5) ecstatic. Another example might be a scale for stress: (1) tension, (2) losing perspective, (3) firefighting, (4) overwhelmed, (5) paralyzed. By regularly measuring your current emotional state, you increase your awareness of it. How aware are you of your daily emotions?

Management. People create their own emotions and are therefore able to regulate them. Emotional regulation is influenced by what a person focuses on, what meaning they assign to events in their inner dialogue, and bodily context like breathing, posture, and social modes. If you focus on what you want, perceive difficulties as opportunities, and focus on how you can influence a situation, your emotional regulation will be further under your control. You can further regulate your internal state if you put a smile on your face, breathe deeply, speak positively, and stand straight. On the opposite end of the spectrum, if you focus on what you don't want, on how bad things are at the moment, and on what you can't influence, you'll find that your emotional state becomes dysregulated. This is all exacerbated by dropping your shoulders and speaking in a complaining tone. Factors like this are why people can react very differently to the same external event.

Clearly there are external factors that can trigger a positive or negative emotional response. The Stoic philosophers, however, argue that humans have the freedom and ability to choose how they respond to that trigger—or even the ability to create their own triggers. The

COVID-19 pandemic is an example of how such worldviews can manifest. All economic, medical, and social factors being equal, some individuals chose to respond very differently to the stresses of the pandemic. Some felt that the COVID-19 pandemic was a great opportunity to recalibrate their lives, while others became depressed about what they were unable to do rather than acknowledging the time for reflection and the freedom from certain obligations. If you don't want to be taken hostage when your emotional procedures are activated by random external events, it's important to designate which emotions you want to feel—almost regardless of the circumstances. There are, then, many ways to induce certain emotions regardless of external events. These practices might include starting your day with three aspects of your life for which you are grateful, listening to uplifting music, using positive affirmations, reading or watching something meaningful, or spending time with people who lift you up. Are you managing your emotions, or are your emotions managing you?

3. Mental Strength

Harnessing your mental power and toughness is key when you are enacting a transformation. Setbacks and challenges as you chart your way in new territory are always part of any transformational journey. Prof. Peter Clough and Dr. Keith Earle of Manchester Metropolitan University have been conducting leading research on the topic of mental toughness for decades. Their study defines *mental toughness* as a leader's capacity for dealing with stressors, challenges, and pressures while continuing to present their best performance, irrespective of the circumstances in which they find themselves.[93] Mental toughness is the ability to conquer adversity and emerge stronger.

How would you rate your mental strength?

---

[93] P. Clough et al., "Mental Toughness: The Concept and Management," in *Solutions in Sport Psychology*, ed. I. Cockerill (2002).

- **Weak Inner Game:** You do not currently possess a lot of mental fortitude.

- **Some Inner Game:** You have moments of mental power but only in specific circumstances.

- **Good Inner Game:** You have good mental power in most situations.

- **Outstanding Inner Game:** You have exceptional mental power, especially when the going gets tough.

If you want to further harness your mental toughness, Clough and Earle identified four proven areas that enhance your mental toughness and strengthen your performance, resilience, and well-being: control, commitment, challenge, and confidence (the 4Cs model):[94]

Control. Leaders who believe that they have control over their destiny, their life, and their circumstances have a higher mental strength. They tend toward viewing the glass as being half full, not half empty. They also believe that there are always other ways to try in the event that something doesn't work out. They prioritize and don't easily get overwhelmed. They use positive language and focus more on solutions and less on problems. They are willing to work hard to tackle blockages and have a can-do attitude.

Commitment. Mentally strong leaders are more goal and achievement oriented. They visualize their goals clearly and have a high sense of commitment to these goals. They try to look at things objectively. They break tasks and challenges down into manageable chunks. They celebrate successes, set high standards, and take responsibility.

Challenge. Those with a high level of mental toughness see challenges as opportunities. They have a tendency to provoke change,

---

[94] D. Strycharczyk et al., *Developing Mental Toughness: Strategies to Improve Performance, Resilience and Well-Being in Individuals and Organizations*, 3rd ed. (2021).

commit easily to new projects, and don't like to be in a status quo for too long. They seek new experiences, love to learn, and accept that there will be mistakes while also believing that failure is not final. They tend to reflect not only when things go wrong but also when things succeed.

Confidence. Leaders with confidence are less reliant on the validation of others and see criticism as feedback rather than as detraction. They are happy to present their position and to answer questions. They see excellence and the success of others not as a threat but as something to strive for. They stand their ground when challenged, are not easily embarrassed, and are happy to ask for support and help.

Are you mentally strong enough to work on the strength-enhancing 4C system?

4. Knowing Yourself

"Know thyself" was one of the maxims of the ancient Delphic oracles. A strong inner game involves understanding your true strengths and weaknesses, your specific personality traits, and your hot buttons and examining how all these might support or hamper the transformation at hand. Investing in knowing yourself will allow you to lead with effectiveness. It leads to less inner conflict, better resistance to social pressure, understanding others better, and better decision-making (among other benefits).[95] This, of course, takes life experience and reflection—and it will always develop and evolve—getting to know yourself is a never-ending journey. A framework you might consider in order to gain greater self-knowledge is that of the six vitals of knowing

---

[95] M. Selig, "Know Yourself? Six Specific Ways to Know Who You Are," *Psychology Today*, 2016.

yourself: values, interest, temper, around-the-clock activities, life missions and goals, and strengths. Let's describe each of these.

Values. Being aware of your most important values at this stage of your life is one of the six vitals of self-knowledge. What do you want to stand for, and what values are important to you? There is a long list of concepts humans value: health, creativity, connection, success, kindness, freedom, serving, learning, power, calmness, excitement, adventure, etc. Writing down and calibrating your focus on your, say, top ten values will help you take targeted action and make decisions that embody and strive toward that which you value.

Interests. What engages you? What catches your interest and sparks fascination? What bores you? This differs widely depending upon the person, but creating a focus on these interests is vital. Consider your activities across the last few years—what do you read first when reading a newspaper or magazine? In your work, what do you love to do? What topics give you energy? Figuring out your passions and interests allows you to see which opportunities you can engage with best and which ones should be pursued by others who are more passionate in that area.

Temperament. This vital aspect describes your inborn preference on how to engage with the world around you. Are you more spontaneous, or do you want to make plans first? Are you more introverted or extroverted? Do you like to make decisions based on gut feel or on facts? There are many more dimensions you can measure yourself against. Knowing your temper allows you to better determine which situations you thrive in and who could best complement you in a team. If you are introverted, for instance, you might want to take time before a meeting to read things first. If you are an extrovert, you might seek more room for open brainstorming on a whiteboard.

Around-the-Clock Activities. This refers to your biorhythms and when you prefer to do things. For example, are you a night owl or a morning person? When in the day do you think most clearly? When are you the most social? When is it best for you to eat? When do you like to exercise? Thinking carefully about your internal clock and aligning your daily activities with your personal preferences substantially enhances your effectiveness.

Life Mission and Meaningful Goals. It is important to discover and define your purpose and your major goals at this stage in your life. Regularly reflecting upon this and reviewing your commitments deepens your self-knowledge and strengthens your ability to engage with life instead of merely responding to events.

Strengths. Your strengths can include many things. They can include not only your abilities, experiences, and skills but also things like emotional intelligence and character traits that stand out—your drive, intelligence, and confidence. Doubling down on your strengths rather than focusing on resolving your weaknesses can be a better strategy for making progress toward your goals.

How would you rate your level of self-knowledge?

- **Weak Inner Game:** You have limited awareness of your vital traits and try to take on challenges that are not aligned with these traits, which causes tension and ineffectiveness.

- **Some Inner Game:** You have some understanding of yourself, but getting a clear sense of your vitals is not currently a priority. You are often reacting to life rather than living with agency.

- **Good Inner Game:** You have worked on understanding your vitals better, but you don't always consider these ideas as you engage with life.

- **Outstanding Inner Game:** You have done a lot of work and self-reflection that has led to clarity regarding your vital traits. You leverage these insights to be a more effective leader.

If you want to actively invest time and energy in knowing yourself better, there are multiple ways to do this. There are tests like Myers-Briggs, Enneagram, and DISC that can aid in evaluating your vitals. Taking quality time for solitude and reflection can also be helpful in determining your current state and your path forward. You can also engage in coaching and solicit full-spectrum feedback regarding your personality and methodology.

5. Empowering Beliefs

Don't let your beliefs limit you. Beliefs are perceived assumptions about oneself, others, or the world around us. These can take on a feeling of certainty, so unexamined beliefs can become extremely limiting when they are negative or pessimistic.

Why do we create beliefs? The world is complex and constantly changing, and we have a limited ability to process information. In order to preserve mental bandwidth, we create beliefs to compress the information we receive from the world into a manageable process. The world is polysemic—it lends itself to multiple interpretations, and many people hold different beliefs that arise from the same facts. And they hold them without absolute certainty. Individuals facing a life change, for instance, might live in a completely different reality. One person might see change as a threat to be avoided while another views the exact same change as an opportunity for growth and education.

Once someone has created a belief, this becomes their world, and they act accordingly. As you believe it, so you see it. If you, for instance, believe that a person can grow and develop, you will coach them, give them opportunities in a committed way, and see every small step of progress as evidence supporting your belief in them. Conversely if you believe that this person can't change and grow, you don't even try to coach them or give them opportunities—furthermore, you'll see every mistake as a proof point of your belief.

A strong inner game means that you are aware of your key beliefs and that you have taken efforts to ensure that they are empowering rather than limiting. Your beliefs regarding yourself, your team, the organization, or your industry are powerful and inspiring.

How would you rate the inner game of your empowering beliefs?

- **Weak Inner Game:** You are not aware of the beliefs you choose to hold, and there are many disempowering ideas that unnecessarily limit.

- **Some Inner Game:** You have a limited awareness of your beliefs. You have a number of empowering beliefs, but these exist alongside limiting ideas.

- **Good Inner Game:** You have some awareness of your beliefs, most of which are empowering. Despite this, you are not actively taking charge of your beliefs.

- **Outstanding Inner Game:** You are aware of your beliefs and deliberately manage your worldview. They are empowering and make a positive difference in your actions and attitude.

If you want to increase your inner game by creating more empowering beliefs, there are certain steps you can consider. First, make yourself aware of your beliefs explicitly by writing them down. Research shows that every belief can be boiled down to two types of statements; namely, A=B (if something can be classified as A, it also means that thing is equivalent to B) and A=>B (when you observe A, you expect that it causes something else to manifest as B).

Once you've identified your limiting beliefs, you can ask yourself questions that undermine these beliefs. "When and how did I come up with this? Who says such a thing is true? Could I be incorrect? Was there a time I didn't have this belief? What are the negative consequences of seeing the world through this belief?"

Then once your sense of certainty has been weakened, you can formulate a more empowering version of these ideas. Reframe "My team doesn't take action" as "I need to learn how to show my team how to take action." This reconstructs the idea so that you are the one responsible for the situation, which also means that you have control. A limiting belief about your team has now become an opportunity for growth and change. An empowering belief will always be underpinned by benefits and the potential for positive results.

6. Motivation Force

To lead a transformation, you need a high level of motivation. Motivation is one's reason for behaving in a particular way. You can, of course, have more or less motivation to do something. Winning the inner game in terms of motivation means that you have created a high sense of drive, eagerness, and determination to make a transformation happen. Since leading a transformation can take several years and be an experience filled with challenges and setbacks, having a high sense of motivation will make you more resourceful and increase your ability to positively impact the people around you. If you have a high level of motivation, you find better solutions, convince others more successfully, deal with setbacks and obstacles easier, and are on a mission.

How would you rate your inner game in terms of motivation?
- **Weak Inner Game:** A true lack of the motivation needed to make a transformation happen

- **Some Inner Game:** Some motivation to work on a transformation but also doubt characterized by a "wait and see" sentiment and an unwillingness to make sacrifices

- **Good Inner Game:** Positively motivated and seeing many good reasons to deliver the transformation but accompanied by more head than heart

- **Outstanding Inner Game:** Unstoppable motivation with head and heart fully aligned to make the change effort successful and a willingness to do whatever it takes

How to raise motivation-related inner game to the next level? There are many different motives for undertaking something in a work context. In the seminal book *Intrinsic Motivation and Self-Determination in Human Behavior* by Edward L. Deci and Richard M. Ryan, the authors define six key motives[96] that drive work. These concepts work well alongside the ideas of Neel Doshi and Lindsay McGregor, who identify six forces that drive performance in their book *Primed to Perform*.[97] Three of these forces are closely related to the work itself: play, purpose, and potential. Three others are further removed from the act of working and are more indirect: emotional pressure, economic pressure, and inertia.

- **Play.** The greatest motivator is finding enjoyment and fascination in the actual tasks you need to do. When you see your work as play or find ways to make it more playful, you will find yourself to be more motivated.

- **Purpose.** When you do something because you value the outcome and effect of the work, you will have purpose even if

---

96   E. Deci et al., *Intrinsic Motivation and Self-Determination in Human Behavior* (Plenum Press, 1985).

97   Neel Doshi et al., *Primed to Perform: How to Build the Highest-Performing Cultures through the Science of Total Motivation* (HarperCollins Publishers, 2015).

the work isn't enjoyable. The work can be challenging, but the opportunity to help others or work toward a greater purpose is motivating enough to push through.

- **Potential.** This is when you do a task in pursuit of an indirect result. An action might, for example, lead to a desired promotion, lead you to learn new skills, or help expand your network. Identifying future opportunities that result from a transformation effort will only increase your motivation.

- **Emotional Pressure.** This is the motive force that results when one is being pressured by their own expectations or those of others. An individual is motivated by the notion that they will be judged should they fail to complete an endeavor.

- **Economic Pressure.** This is when one does something to get a reward or to avoid a direct loss of assets or earning power. An example of this would be when one works to avoid losing one's salary.

- **Inertia.** Inertia is the law of physics describing how a force will try to stay as it is. A moving object will try to continue moving. A stationary object will try to stay at rest. A worker also has inertia. The motivational force of inertia describes how a worker might be motivated to continue working because work has become their status quo. They work because they have always worked. It is preferable to work because one is mindful and directed, but inertia might still serve as a force of motivation where the other forces are not active.

Research proves that the most motivated leaders are the ones who score high on the first three and low on the last three, creating what is described as "total motivation." This describes a state where you can make your work more playful and purposeful and see your future growth potential. Working in a state of total motivation reduces the emotional pressure, economic pressure, and inertia motive forces at work in your transformational effort. These conditions will significantly improve your motivation.

Are you motivated to work on your motivation and raise your inner game?

13.3 Harnessing Your Inner Game

How do you currently rate yourself on the individual elements of your inner game? Would these scores be better or worse during a different moment in your career? What are the prime areas where you might improve your inner game? Mark the appropriate fields in the table on the next page in order to track your assessment of your inner game.

CHAPTER 13: THE INNER GAME

WHAT IS YOUR SCORE?

	OVERALL	1. HEALTH & FITNESS	2. EMOTIONAL FUEL	3. MENTAL POWER	4. KNOWING YOURSELF	5. EMPOWERING BELIEFS	6. MOTIVATIONAL FORCE
LEVEL 4 — OUTSTANDING INNER GAME							
LEVEL 3 — GOOD INNER GAME							
LEVEL 2 — SOME INNER GAME							
LEVEL 1 — WEAK INNER GAME							

References

James, G. "How Steve Jobs Trained His Own Brain." *Inc.*, 2015. https://www.inc.com/geoffrey-james/how-steve-jobs-trained-his-own-brain.html.

"Bob Iger: Daily Routine." Balance the Grind, 2020. https://www.balancethegrind.com.au/daily-routines/bob-iger-daily-routine/.

Stieg, C. "Microsoft CEO's Two Morning Rituals to Help 'Orient Yourself for the Day.'" CNBC, 2019. https://www.cnbc.com/2019/12/11/microsoft-ceo-satya-nadellas-morning-rituals.html.

"Life Advice from Marc Benioff." Meaning Ring, 2019. https://meaningring.com/2019/09/07/life-advice-from-marc-benioff/.

Hogan, C., J. Mata, and L. Carstensen. "Exercise Holds Immediate Benefits for Affect and Cognition in Younger and Older Adults." *Psychology and Aging* (2013). https://pubmed.ncbi.nlm.nih.gov/23795769/.

McDowell-Larsen, S., L. Kearney, and D. Campbell. "Fitness and Leadership: Is There a Relationship?: Regular Exercise Correlates with Higher Leadership Ratings in Senior-Level Executives." *Journal of Managerial Psychology* (2002). https://www.researchgate.net/publication/235310303_Fitness_and_leadership_Is_there_a_relationship_Regular_exercise_correlates_with_higher_leadership_ratings_in_senior-level_executives.

Lally, P., C. van Jaarsveld, H. Potts, and J. Wardle. "How Are Habits Formed: Modelling Habit Formation in the Real World." *European Journal of Social Psychology* (2010). http://citeseerx.ist.psu.edu/viewdoc/download?doi=10.1.1.695.830&rep=rep1&type=pdf.

Haver, A., K. Akerjordet, and T. Furunes. "Emotion Regulation and Its Implications for Leadership: An Integrative Review and Future Research Agenda." *Journal of Leadership and Organizational Studies* (2013). https://www.researchgate.net/publication/235916037_Emotion_Regulation_and_Its_Implications_for_Leadership_An_Integrative_Review_and_Future_Research_Agenda/citation/download.

Lewandowski Jr., G., and M. Lenneville. "Is a Bad Mood Contagious?" *Scientific American Mind* (July 2012). https://www.scientificamerican.com/article/is-a-bad-mood-contagious/.

Sy, T. "Contagious Leaders and Followers: Exploring Multistage Mood Contagion in a Leader Activation and Member Propagation (LAMP) Model." *Organizational Behavior and Human Decision Processes* (November 2013).

Clough, P., K. Earle, and D. Sewell. "Mental Toughness: The Concept and Management." In *Solutions in Sport Psychology*, edited by I. Cockerill, 2002.

Strycharczyk, D., P. Clough, and J. Perry. *Developing Mental Toughness: Strategies to Improve Performance, Resilience and Well-Being in Individuals and Organizations*, 3rd ed., 2021.

Selig, M. "Know Yourself? Six Specific Ways to Know Who You Are." *Psychology Today*, 2016. https://www.psychologytoday.com/us/blog/changepower/201603/know-yourself-6-specific-ways-know-who-you-are.

Deci, E., and R. Ryan. *Intrinsic Motivation and Self-Determination in Human Behavior*. Plenum Press, 1985.

Doshi, N., and L. McGregor. *Primed to Perform: How to Build the Highest-Performing Cultures through the Science of Total Motivation*. HarperCollins Publishers, 2015.

INNER GAME POWER

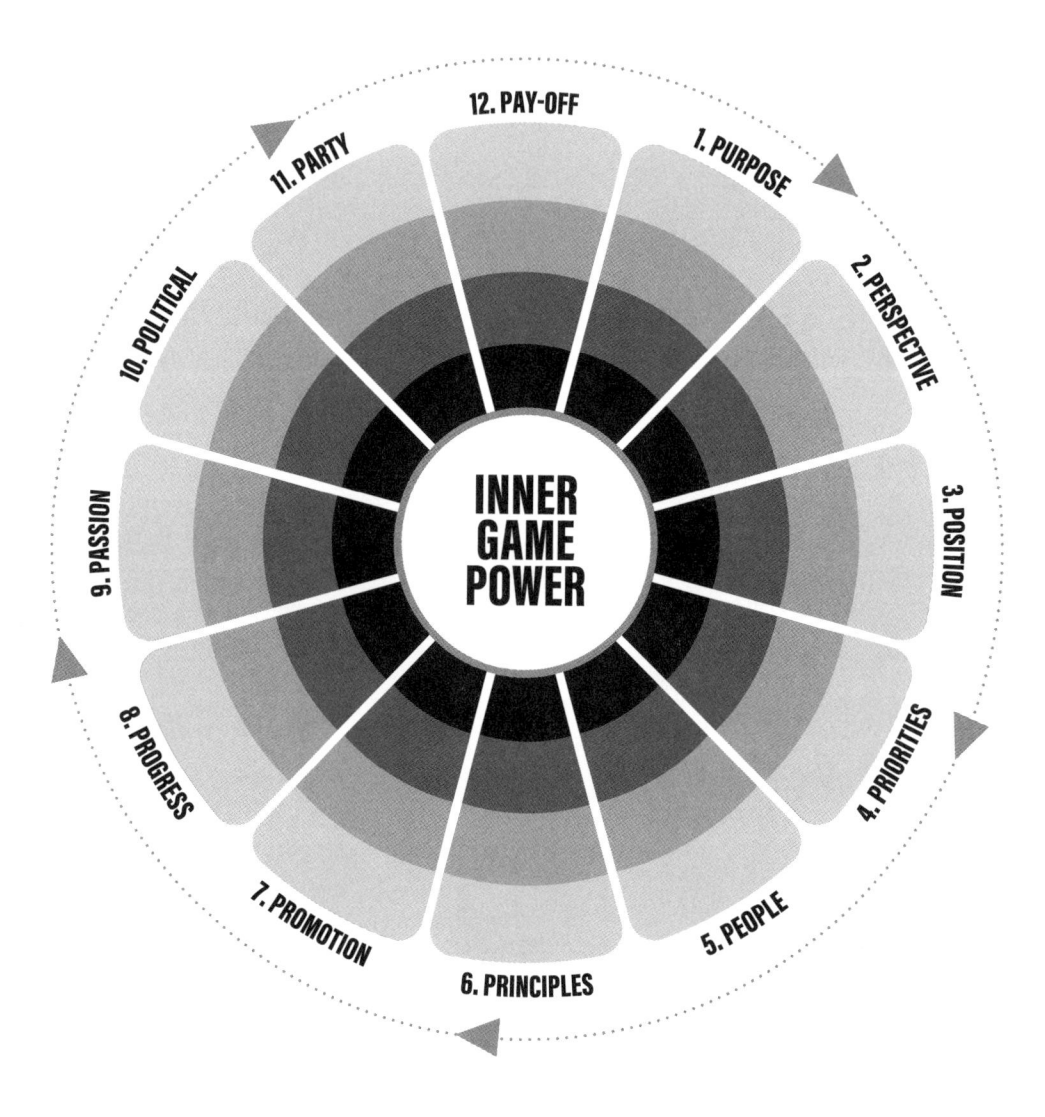

- 1. PURPOSE
- 2. PERSPECTIVE
- 3. POSITION
- 4. PRIORITIES
- 5. PEOPLE
- 6. PRINCIPLES
- 7. PROMOTION
- 8. PROGRESS
- 9. PASSION
- 10. POLITICAL
- 11. PARTY
- 12. PAY-OFF

CHAPTER 14

CONCLUSION: END OF THE BOOK, START OF THE JOURNEY

You're pushing no harder than during the first rotation, but the flywheel goes faster and faster. Each turn of the flywheel builds upon work done earlier, compounding your investment and effort. A thousand times faster, then ten thousand, then hundred thousand.
—JIM COLLINS

14.1 Introduction

As we shared in the introductory chapter at the start of this book, we wrote this book as part of a shared quest to find the factors that drive successful transformations. Many organizations need to transform regularly to stay relevant to society and ahead of a dynamic market.

The market is subject to key trends like digitalization, globalization, and the increasing importance of environmental, social, and governance as factors that impact investment. This includes macroshocks like the internet bubble burst in 2001, the financial crisis in 2008, and the COVID-19 pandemic in 2020.

Reality has proved that making change happen is difficult. Making a full transformation can even look impossible. One striking sign of this trend is that many organizations that previously ranked in the top twenty of the *Fortune* 500 in the past two decades no longer appear on the list at all. The ability to transform is perhaps the main factor that determines whether or not an organization will be able to stand the test of time. This is as true for smaller businesses as it is for corporate juggernauts. Change is ironically a constant—and it's a filter through which many organizations cannot pass.

This somewhat grim reminder of reality does not indicate that all businesses fail in their change and transformational efforts. There are inspiring examples of leaders and leadership teams who were able to transform their organizations. What are their keys to success? Is there a pattern in their common practices? What does the latest research say, and how can you use these insights effectively? Is there a secret code that can be revealed with enough reflection and research?

After years of practicing, studying, and advising transformations, we became convinced that a sacred code of successful transformations does, in fact, exist. In the book, which has been several years in the making, we have tried not only to excavate this code but also to make this information into an actionable methodology a leader can use to assess, track, and direct their transformation plan for their organization—thereby giving themselves a much better chance of success. Before concluding this book, we would like to give you a short recap you can use as reference for both the twelve wings of the Flywheel of Transformation and the case studies that illustrate their practical application.

14.2 Introduction: A Short Recap of the Flywheel

In a transformation there are no quick fixes or simple tricks. Making a transformation work requires active effort on multiple fronts. Based on our quest, we concluded that there are at least twelve key drivers to get it right, each of which is captured in the Transformational Flywheel concept. This model brings you a clearer mental picture of the individual levers and acts as an actionable tool for you to evaluate and direct your change effort.

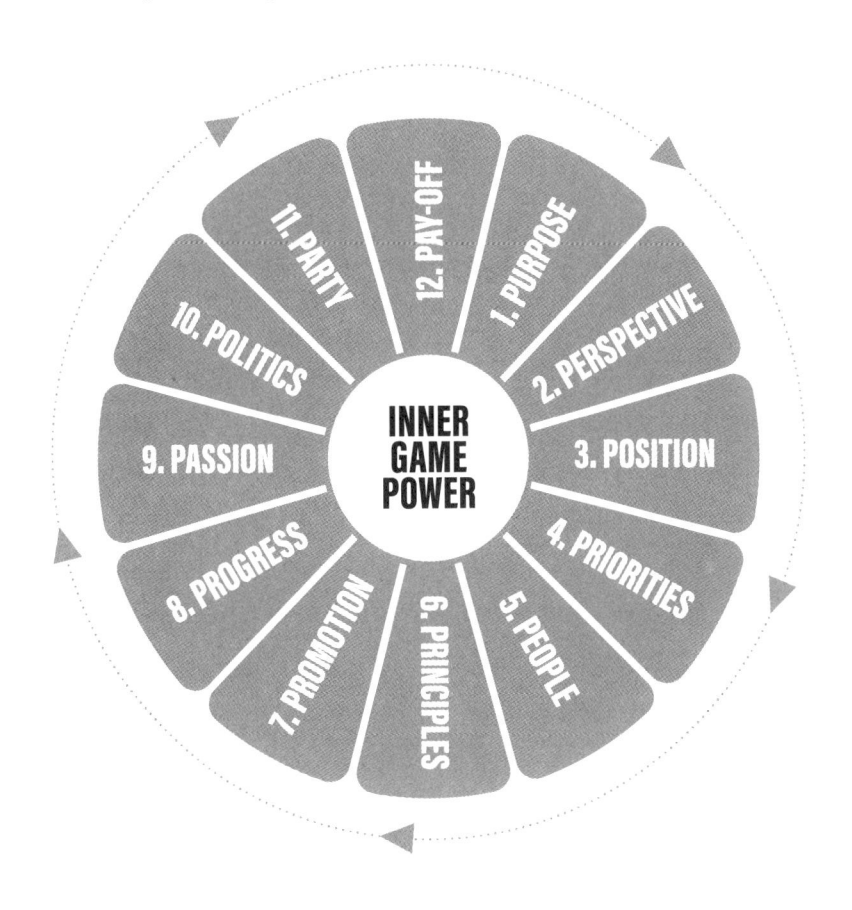

Let's briefly recap each of the wings of the flywheel. Each chapter provides case studies and insights into the what, why, and how of each of the specific wings.

1. **Purpose (Apple - Steve Jobs).** Purpose is the foundation for a successful transformation. A strong purpose is the reason an organization exists, and it can often be captured in a sentence with the following structure: "We do X to help others do Y." Can your purpose be captured in this format? Is your purpose clear and compelling? Is your team and organization working to transform the business in service of a higher cause?

2. **Perspective (Tesla - Marc Tarpenning and Martin Eberhard).** Perspective is how accurate your beliefs are on the business, market, competitor, and broader social trends. How accurate are the beliefs with which an organization and its leadership operate? Are these beliefs based on insightful views of how the market is changing and what this shift means, or are they clouded by outdated biases?

3. **Position (Starbucks - Howard Schultz).** Every organization has an implicitly or explicitly defined target market position for the future. Your future position is a combination of the answers to these two questions: "Where to play?" and "How to win?" If a future position is not defined, it is, then, by default an assumption that the current position will be the future market position. The more clear and compelling this future position, the more power this wing has in the flywheel.

4. **People (Microsoft - Satya Nadella).** This wing is all about getting the "right people in the right seats on the bus and the wrong people off the bus," as Jim Collins described in his book *Good to Great*. Does the leadership of your organization consist

of the right inside and outside talent? Is it operating as a high-performing team, or is every person fighting for their own part of the business?

5. **Priorities (Disney - Bob Iger).** Setting priorities is absolutely key to a transformation effort. Successful leaders in a transformation set only a handful of priorities and make these clear and compelling and ensure that they are communicated often. How powerful is your priority wing? Does everybody in your organization understand these priorities and invest energy in them with force and commitment?

6. **Principles (Zappos - Tony Hsieh).** *Principles* are defined as the key values and behavioral changes in an organization to support its transformation. These principles ultimately are a company's culture. Principles can be a thriving force, or they can put a hand brake on change. As Peter Drucker once said, "Culture eats strategy for breakfast." Leaders of successful transformations have a clear view of where and how their values need to shift to make their organization fit for the future. Are your current principles future fit?

7. **Promotion (Salesforce - Marc Benioff).** We have defined *promotion* as both the internal and external communications of the what, why, and how of the business undergoing a transformation. In a successful transformation, leaders invest heavily in communicating these concepts to all employees and stakeholders, not just once in a presentation or a newsletter but also consistently throughout the transformation process. The more this approaches a ridiculous level of communication, the better. How effectively do you communicate with your organization and its stakeholders?

8. **Progress (3G - Jorge Paulo Lemann, Marcel Telles, and Beto Sicupira).** *Progress* is defined as the power of execution. You can have a great purpose, a clear perspective, a magnetic future position, a great leadership team, a well-defined culture, and great communication, but the rubber truly hits the road with execution. The strength of this wing in the flywheel can range from weak execution to progress powerhouses. How relentless is your organization at getting things done?

9. **Passion (Nike - Phil Knight).** Passion is the fuel of any great transformation. Passion is needed to convince others to join the transformation journey and leave their comfort zones. Passion creates the drive to continue even when facing hurdles or setbacks. How passionate is your organization about what they do for their customers? Is it unstoppable?

10. **Politics (Instagram - Kevin Systrom/Mike Krieger).** Politics is the management of the interests and goodwill of important stakeholders in support of the change journey, as well as managing the internal power allocation within an organization. Successfully managing politics is an essential part of creating the sustained momentum necessary to transform. How well are you aligning with the key stakeholders in your organization? How much goodwill have you amassed with each of them?

11. **Party (Virgin - Richard Branson).** Celebrating progress and achieving milestones is important in any transformation. Just like in soccer, players celebrate every goal in a game and every game won instead of waiting until the end of a season. Successful transformations are more likely when an organization frequently celebrates the progress they've achieved. Do you celebrate small wins as well as larger successes?

CHAPTER 14: CONCLUSION: END OF THE BOOK, START OF THE JOURNEY

12. **Pay-off (Union Square Hospitality Group, Danny Meyer).** We have defined *pay-off* as how well the transformation creates value for all key stakeholders including customers, employees, suppliers, investors, society, and beyond. If a transformation doesn't create value for these groups, it will be difficult for the effort to succeed.

For each of the twelve wings, we have defined four measurable levels of power, which you can assess yourself. In each of the chapters, there is a description for each of the levels that you can use as a reference for your own self-assessment.

	WING-POWER LEVEL	YOUR SCORE?
LEVEL 4	TRANSFORMATIVE POWER	
LEVEL 3	GOOD POWER	
LEVEL 2	SOME POWER	
LEVEL 1	NO POWER	

FLYWHEEL WING

To get a sense of your current flywheel power, you can plot the score of each individual wing in the graph on the following page by coloring the level/ring that corresponds with your current score.

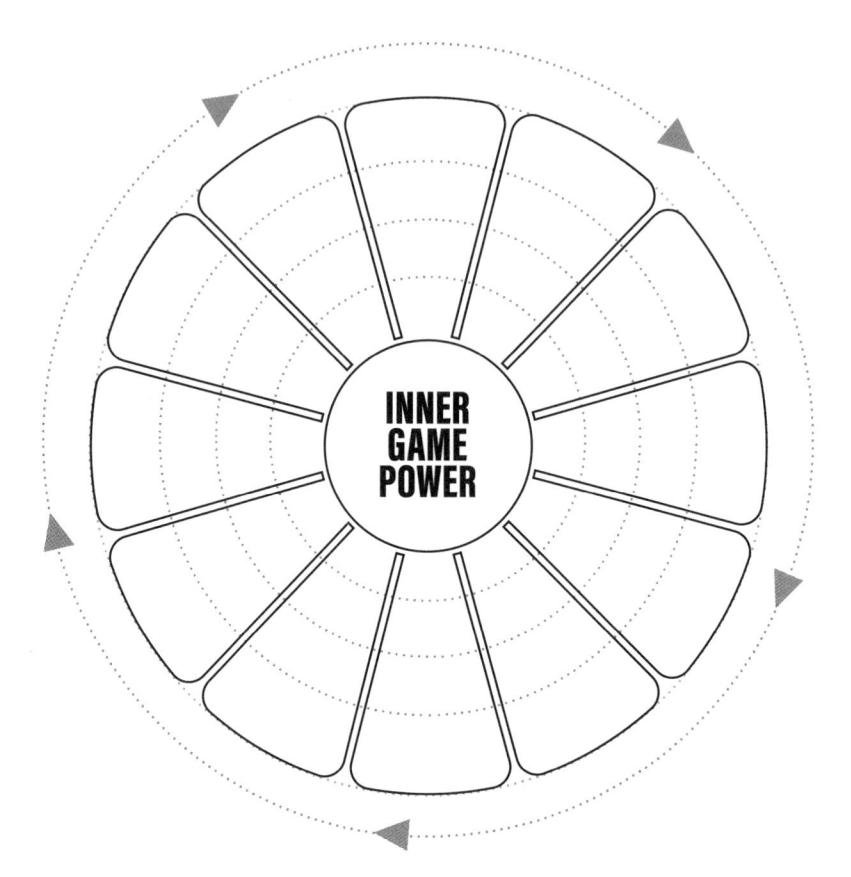

What is your flywheel's pattern? Is there strength across all wings, or is there room for improvement? Are there perhaps several strong wings and a few weaker ones? Is there a theme across the areas that can be improved?

We hope that if you have gone through each of these chapters, made the assessment, and plotted it on the graphic above, you can see the areas that have the biggest potential for improvement.

14.3 Your Inner Game

As we shared in the chapter "The Inner Game," it's helpful to assess the Transformational Flywheel of your business and define an action plan, but it's often just as important to strengthen your own inner game. Transforming is challenging and often requires a leader and their leadership team to bring their A game. Does your inner game have full transformation power, or are there areas you can improve?

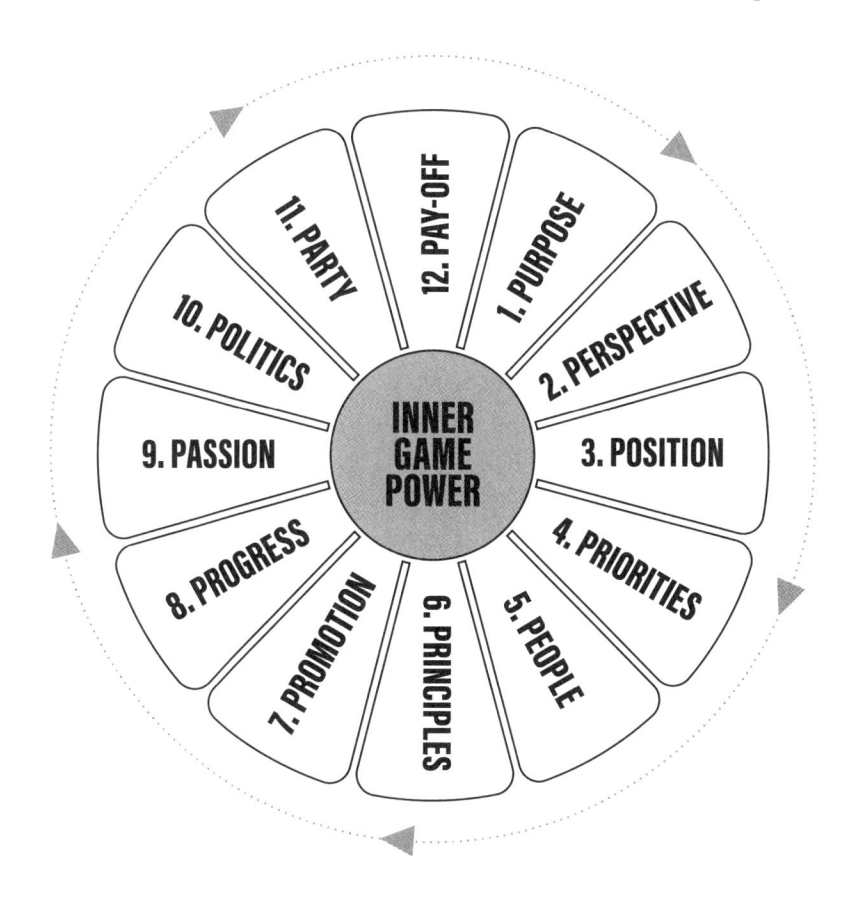

We have found that focusing on the "big six" forces of the inner game is a practical way to enhance your readiness for transformation. In chapter 13 we have described these in more detail. Each of these always starts with an increased sense of your awareness and pattern recognition before you can shift and expand.

1. **Health and Fitness.** Most successful leaders prioritize their physical health and vitality. Whether it's through fitness, nutri-

tious eating, or other healthy behaviors, these leaders who invest in their physical well-being will reap rewards. By investing in your health, fitness, strength, flexibility, and resulting vitality, you can optimize your energy and endurance. How strong are your health, fitness, strength, and flexibility? How would you rate the vitality your lifestyle grants you?

2. **Emotional Fuel.** How are your emotional fitness and your vitality? Leaders who are able to operate in a positive and productive emotional state can deal with challenges more positively and better motivate the people around them. If you are frequently stressed, worried, and angry, then it is challenging to succeed in driving a change program forward. Are you consistently living in an empowered state?

3. **Mental Strength.** Mental toughness as a leader is important in a transformational situation. It's the capacity as a leader for dealing with stressors, challenges, and pressures while continuing to present their best performance, irrespective of the circumstances in which they find themselves.[98] Mental toughness is the ability to conquer adversity and emerge stronger. Do you have ways to enhance your mental strength?

4. **Knowing Yourself.** Every person has a unique personality. Are you aware of your personality characteristics as well as those of the key people around you? Are you aware of what parts of those personalities will be helpful for succeeding with the change program? Are you able to anticipate those traits that might harm the effort?

5. **Empowering Beliefs.** We, as human beings, are inherently biased. When we embark on any kind of transformational journey, we begin it with all kinds of beliefs and values. How do you judge and

---

[98] Clough et al., "Mental Toughness."

interpret the world? Do you hold empowering beliefs regarding yourself, your team, the business, your industry? Or do you hold limiting, disempowering beliefs?

6. **Motivation Force.** How strong and empowering are your motivations and your drive to make your transformation happen? Are you fully committed and empowered? As a leader, you can work on enhancing your motivation by, for instance, focusing on the benefits your transformation will create for both yourself and your stakeholders.

How is your inner game? How would you rate your current overall inner game strength from 1 to 10? What shifts can you make on a daily/weekly basis to enhance your inner game even more?

14.4 How to Shift Gears with Your Flywheel

Where to go from here? We hope that after reading the final chapter of this book, you don't see this as the end but rather as the beginning of strengthening your Transformational Flywheel and inner game. How can you go about it? We have experienced that a logical approach, as described below, can be a helpful step-by-step journey.

1. Make it *Chefsache*, a top priority. Also, take regular moments to step back from the day-to-day grind.

2. Conduct the assessment of the current power in your flywheel, define if there are areas where strength can be increased, and reflect on these. It might be good to not only depend on your own assessment or your team's but also include other perspectives on how the wings are powered, for example, employee surveys.

3. Define three clear priority goals for the next quarter and the next twelve months to improve your flywheel. How will you define *success*? Which wings do you want to score strong or transformative?

4. Make a concrete plan of action. In each of the chapters, we have provided some ideas on what actions you might take. They are, of course, not complete lists, but they can serve as points for inspiration and contemplation. Ask yourself, "Which of these would be most authentic in my organization?"

5. Assign milestones and responsibility to each of the actions and track them through completion. Make them an agenda item at your monthly leadership meeting. Celebrate progress moments.

6. Continue your awareness by, for example, placing the flywheel picture at your desk or setting it as your screen saver.

7. Assess your flywheel score at regular intervals—every six months, for instance. Celebrate progress and define intervention actions where needed.

Next to the business flywheel, it might be good to set up a similar assessment and, if needed, action plan for strengthening your inner game.

14.5 Thank You

We sincerely thank you for having spent time engaging with the content of this book. We hope it provided you some new or refreshed insights. More importantly we hope it gives you the motivation and tools to make your transformation happen.

ACKNOWLEDGMENTS

Marco van Kalleveen

While creating this book, I have relied strongly on many for support and inspiration. Before anyone else, I am grateful for the writing collaboration with Peter Koijen, whom I was able to convince to join this book project and to inject the "inner game" lens. What started as an idea became a three-year intense and inspiring journey. Sadly, just before we could finish dotting the i's and crossing the t's, Peter was taken from us after a short illness.

Second, I would like to thank my lovely wife, Birgit, and my daughter, Marie, for all their patience and encouragement. Writing a book next to a busy international CEO job required many weekends and vacation days for several years—without their incredible support, this would not have been possible.

Third, I am grateful for the many senior leaders whom I could observe and work with, and some of whom were mentors along the different phases and moments of my career until now. The list is too long to mention everyone, but I would like to thank the following people who have become role models and reference points for me:

Asim Abdullah; Jill Ader; Buford Alexander; Prof. David Bell; Jan Bennink; Jan Boomaars; Ivo Bozon; Chris Britton; Wiet de Bruijn; Antony Burgmans; Heang Chhor; Alex Dibelius; Wiebe Draijer; Pat O'Driscoll; Tarek Elmasry; Michael Farello; Jan Fischer; Mike George; Stuart Gent; Duncan Gillis; Marc McGrath; Max Groeneveld; Tex Gunning; Wilfred Griekspoor; Mary Harris; Stefan Heck; Mickey Huibregtsen; Jorgen Johansson; my father, Ron van Kalleveen, whom I learned so much from; Graig Knoche; Adriaan Nuhn; Sally Pofcher; Robert Reibestein; Margot Scheltema; Dick Sluimers; Sven Smit; Olivier Sibony; Marc Singer; Fred Stokvis; Jos Streppel; Marc Valentiny; Peter Ventress; Prof. Willem Verbeke; Ben Verwaayen; Sjoerd Vollebregt; Maarten de Vries; Sue Whalley; Eric Wiebes; and many more.

Fourth, I am also grateful to all the incredible leadership talent I had the privilege to work with at McKinsey and later at TNT, LeasePlan, and DKV Mobility. The list would be too long for this book—so I can only mention a few beyond those already listed.

- At McKinsey, particularly Bjorn Annwall, Wouter Aghina, Rajiv Ball, Bas Becks, Doug Bewsher, Roberto Cirillo, David Doctorow, Jevin Eagle, Gerritjan Eggenkamp, Arne Gast, Michael Gregg, Teun Hermsen, Martin Heijnsbroek, Aafke Keijzer, Dymfke Kuijpers, Michiel Kruyt, David Lee, Alex Liu, Joe Nastasi, Gordon Mowat, Reinier Musters, Jasper van Ouwerkerk, Jean Park, Olivier van Riet Paap, Jurriaan Ruys, Martin Scheepbouwer, Markus Schroder, Kim Spalding, Rob Theunissen, Madeleine Tjon Pian Gi, Tom Voskes, Rutger Vrijen, Heleen Wachters, Marijn de Wit, and Annelies van Zutphen

- At Bain Capital, particularly Yvonne Hao, Jerome Bertrand, Frederic Gren, Nick Isbouts, and Brian Murphy

ACKNOWLEDGMENTS

- At TNT Express, my leadership team consisting of Christophe Boustouller, Marianne Culver, Ignacio Garat, Martin Gussinklo, Tony Jakobsen, Peter Langley, Alex Noomen, Thierry Miremont, Jan Renieri, Nicky Stevenson, and David Walker and also my fellow management board members Ian Clough, Michael Drake, Chris Goossens, Tex Gunning, Joost Otterloo, Martin Sodergard, Maarten de Vries, and Tjeerd Wassenaar and the supervisory board

- At LeasePlan, my leadership team consisting of Ignacio Barbadillo, Jesper Erichsen, Ewout van Jarwaarde, Berno Kleinherenbrink, Paul Lejeune, Onno Maliepaard, Anders Ree-Pederson, and Philipps Zagorianakos, as well as my fellow management board members Tex Gunning, Yolanda Paulissen, Franca Vossen, and Gijsbert de Zoeten and the supervisory board

- At DKV Mobility, my executive board consisting of Jana Eggerding, Jesper Erichsen, Till Kreiler, Jerome Lejeune, Sven Mehringer, and Markus Praßl and my fellow management board member Peter Meijer but also the broader executive committee and the supervisory board

Fifth, all my HBS classmates and faculty members whom I learned from and who inspired me, in particular Professors Bell, Bowen, Heskett, Ibarra, Light, Koehn, Pisano, Poorvu, and Thomke but also my classmates Pablo Antonini, Gideon Agar, Randall Bone, Jerome de Chassey, Igor Da Costa, Hadriano Dominques, Pedro Esquivias, Caio Gilberti, Thomas Kermorgant, Steve Krognes, Gustavo Laforte, Memo Lanusse, Christian Laub, Angel Munoz, Dalton Philips, Thomas Pichler, Luis Plata, Chris Po, Scott Powell, Barney Quinn, Jan Reinhart, Scott Rudmann, Omar Saeed, Nuno

Santos, Neil Shepherd, Amar Singh, Juan Carlos Velten, Carina and Steve Walker, and Branny Zavala.

Sixth, from my studies and early career phase, I am grateful for my EFR board members Harmen Geerts, Hans den Hoedt, Marloes Roelands, Margot van der Velden, Erwin van der Voort, Robert Willemse, and Onno Zijderveld (in memoriam). Further, I am grateful for Jacco Heemskerk, Dick van't Hof, Charles Laurey, Robert Spieker, Bert van der Velden, and Lex Verweij, as well as Steven Le Poole, Frederik Nieuwenhuys, Alex Shivananda, and Lodewijk Westerling.

Seventh, I want to thank the different business leaders who have already completed the journey of writing a book and who generously shared their lessons learned and best practices: Barney Quinn, Martin Scheepbouwer, Olivier Sibony, Sven Smit, and Arne de Vet.

Finally, I would like to thank Joseph Simpson for his writing and editing support and the publishing team of Advantage|ForbesBooks for the excellent professional support.

Peter Koijen*

I want to thank my wife, Ligia Koijen de Oliveira Ramos, as my biggest inspiration. My children—Adriana, Alicia, and Adam—are also my love and inspiration. I would also like to thank my parents, brother, and all my important family and friends.

I would like to thank Marco van Kalleveen for the partnership, the friendship, and this great cooperative endeavor. I would also like to thank Joseph Simpson for editing and working together on our text.

Thank you to all my clients, partners, and employees at in2motivation all these years. Thank you to all the people there who were inspirational—people like John Grinder and many others.

*Peter wrote this text before he passed away.

ABOUT THE AUTHORS

Marco van Kalleveen

Marco van Kalleveen is passionate about growing and transforming organizations. For over thirty years, he has been dedicating his professional career to mastering the science and art of transformations, as well as leading large business transformations on an international scale.

In recent years Marco has led several multibillion-dollar transformations as a management board member and as a CEO. He helped transform TNT Express, the public global overnight package delivery company, where he was responsible for a $3 billion global division with over thirty thousand employees, covering Europe, Brazil, and Australia. He was COO of the largest European car-leasing company LeasePlan, where he had P&L responsibility for the $6 billion European business. Marco is currently CEO of DKV Mobility, the leading European B2B road payment and services platform with presence in forty-five countries.

Before his active executive roles, Marco worked for a decade at McKinsey & Company in their Chicago, San Francisco, and Amsterdam offices, where he spent the last four years as partner. He supported clients ranging from Silicon Valley tech start-ups to *Fortune* 500 companies in realizing transformations. He has also worked for Bain Capital, one of the leading private equity firms, supporting the management teams of various portfolio companies.

Marco earned an MBA from Harvard Business School and an MSc in business economics from the Erasmus University Rotterdam in the Netherlands. Marco is regularly asked to speak about transformational leadership. He and his wife, Birgit, live with their daughter in Amsterdam.

www.marcovankalleveen.com

Peter Koijen

Peter was an experienced coach for senior executives and international companies. He also made a difference in the fields of training, HR, and motivational speaking.

After receiving his MBA from the University of Tilburg, Peter began his career at various multinational companies including Manpower, Oracle, and ABN AMRO, focused on facilitating change from an HR perspective. At ABN AMRO he facilitated many change projects in a variety of roles in several countries. He was, for example, responsible for a major cultural integration and change program in Italy when the company acquired a leading Italian bank. After returning to the Netherlands, he decided to follow his passion and started his own coaching and consultancy company, in2motivation, which he successfully built and ran for thirteen years. He and his team helped leaders and companies with change and their motivation. He incorporated many different change skills, such as NLP, in which he was personally trained by one of NLP's founders, John Grinder. He also wrote a book on human superpowers together with his wife, Ligia Koijen Ramos. Very sadly Peter passed away in 2021 after a short illness just before the book was completed.

His credo was "Live your life and do it your way."